Learning to Sell Sex(ism)

D1739489

Aileen O'Driscoll

Learning to Sell Sex(ism)

Advertising Students and Gender

palgrave
macmillan

Aileen O'Driscoll
Dublin City University
Dublin, Ireland

ISBN 978-3-030-06825-7   ISBN 978-3-319-94280-3   (eBook)
https://doi.org/10.1007/978-3-319-94280-3

This Palgrave Macmillan imprint is published by the registered company Springer Nature Switzerland AG
The registered company address is: Gewerbestrasse 11, 6330 Cham, Switzerland

Acknowledgements

This book represents the culmination of a number of years of research, kindly funded by the School of Communications at Dublin City University. I am especially grateful to my colleagues Debbie Ging, Neil O'Boyle, and Pat Brereton for their invaluable encouragement, advice, and feedback throughout the process. More generally, the intellectually stimulating environment and inspiring research outputs at the School of Communications provided the conditions needed to undertake and thoroughly enjoy the whole process. Additionally, I wish to acknowledge and express my gratitude to the people who participated in this study, without whom it would have been impossible for the research to progress.

Special thanks to Dawn Wheatley, in particular, for her constant friendship and availability for chats, cups of coffee, and something stronger when required. Special mention also goes to both Katayoun and Caspar for practical help with this project, it is much appreciated. I further wish to extend my gratitude to Amelia Derkatsch, at Palgrave Macmillan, for always providing quick and efficient responses to various queries in the months before completing the final manuscript.

Final thanks go to my family. To my wonderful parents, John and Bridget, who taught me the value of hard work and integrity. I could not have succeeded in completing this project without their love and enthusiasm. Huge gratitude goes to my sisters, Ciara and Clare, and my brother-in-law, Richie, who are always so generous and kind. Here's to spending much more time with my lovely nieces, Olive and Ida.

This work is dedicated to my brother, Barry O'Driscoll, who played no small role in motivating me to undertake and complete the writing of this book. Massive thanks to him for time spent proofreading, asking insightful questions, and providing constructive advice. In particular, his unwavering support, friendship, curiosity, and good humour mean everything to me.

Contents

List of Tables

1

Introduction

On the day that I interviewed Pauline,[1] an advertising art director, who told me that her male creative director 'hates the way men are always or quite often perceived to be the bumbling idiot in ads next to the woman …who is the smart, logical one', the comment was significant for the fact that it mirrored a belief expressed by a number of the advertising students who participated in this study, and who likewise felt that advertising's representation of men has become increasingly problematic. Indeed, these students referred to the trend of misandrist advertising as one of notable concern. Such a conviction, among others, clearly warranted closer scrutiny.

This book has come about as a result of two questions that germinated in my mind for a considerable time. Firstly, why does advertising seem to be central in pushing an aggressive 'war of the sexes' cultural narrative, intent on positioning men and women as opposites (albeit a 'war' constructed in ways to suggest sexual frisson as well as tension and difference between the two)? And, secondly, *who makes these ads*? While both questions began more as casual talking points, before tackling them through academic enquiry, they did point to an intense concern with what I saw as the advertising industry's continued trotting-out of sexist and

© The Author(s) 2019
A. O'Driscoll, *Learning to Sell Sex(ism)*,
https://doi.org/10.1007/978-3-319-94280-3_1

old-fashioned assumptions about women and men. This niggling need to find out more about the people behind the making of adverts turned into a desire to discover if there was some correlation between advertiser's personally held attitudes and opinions about gender and the content we see on our televisions, hear on the radio, flip through in the magazines we read, and rush past on the billboards that occupy our streets.

That curiosity led to me thinking about whether the educational sphere might offer some insights into the gendered work practices and texts produced by the advertising industry. In other words, were advertising students entering the industry with certain gendered attitudes already in tow? It was apparent that if I wanted to explore this in a concerted way then a number of questions would have to be answered: How do advertising students understand gender and related issues? What are their predominant attitudes to representations of gender, gender roles, and sexism in advertising texts? What are their perceptions of working in an advertising agency, and do they believe there is room to be gender critical in designing and creating adverts? Finally, some consideration was given to the extent to which the topic of gender is currently incorporated into third-level advertising communications degree courses. These pressing questions kicked off the study that underpins this work. This book, therefore, is an attempt to shed light on these considerations and comes, I would argue, at an opportune time. In the wake of the sexual assault charges laid at the feet of Hollywood executive and film producer Harvey Weinstein, conversations about the problem and prevalence of predatory, intimidating, and indeed more seemingly benign but nevertheless sexist behaviours against women by their male colleagues and superiors has spilled over from the media and entertainment industries to politics, academia, and those who work in the services industries. Such industry-wide soul-searching must also involve scrutiny of smaller-scale domains and dynamics in order that sexism against women and girls may be better tackled. Consequently, this book explores what the typical gendered attitudes of a group of advertising students might reveal about their opinions towards the sexes and how that may be mirrored in the kind of content created by the advertising industry. In other words, although this study's cohort is modest in terms of numbers of advertising students surveyed and interviewed, extrapolation of the findings is useful when considering whether proactive measures are needed in order to address the persistent issue of gender stereotyping and sexism in advertising.

The emphasis of this book on the future producers of media content is predicated on an acknowledgement that careful critique must continue to be carried out on how the sexes, gender roles, and gender norms are represented and perpetuated by such media texts as film, television programmes, and advertising in particular. Such feminist campaigning groups as OBJECT, among others, persist in raising awareness about stereotypical and reductive representations in the media and advertising. This attentiveness is echoed in the academic sphere with Rosalind Gill (2007) arguing that '[s]tarting from the proposition that representations matter, feminist analyses of the media have been animated by the desire to understand how images and cultural constructions are connected to patterns of inequality, domination and oppression' (p. 7). The focus of present-day feminist campaigns draws heavily on second-wave feminist discourse, which in the 1970s developed an understanding of the interplay between culture, gender,[2] and power (Williamson 1978; Goffman 1979; Kilbourne 1979) by accounting for both substantive and symbolic challenges facing women.

Those critiquing representations of the sexes and associated gender roles have long pointed the finger at the advertising industry. Theorists have explained the emergence of advertising from a number of different perspectives. Since the Industrial Revolution ushered in a phenomenon of mass production, the manufacturing of products in large bulk needed to take place in a context where producers could be confident that demand would keep up with supply. As a result, advertising emerged as a strategy in order to allay the fears of producers. The role of the advertiser was, and is, to develop and implement strategies that predict and influence consumer behaviour. However, Lury and Warde (1997) posit the view that advertising exists more to assuage the anxieties of the producer of goods, rather than to nudge the consumer to make certain decisions. Advertisers do this through assertions that they have a unique insight into the consumer's psyche. The ability of advertising to predict and manipulate consumer behaviour and choice is a hotly debated topic. Perhaps it is more accurate to think of the advertisers' function as 'a kind of modern witch doctor … to calm the worried spirits of the producers of potentially unwanted commodities' (Lury and Warde 1997, p. 96).

Notwithstanding the contested *raison d'être* of advertising, the fact remains that companies producing goods and services for commercial sale do turn to advertisers to promote their products. The advertising industry achieves this through a number of different functions, broadly split between executive and creative activities. The executive roles within the advertising industry fulfil such functions as the management of client portfolios by the account handler; the strategic planners, who have responsibility for providing insight into the particular consumer markets; and the media planner, who devises strategies concerning media and marketing. The creative department includes the art director, who creates and develops the vision, the images, and the overall feel and tone of the advertising campaign; the adverts text is devised by the copywriter in conjunction with the art director, and their work is overseen by the creative director. All three roles are collectively referred to as 'creatives'.

Following consultation with clients, the executive side of the agency delivers a 'brief' to the creatives, which outlines the product or products to be advertised, the objectives of the campaign, the target audience, as well as, sometimes, broader requirements about the overall message and company ethos to be communicated by the campaign. While there are many different objectives, aims, and functions that come together in the design and dissemination of an advertising campaign, and indeed often competing visions and ideas between client and advertising agency, and sometimes disagreement between executive and creative practitioners about the direction of campaigns, the role of the creative department within the advertising process represents the sphere where there is most influence and control over the choices made in *how* to fulfil the brief (Soar 2000). In other words, while allowing for the fact that the client is ultimately in the more powerful position of being able to reject a proposed advertising campaign as put forward by the agency, the creative retains the power of choosing certain images, ideologies, and discourses in planning and designing the campaign in the first place. For this reason, the creative function within advertising practice is here afforded dominant status in shaping advertising content. Furthermore, and more generally, although numerous factors are relevant to any analysis and study of advertising and the industry, this book, rather than focusing on how effective various strategies are in driving up sales for the clients of advertisers, is concerned with the social implications of using gendered images, narratives, and discourses as a selling strategy.

This concern is driven by recognising that such is the reach and influence of the advertising industry in contemporary society that it is positioned as one of the most controversial of media industries (Cook 2000). It is argued (James et al. 1994) that no other industry has, throughout its existence, received such criticism. Advertising is a particularly potent form of communication in multimedia, which goes beyond simply promoting and selling products. In addition to creating collective unease (Pollay 1986; Cook 2000; Lazar 2006), it is thought to manipulate already existing social anxieties (Jhally 2011). Advertising prompts all consumers, not just those to whom a particular advert is targeted, to 'read' and interpret the ad. Given, as Baudrillard suggests, that society is 'hierarchically ordered' (p. 34), our reading of adverts results in individuals positioning themselves within this socially sanctioned hierarchy. Thus, in engaging—consciously or unconsciously—with advertising texts, it urges one to assess how we measure up: Are we attractive enough or suitably successful enough? If we purchase and consume the products being advertised, are we trendier or cooler than our peers who do not? Do our lived realities as women and men mirror those of the figures we see in adverts? Advertising, therefore, 'imposes a consensus' (p. 125) and works to uphold a *status quo*, since everyone is held, and holds themselves and others, to the same standard. Moreover, the normative and prescriptive nature of advertising texts and 'the fact that the consensus produced by advertising can then result in attachment to objects, acts of purchase and implicit conformity to the economic imperatives of consumption is certain, but it is not the essential point' (Baudrillard 1998, p. 166). In other words, advertising's ability to result in increased sales of a product is secondary to its efficacy at compelling society at large to adhere to expected norms and thereby uphold established social and gendered relations.

Commonly, advertising is disparaged for its promotion of consumerism. In the 1940s, Horkheimer and Adorno of the Frankfurt School took issue with the 'ideology of consumerism' (Kelly 2008). By playing on and manipulating our most deep-seated insecurities, by shining a light on our failings at not being 'successful' enough, or attractive enough, or wealthy enough, advertisers propose a solution through the consumption of goods and/or services (UNESCO report 1980; referenced in Pollay 1986). According to Pollay, humanities and social science scholars position advertising and its negative consequences 'as reinforcing materialism, cynicism, irrationality, selfishness, anxiety, social competitiveness, sexual preoccupation, powerlessness, and/or a loss of self-respect' (1986, p. 18). Indeed, this 1980 UNESCO report charged the advertising industry with reinforcing sex-role stereotypes[3] (Pollay 1986). Almost 30 years later, the Council of the European Union (Council of the European Union 2008) continued to recognise the role that multimedia often play in perpetuating gender stereotypes, and consequently adopted Council Conclusions on Eliminating Gender Stereotypes in Society. In September of the same year, the European Parliament (European Parliament 2008) set out its position in relation to how marketing and advertising, through the perpetuation of gender stereotypes, can negatively impinge on progress towards greater equality between women and men by passing a resolution attempting to counter that trend. Additionally, in 2010, the European Commission published a report outlining its official position on 'Breaking Gender Stereotypes in Media', noting that the Beijing Platform for Action, which was drawn up at the Fourth World Conference on Women in 1995, explicitly recognises that advertising's dissemination of images that depict gender stereotyping upholds inequality between the sexes.

In considering the intersection of gender and advertising, one must be aware that the current gender landscape is characterised by various disturbances and anxieties. Such unease has emerged as a result of a number of social upheavals. For instance, the real and perceived gains of both second-wave feminism and the gay rights and marriage equality movements, the acknowledgement that patriarchy can no longer be justified, the rendering visible of both a White and performative masculinity have all contributed to a push and pull within the gender order. Reactions to such changes in the gender order have manifested in various ways. In response to material social changes, such as male unemployment resulting from the neoliberal restructuring of the labour force (Messner and Montez de Oca 2005) and the 'feminization of the workplace', backlashes have occurred in the guise of men's rights movements and more recently men's rights activists (MRAs). Social and cultural manifestations to the disruption of long-established gender roles include a shift from the discourse and politics of feminism to the cultural rhetoric of postfeminism (Tasker and Negra 2007) and back to feminism again; the associated emergence of Lad Culture with its attendant tropes of ironic sexism (Whelehan 2000); the increased 'pornification' or sexualisation of society (Levy 2006; Coy and Garner 2010, 2012), seen as both a progressive and a regressive phenomenon; a new cyber backlash in the form of overt misogyny in violent pornography and hacker and gaming culture (Nagle 2017); and a more highly charged, antagonistic discourse around relations between the sexes, which is amplified by the tacit approval of Donald Trump's sexism by way of his election to the US presidency. Amidst all of this, advertising remains influential in the formation and enactment of gendered norms and worldviews, since advertising 'require[s] the work of symbol creators' (Hesmondhalgh 2007, p. 13). This dominance of the symbolic and the cultural, rather than the political, in new gender formations and discourses (Tasker and Negra 2007) is one of the reasons it is so important to scrutinise advertising. Consumers and advertisers may not consciously understand pervasive gender ideologies in the way that feminist theorists do, but almost everybody recognises them, speaks their language, and knows how to use them.

There is a scarcity, however, of studies that bring together a consideration of gendered beliefs with the cultural production of advertising in order to examine the process of encoding gender in advertising texts. Furthermore, in considering the potential impact of a feminist-infused sensitivity and awareness on the creation and production of advertising texts[4] that resist rather than promote gender stereotypes, the intersection of education and professional practice is a critical juncture that has not been explored before. Consequently, this book represents an empirical study of how gender is constructed and understood in the educational cultures of advertising students in Ireland. It is guided by Nixon's (2003) study into advertising cultures, which was anchored in qualitative interviews with creative advertising practitioners. Nixon found an adherence to discourses among creative advertisers that promote traditional gendered working practices and organisational cultures hostile to equality.

Building on his research, among others (see Gregory 2009), this work likewise considers the cultural production processes that create advertising texts, along with the gendered experiences of those working and creating in that field. As a point of departure, however, I contextually foreground feminist critiques of postfeminism and consider the impact of postfeminism on advertising imagery.[5] In addition, I draw on marketing and advertising academic research to highlight the underexplored and underresearched sphere of advertising education and gender. Central to this book is an exploration of student attitudes and understandings of gender as they relate to the social world and to representational ideologies, their perceptions of advertising work, as well as their opinions regarding desired roles in the industry. Examining the gendered attitudes and worldviews expressed by advertising students necessitated ascertaining the prevalence and indeed absence among students of feminist, postfeminist, masculinist, and androcentric discourses that may impact on attitudes towards the sexes. Such a focus is predicated on Nixon's (2003) contention that the 'informal cultures' and subjective gendered identities and experiences of advertising practitioners, and advertising creatives especially, are crucial in how they approach advertising production and practice. The same may be said for advertising students.

In order to shed light on the issues being investigated and to illuminate 'what is going on and why' (Maxwell 2013, p. 28; cited in Bazeley 2013, p. 7), a mostly qualitative methodology was implemented. The data comprising the study that forms the basis for this book includes student responses to 30 questionnaire questions ($n = 107$); student responses to 5 open-ended survey questions, as devised and distributed in class by one lecturer ($n = 57$); one-on-one interviews with students ($n = 12$); non-participant observational attendance at several first-year undergraduate lectures; attendance at student's end-of-year showcases at undergraduate and postgraduate levels; examination of course modules; and interviews with advertising practitioners ($n = 4$). Although the study was developed to be mostly qualitative in nature, a secondary, quantitative analysis was carried out on the questionnaire and survey responses in order to ascertain relevant sex-disaggregated data. I employ a methodologically and analytically robust thematic analysis, which allows prevalent discourses to be discussed through the identification of dominant themes along with an interpretive understanding and in-depth knowledge of the data.

Being cognisant of one's reflexive and subjective position as a researcher and also conceding that knowledge is always situated, the position taken herein is that I locate myself as politically, socially, and ethically invested in the research in order to 'critiqu(e) discourses which sustain a patriarchal social order' (Lazar 2007, p. 145). This is done with a view to adding to the canon of radical feminist thought that is concerned with challenging preconceptions about 'natural' gender roles, and the supposed inevitability of the polarisation of the sexes. In other words, this work is aligned to a radical feminist tradition, which is concerned with the socially constructed nature of gender, and its inculcation through a process of socialisation and cultural expectations (Rubin 1975). Although emerging as a strand of feminist philosophical thought during the time of second-wave feminism, references throughout this book to radical feminism do not refer to a historical movement but, rather, as a way to conceptualise and understand 'gender' as fundamental to the continuation of the sex/gender system that operates under patriarchy. This system works to hierarchically value women and men in such ways that legitimate the subordination of women as a sex class to men as a sex class by virtue of assigning differential gender roles to males and females accordingly. The radical feminist-aligned objectives of this research to add further strain on the legitimacy of the concept of gender as operationalised under patriarchy ultimately argues for sensitising advertising students—and hence future practitioners—to sexist, stereotypical gender essentialist content, thereby potentially leading to a shift in the symbolic representation of women and men.

Such an objective is accompanied by a contention that identifying, decoding, and critiquing gender in advertising may be aided by an awareness of the beliefs held by practitioners. That said, there are limitations implicit in this research, since problematic gendered content of advertising texts cannot be simply chalked up to the gendered beliefs and opinions of advertisers. Nevertheless, the value of this research is in setting out predominant gendered attitudes of students in order that the third-level educational sector and the advertising industry engage with the findings and respond with policies and action plans that aim at creating a future industry populated by practitioners who resist the use of gender stereotypical and sexist images and tropes in adverts. Indeed, when considering that the European Commission's Advisory Committee on Equal Opportunities for Women and Men advises that 'in order to ensure a long term impact, gender equality should be a compulsory module for training in university studies of journalism and communication' (European Commission 2010, p. 13)', it is clear that the training of future advertisers must be included in that assertion.

Contemplating the nature of advertising and its relationship to consumer capitalism also poses a challenge and represents a tension throughout this book. For instance, advertisers have responded to feminists' calling-out of sexist and one-dimensional representations of women by co-opting feminist values to suit their own aims. Advertisers have been found to incorporate feminist language by using terms such as 'empowerment' and 'take control' in order to sell everything from wrinkle creams to car insurance. Referred to as 'commodity feminism' by Goldman et al. (1991) and 'power femininity' by Lazar (2006), such a strategy is testament to the challenge of engaging advertisers and clients in an uncynical concern for the social implications of the adverts produced and circulated by them. This issue, coupled with a consideration of what would constitute a more 'real' or accurate depiction of the sexes and its associated risk of falling into the trap of essentialism, begs the question of where this research converges with a feminist politics. The justification for this work lies in having hard data about student perceptions of gender in order to strengthen the case for adequately incorporating and teaching associated issues at the educational level. This could have a transformative impact on the students studying and training for a career in advertising, and, by extension, allowing for mitigating factors, the industry.

A further limitation of this research is that it is beyond its scope to apply an intersectional approach in terms of fully incorporating and exploring issues of social class, age, ethnicity, disability, and other social categories of privilege and oppression. However, I do acknowledge that an intersectional approach to the research would have been desirable in terms of more fully exploring how gendered attitudes cut across and differ when compared to students' age and socio-economic backgrounds. Nevertheless, as argued by Eckert (1989: referenced in Lazar 2007), an explicit emphasis on gender and sex in social research can be justified on the basis that, although class and race are indeed sites of discrimination, sex-based oppression involves systems of domination and subordination at such close quarters in people's daily lives that it is vital to treat it separately.

The following chapters build on the findings of this extensive study. Chapter 2 contextualises the key advertising shifts that have occurred amid the socio-cultural 'genderscape' brought on by second-wave feminism. This covers some theorisation of advertising work by considering advertisers as taste-makers, as shaping culture, and as reaffirming already established social gendered relations. In order to expand the discussion of why it is hugely important to pay attention to the social attitudes and worldviews of the people who populate (and will in future populate) the cultural industries, research that explores the topic of class and race, as well as gender, is also explored. Consideration is also given to the organisational cultures which produce gendered advertising texts by referencing studies that have discovered advertising departments to be homosocial environments, often hostile to women. Furthermore, since the concept of creativity and creative endeavour is very often understood in gendered terms and as reserved for a male sensibility and expertise, this is afforded examination, as is the intersection of practice and education which is explored through an understanding that both students and practitioners undergo a process of adaptation and socialisation into advertising agencies and working practices.

Chapter 3 presents the first of three chapters outlining the findings of this study. It offers a deconstruction of student attitudes to gender, gender roles, and feminism, in addition to exploring the ways in which they talk about women and men and relations between the sexes. It is found that salient attitudes to women and men work to construct a gender discourse that is androcentric and thereby, in the main, unsympathetic and lacking in empathy for women. In Chap. 4, student attitudes to pertinent issues concerned with gender in advertising texts are addressed. While there is strong awareness, particularly among female students, that sexual objectification of women in advertising remains problematic, such a position is more precarious when analysing the various responses from male students. Discussions of such problematic imagery was often greeted with a 'yeah, but what about men?' response. This calling for attention to be paid to men and boys results, among some of the students, in misguided assertions that misandry is a newly emerging and unwelcome trend in contemporary advertising texts. Less contradictory or complex is the finding of an almost total lack of interest or investment in depictions of exclusively women involved in domestic activity in adverts.

Chapter 5 deals with attitudes that relate to advertising practice, generally, and more specifically considering what might be done to promote representations that offer greater diversity and less gender stereotyping. When moving from the level of 'surface' or abstract avowal of the continued need to strive for genuine equality between the sexes, to concrete discussions of bringing that reality about, attitudes counter-productive to that struggle emerge. Additionally, it was found that creativity and its associated concept of humour are discursively constructed as male skills and attributes, and in reality manifest as roles reserved for male students in the educational setting. This thereby implicitly and explicitly discourages female students from taking up these creative roles. Chapter 6 offers some concluding thoughts. While there is not a malicious sexism running through the opinions, attitudes, and behaviours of this study's participants, and students were found to be articulate, thoughtful, intelligent, and engaging research subjects, there is a sort of sexism apparent through taking up a stance of keeping ethical and moral considerations at arm's length, as well as a sexism borne out of an exasperation and boredom with feminist concerns.

Notes

1. Pseudonyms are used throughout for all research participants, unless otherwise stated.
2. From the outset, it should be noted that the position taken herein in relation to 'gender' is one of critique, and sits within a radical feminist interrogation of the concept. As such, where the concept of gender is used and referred to, it is not value free; rather, inherent in its use is a challenge to the concept. Radical feminism's theorisation of gender is further discussed elsewhere.

3. According to UNESCO (2012), gender stereotypes relate to 'socially con-structed beliefs about men and women, often but not necessarily sexist and negative, which ignore complexity and serve to rule out exceptions and choices' (p. 54). These constructions will vary depending on cultural frame, but, for the purposes of this study, the term refers to contemporary Western society.
4. Allowance, of course, needs to be made for outside influencing factors, such as the desired approach of the client company.
5. Rosalind Gill's (2007, 2008, 2009a, b) work in this area forms the corner-stone in this book's consideration of postfeminist gendered imagery in contemporary advertising.

References

Baudrillard, J. (1998). *The Consumer Society: Myths & Structures*. London: Sage.

Bazeley, P. (2013). *Qualitative Data Analysis: Practical Strategies*. Los Angeles: Sage.

Cook, G. (2000). *The Discourse of Advertising* (2nd ed.). London: Routledge.

Council of the European Union. (2008). *Council Conclusions on Eliminating Gender Stereotypes in Society*. Retrieved from http://www.eu2008.si/si/News_and_Documents/Council_Conclusions/June/0609_EPSCO-Gender.pdf

Coy, M., & Garner, M. (2010). Glamour Modelling and the Marketing of Self-Sexualization: Critical Reflections. *International Journal of Cultural Studies, 13*(6), 657–675.

Coy, M., & Garner, M. (2012). Definitions, Discourses and Dilemmas: Policy and Academic Engagement with the Sexualisation of Popular Culture. *Gender and Education, 24*(3), 285–301.

European Commission. (2010). Advisory Committee on Equal Opportunities for Women and Men. Opinion on *Breaking Gender Stereotypes in the Media*. Retrieved from http://ec.europa.eu/justice/gender-equality/files/opinions_advisory_committee/2010_12_opinion_on_breaking_gender_stereotypes_in_the_media_en.pdf

European Parliament. (2008). *How Marketing and Advertising Affect Equality Between Women and Men*. Retrieved from http://www.europarl.europa.eu/sides/getDoc.do?pubRef=-//EP//TEXT+REPORT+A6-2008-0199+0+DOC+XML+V0//EN

Gill, R. (2007). *Gender and the Media*. Cambridge/Malden: Polity Press.

Gill, R. (2008). Empowerment/Sexism: Figuring Female Sexual Agency in Contemporary Advertising. *Feminism & Psychology, 18*(1), 35–60.

Gill, R. (2009a). Beyond the 'Sexualization of Culture' Thesis: An Intersectional Analysis of 'Sixpacks', 'Midriffs' and 'Hot Lesbians' in Advertising. *Sexualities, 12*(2), 137–160.

Gill, R. (2009b). Supersexualise Me! Advertising and "The Midriffs". In *Mainstreaming Sex: The Sexualization of Western Culture*. London/New York: I.B. Tauris.

Goffman, E. (1979). *Gender Advertisements*. London: Macmillan.

Goldman, R., Heath, D., & Smith, S. L. (1991). Commodity Feminism. *Critical Studies in Mass Communication, 8*(3), 333–351.

Gregory, M. R. (2009). Inside the Locker Room: Male Homosociability in the Advertising Industry. *Gender, Work and Organization, 16*(3), 323–347.

Hesmondhalgh, D. (2007). *The Cultural Industries* (2nd ed.). Los Angeles: Sage.

James, E., Pratt, C., & Smith, T. (1994). Advertising Ethics: Practitioner and Student Perspectives. *Journal of Mass Media Ethics, 9*(2), 69–83.

Jhally, S. (2011). Image-Based Culture: Advertising and Popular Culture. In G. Dines & J. M. Humez (Eds.), *Gender, Race, and Class in Media. A Critical Reader* (3rd ed.). Los Angeles: Sage.

Kelly, A. (2008). *Mediators of Meaning: A Critically Reflexive Study of the Encoding of Irish Advertising*. Doctoral Thesis, Dublin Institute of Technology. https://doi.org/10.21427/D7Q013.

Kilbourne, J. (1979). *Killing Us Softly: Advertising's Image of Women*. Retrieved from http://www.jeankilbourne.com/videos/

Lazar, M. M. (2006). Discover The Power Of Femininity! *Feminist Media Studies, 6*(4), 505–517.

Lazar, M. M. (2007). Feminist Critical Discourse Analysis: Articulating a Feminist Discourse Praxis. *Critical Discourse Studies, 4*(2), 141–164.

Levy, A. (2006). *Female Chauvinist Pigs: Women and the Rise of Raunch Culture*. London: Pocket.

Lury, C., & Warde, A. (1997). Investments in the Imaginary Consumer: Conjectures Regarding Power, Knowledge and Advertising. In M. Nava, A. Blake, I. McRory, & B. Richards (Eds.), *Buy This Book: Studies in Advertising and Consumption* (pp. 87–102). London/New York: Routledge.

Messner, M. A., & Montez de Oca, J. (2005). The Male Consumer as Loser: Beer and Liquor Ads in Mega Sports Media Events. *Signs, 30*(3), 1879–1909.

Nagle, A. (2017). *Kill All Normies: Online Culture Wars from 4Chan and Tumblr to Trump and the Alt-Right*. Winchester/Washington, DC: Zero Books.

Nixon, S. (2003). *Advertising Cultures: Gender, Commerce, Creativity*. London: Sage.

Pollay, R. W. (1986). The Distorted Mirror: Reflections on the Unintended Consequences of Advertising. *Journal of Marketing, 50*(April), 18–37.

Rubin, G. (1975). The Traffic in Women: Notes on the "Political Economy" of Sex. In R. R. Reiter (Ed.), *Toward an Anthropology of Women*. New York: Monthly Review Press.

Soar, M. (2000). Encoding Advertisements: Ideology and Meaning in Advertising Production. *Mass Communication and Society, 3*(4), 415–437.

Tasker, Y., & Negra, D. (2007). *Interrogating Postfeminism: Gender and the Politics of Popular Culture*. Durham: Duke University Press.

UNESCO. (2012). *Gender-Sensitive Indicators for Media: Framework of Indicators to Gauge Gender Sensitivity in Media Operations and Content*. Paris: UNESCO.

Whelehan, I. (2000). *Overloaded: Popular Culture and the Future of Feminism*. London: Women's Press.

Williamson, J. (1978). *Decoding Advertisements: Ideology and Meaning in Advertising*. London: Marion Boyars Publishers Ltd.

2

Gendered Advertising: From Text to Industry to Classroom

Examining and analysing the gendered attitudes and opinions of advertising students cannot occur without considering both the gendered cultures that operate in advertising practice and the advertising texts that the sector produces—both of which will shape their future professional lives. It is crucial, therefore, to survey the key trends in advertising's representations of femininity and masculinity through the critiques offered by second-wave feminism in the 1970s up to the contemporary period of the 2000s, and also to scrutinise how industry responses to feminism influenced recurring motifs in advertising imagery, particular since the onset of postfeminism in the 1990s. Further discussion must also focus on how creative and cultural workers can be conceptually and theoretical understood, on the hypermasculine working cultures and practices that proliferate in advertising agencies, and on the insight provided by academics into the creative advertising practitioner as a gendered subject. Additionally, attention is afforded to positioning the advertising student as a future practitioner 'in training'—one who will be tasked with making ethical and moral, as well as professional, decisions with regard to depicting the sexes in particular ways. All of these are given consideration in this chapter before the study's findings are outlined in the following three chapters.

© The Author(s) 2019
A. O'Driscoll, *Learning to Sell Sex(ism)*,
https://doi.org/10.1007/978-3-319-94280-3_2

Advertising Texts: From Second-Wave Feminism to Postfeminism

In part response to aggressive advertising directed at housewives, Betty Friedan's *The Feminine Mystique* (1963) sought to expose the 'problem that has no name'. Although much criticised for its exclusive focus on White, middle-class, suburban America, Friedan's work aimed to reveal that the 'domestic dream' that women were being sold was a form of enslavement and confinement to the home. The 1950s and 1960s advertisements for domestic appliances were imbued with symbolism that tied women to working in the home by equating her entire identity to her role as housewife and mother. Friedan's dispelling of the myth of the 'happy housewife', so regularly portrayed in US advertising at that time, is credited with igniting the flame that sparked the beginning of the second-wave feminist movement. Where the first-wave of feminist activism during the nineteenth and early twentieth centuries was mobilised around material concerns and issues of political, legal, and voting rights, the second wave of the 1960s and 1970s was characterised by an increased focus on cultural issues, such as workplace sexism, insidious stereotyping, and the representation of women in the media and in advertising, in particular.

Fifteen years after Friedan had mobilised a new generation of women to pay attention to feminist issues, Williamson's (1978) semiotic study of over one hundred advertising images broke new ground. In her work, she paid attention to the matter of ideology and meaning, significations and representations, and sought to offer ways to deconstruct advertisements. She exposed the visual cues evident in advertisements, which reduce the person portrayed in an advert from a human being to a symbol or concept—be that power, prestige, rebellion, for example, or vulnerability, narcissism, vanity. She surmised that domesticity, nature, and animalism are all signifiers used by advertisers as shorthand for femininity and, by extension, the woman—thereby reducing women to fragmented and one-dimensional representations. Kilbourne likewise drew attention to the advertising text itself, and came to prominence as a result of her 1979 film *Killing Us Softly: Advertising's Image of Women*. In the documentary she singles out the advertising industry for special attention when examining culturally sanctioned modalities of masculinity and femininity. She focused primarily on beauty and image, on gender stereotypes and their effect on gender relations, as well as on the emerging trend in the 1970s of conflating sexual and violent imagery. This is a trend which continues unabated in contemporary adverts, particularly in fashion advertising. As Kilbourne has argued (1999), ads depicting either explicit or implied violence wrapped up in sexualised imagery allow for the ongoing objectification of women which is instrumental in facilitating a culture that leads to real-life violence against females—something termed 'conducive context' by Coy and Garner (2012). The prevalence of gender stereotypes in advertising was central also to Goffman's 1979 book *Gender Advertisements*. He was concerned with gender expressions and depictions of gender behaviours in adverts. Through systematic content analyses, he showed that stark differences pertained to women and men in adverts. Women were much more often represented in a sensual manner, for instance, through the sense of lightly, or carefully, touching—connoting sensuality and passivity. In what Goffman calls, a 'hierarchy of functions', men were more frequently shown in positions of authority or expertise, through the activities in which they are engaged. This aspect of authority and superiority is also achieved through the positioning of bodies in advertising imagery. Women were much more often depicted lying down or looking up in ways that suggested vulnerability and weakness, while men will be shown standing over women and/or looking down on them. Almost 30 years later, a study of gender in Irish advertising found a similar trend (Ging and Flynn 2008). Furthermore, on the use of the body in gendered advertising, the trend of women with their hands or fingers covering their lips or mouths, implying silence and, arguably, a lack of value for what women have to say, is not one repeated in representations of men, nor is the tendency for women to be shown seductively and suggestively biting or sucking her finger, accompanied by a coy facial expression.

The sustained 1970s critique of advertising and its problematic representations of gender, and women in particular, continued into the 1980s. During this period, there was a prevailing optimism that the second-wave feminist movement of the 1960s and 1970s had sown the seeds of irreversible change, and there was much-hyped talk of the 'new man', especially in relation to his role as father. In 1987, Polly Toynbee wrote about the supposed enlightened qualities that the 'new man' possessed. These spanned emotional sensitivity and attention to detail, and a self-sacrificing ethos more commonly associated with women and mothers. However, Toynbee (1987) proposed a counter-narrative that aligned to the view that men's forays into the kitchen and the nursery had been wildly overstated. Similarly, the more accurate reality of a mostly unchanged domestic sphere was echoed two years later by Hochschild in her 1989 book *The Second Shift: Working Parents and the Revolution at Home*. She uses the phrase 'stalled revolution' to describe the 1980s phenomenon that saw more and more women taking up their place in the labour market without a corresponding redress of the share of caring and domestic responsibilities in the home between male and female partners and spouses.

Despite the material reality, advertising imagery of the 'new man' cemented his position as a cultural figurehead of the zeitgeist of the time. Emblematic of this 'new man' was the 1985 Levi's 501 'launderette' advert featuring Nick Kamen. The ad brought together two aspects most usually reserved for depictions of women in advertising; that is to say, in the 'domesticity' shown by Kamen doing his own washing, and in the objectification of the male body, represented by the tantalising 'striptease' offered by Kamen, and accompanied by the salacious and lustful glances of the women present in the launderette. As Nixon (1997) notes in his discussion of 'regimes of masculinity' concerning male advertising professionals, the 'new man' in advertising imagery and his displays of variant forms of masculinity were deeply wrapped up in the subjective masculine identities of advertising practitioners and creatives themselves. Whatever the etymology of the 'new man', the unrealised figure of the progressive nurturer and homemaker soon morphed into the narcissistic 'metrosexual'. As Beynon (2002) points out, of the two strands of new mannism that existed up until the 1990s—the new-man-as-narcissist and the new-man-as-nurturer—only the former survived. In the early 1990s, the perceived emasculation and sexual objectification of the new man gave rise to a new set of images and discourses in the form of Lad Culture, which attempted, albeit often through strategies of self-mocking and defensive irony, to repackage modern masculinity through tropes of working-class manhood and ironic sexism. Lad Culture unfolded as a response to the feminism of the 1970s, and the gains made by women in the public sphere throughout the 1980s, and marked a push against 'new mannism' and the style magazines that the 'metrosexual' was reading, as well as railing against the new social adherence to a so-called 'political correctness'.

From the late 1980s and into the 1990s, before postfeminism and Lad Culture took hold, the spotlight began to move away from an exclusive focus on problematic imagery of women, and turn towards constructions of masculinity, through exploring representations of men and masculinity in media and advertising, as well as issues of masculinity, hegemony, and domination (Kimmel 1987; Craig 1992; Fejes 1992; Sedgwick 1995; Pfeil 1995; Savran 1998; Connell 1987, 1990; Hanke 1998). As Barthel (1992) points out, neither masculinity nor femininity are either mysterious or assumed, unchanging givens. Both are bound up in practices of consumption, and have been differentially defined through advertising over time. As definitions of appropriate gender expressions and behaviours change, so too does advertising's reflection of that. Referring to the specifics of the typical 'man's fashion suit' advert, Barthel suggests that its exaggerated associations of masculinity to power and wealth are in response to 'the very real threat of women invading ... centers of power ... [which] makes social construction, and perpetual *re-construction* of masculinity so important' (1992, p. 140). Barthel identifies themes of 'masculine nostalgia', which advertisements evoke through displays of boyhood fantasies of escape, adventure, and sporting success. In essence, this represents a world uncomplicated by the presence of women and girls. Concluding that the 'meaning of masculinity is neither predetermined nor hidden from view... [that it] can be altered, shaped and molded' (1992, p. 153), it is clear that advertising is one of the more influential ways that masculinity and, indeed, femininity are formed and constructed.

The patriarchal constructions of masculinity and femininity found in advertising texts have been retained since the onset of postfeminism, and in fact have cemented a distinct polarisation of the sexes' narrative (Ging 2009). While postfeminism is a slippery concept to define, it is clear that unlike feminism it is not a coherent political movement or a cohesive ideology (Tasker and Negra 2007). Rather it can be understood as a periodising concept—the era after feminism—and/or as a dominant set of gender-political values. A number of key scholars have been to the fore in advancing feminist critiques of postfeminist culture, the most significant being Whelehan (2000), Levy (2006), McRobbie (2007), Tasker and Negra (2007), and Gill (2007, 2008, 2009a, b, 2016). Tasker and Negra (2007) note that the shift from feminism to postfeminism has marked a change in course from the political to the cultural, and that understanding postfeminism entails recognising that the domain of culture is now centre stage in the struggle for gender equality, echoing radical feminist concerns of the 1970s. They contend that postfeminism is a 'concept and a cultural phenomenon (which) repays close interrogation' (p. 6) because of its ubiquity across all media platforms. According to the authors, postfeminism is 'a set of assumptions, widely disseminated within popular media forms, having to do with the 'pastness' of feminism, whether that supposed pastness is merely noted, mourned, or celebrated' (p. 1). Furthermore, the influence of postfeminism must be understood at a time when there is ample evidence of rolling back on women's rights.[1]

Whether it continues to be helpful to apply ideas of postfeminism to the contemporary period, particularly in light of the emergence of feminism's fourth wave (Rivers 2017), is contested. In answer, Gill (2016) defends the concept of postfeminism as an appropriate analytical tool for interrogating the current climate. Consequently, when referring to postfeminism and postfeminist cultures throughout, the term is used in its analytical capacity and on the understanding that it encompasses a number of features that combine to construct this notion—something that Gill contends remains relevant (2016, 2017). Broadly, postfeminism encapsulates a number of key characteristics. In its earliest iteration, postfeminism emerged from what has been called the 'backlash' (Faludi 1992); that is to say, cultural talking points that centred around accusatorially jabbing the finger at second-wave feminists for deluding women about the possibilities for and desirability of societal change. Postfeminism is also simultaneously characterised by a return to assumptions of 'natural', biological, and genetically determined differences between the sexes (in other words, a supposedly tongue-in-cheek 'war of the sexes'), as well as a fervent rejection of women as 'victims', as evidenced, for example, in the hugely popular 'Women Against Feminism' Tumblr that began in 2013, and which repeatedly reiterates the view from the mostly young women contributing to the site that they are against feminism because 'I am not a victim'. This stance sits alongside assumptions that equality for women has already been achieved. Such an assumption is aided by the undeniable gains of women in many fields and professions. However, McRobbie (2004) argues that this masks the problematic reality that women may be afforded such opportunities because it is 'good for business'. In other words, advances made by women are conditional on the basis that they do not challenge the patriarchal structures that tolerate them in previously male-reserved spheres. McRobbie refers to this as the 'sexual contract' and notes that 'the new female subject is, despite her freedom, called upon to be silent, to withhold critique, to count as a modern sophisticated girl' (2004, p. 260). Similarly, her concept of 'double entanglement' refers to the distinctly postfeminist tensions and contradictions inherent in the existence of prevailing conservative social norms with respect to gender roles, sexual relations, and family, alongside discourses of supposed choice and individual freedoms, particularly in relation to an assumed sexual freedom. Postfeminism also asserts that the commodification of feminist principles and self-objectification are empowering—both of which are heavily reliant on a dominant neoliberal capitalist economic, political, and social climate, with its attendant individualisation of people's lived experiences.

All of these complex and—at times—contradictory notions of what constitutes equality and empowerment are elucidated, Gill (2017) suggests, by continuing to apply the benchmark of postfeminism to the contemporary period. In other words, the features that came to define the postfeminism of the 1990s and early 2000s continue to be present. Indeed, some hallmarks of a postfeminist gender climate, such as self-surveillance, have been further consolidated as a result of the invention and uptake of social media platforms like Instagram. Furthermore, Gill refers to the 'affective life of postfeminism', which represents the sustained emotional labour that must be undertaken by women in order for them to negotiate a culture that demands that they be charming, fun, witty, and able to articulate and present their dissatisfaction with the daily sexism they endure in acceptable and good-humoured terms. In addition, and connected to the disavowals of victimhood that were common in the postfeminist environments of the 1990s and 2000s, this continues to be present in something that Gill terms a calling-out of 'toxic insecurity'. Although, for instance, the #metoo movement against industry-wide sexism in various fields offers a counter-narrative and understanding of female oppression to postfeminism's individualised discourse, Gill's concept of 'toxic insecurity' is no less prevalent in letting women know that they must bear sole responsibility for cultivating a self-confidence, and if they fail in this, there are under no illusion that to be 'insecure' or 'needy' is to be unattractive.

As already mentioned, the phenomenon of Lad Culture emerged as a by-product of postfeminism and in response to seismic shifts in attitudes that were concerned with questioning assumptions about male superiority and privilege, and traditional gender roles. The painful renegotiation or reappropriation of masculinity that occurred following changes in gender relations throughout the 1970s and 1980s and into the 1990s places the blame for that turmoil at the feet of the feminist movement (Whelehan 2000). The disruption to traditionally prescribed modalities of masculinity caused by feminism culminated in the pervasion of a form of ironic sexism that is the founding characteristic of Lad Culture. Whelehan's analysis of Lad Culture describes the 'gang mentality of this new/old masculinity' (2000, pp. 58–59) as saturated in humour and irony. The new 'lad' of Lad Culture, in contrast to the 'new man' of the 1980s, is immature, crude, irreverent, unapologetic, and only interested in beer, football, women and sex. The discourse surrounding the emergence of Lad Culture is recognisable for its bantering, tongue-in-cheek tone. Indeed, it is only in the context of postfeminism that Lad Culture's ironic sexism could thrive, since it was premised upon the notion of equality already won as well as on the reversal of some of the core tenets of feminism, for example, in its contention that women could attain power through being sexually objectified (Ging 2009). According to Gauntlett (2002), Lad Culture in the UK emerged as a sort of jokey, ironic, self-aware dialogue with feminism, but gradually lost its ironic edge as successive groups of young men became less and less familiar with this 'backstory', and a broadly postfeminist rhetoric took over. The publication of the 'Lads Mag', with *Loaded* being the first in a string of this genre first appearing in 1994, simultaneously targeted and was responsible for promoting the 'lad'. The exclusively young, White, and heteronormative nature of the magazines came to be reflected more broadly across mainstream media in television shows like *Men Behaving Badly*, which ran on British television right throughout the 1990s and from 1992 to 1998 (Whelehan 2000). The characters and set-ups written into the show exemplify the juvenile, beer-swilling, sexist—yet well-meaning—fun-loving 'lad'. As Ging (2005) notes, 'those who take offence at Lad Culture's sexism are accused of being humourless or of not "getting" its ironic intentions' (p. 41). This defensive, or rather offensive, tactic has served to protect retro-sexist, ironic lad humour from criticism.

Advertising's version of a masculinity heavily influenced by Lad Culture has been constructed in terms that often only make sense as a counterpoint to femininity and women—whether that is through wealth, physical strength, rebelliousness, or cultural capital. Indeed, hypermasculinity, as antithetical to femininity, remains a mainstay in advertising. Vokey, Tefft, and Tysiaczny (2013), through a content analysis of US male-targeted magazine advertising, sought to investigate the presence of hypermasculine tropes in adverts. Using Zaitchik and Mosher's (1993) understanding of hypermasculinity as characterised by 'toughness as emotional self-control, violence as manly, danger as exciting, and calloused attitudes to women and sex' (Vokey et al. 2013, p. 562), they found it to be a recurring theme, present in the majority of adverts printed in male-targeted magazines. This widespread hypermasculine motif accounted for as high as 90% of the adverts appearing in certain magazines, and more often in those magazines with a younger readership of a lower socio-economic status. As the authors note, advertising's adherence to this strong narrative is not without consequence for both men and women, primarily in terms of its sanctioning and encouragement of risk-taking and aggressive behaviours. In general, academic literature concerning representations of contemporary masculinity in advertising has tended to find evidence of a strong reaffirmation of men's superior status that is markedly counter to the social position of women (Gill 2007, 2009a; Ging and Flynn 2008; Hanke 1998).

Rosalind Gill's work on contemporary advertising, postfeminism, and sexualisation is fundamental to an understanding of the impact of postfeminist tropes on advertising imagery. It is often taken for granted that 'sex sells', and 'for almost as long as it has existed (advertising) has used some sort of sexual sell, sometimes promising seductive capacities, sometimes more simply attracting our attention with sexual stimuli, even if irrelevant to the product' (Pollay 1986, p. 28). However, in the 1990s, as a result of the emergence of postfeminism alongside feminist critiques of women depicted as vapid, stereotypical sex objects, changes in advertising were becoming apparent. The sexual *agency* of women became the new way to represent female sexuality and the female body. This has meant that 'since 1994 there has been a marked shift in the manner that women's bodies are depicted sexually, in ways that emphasise pleasure, playfulness and empowerment rather than passivity or victimisation' (Gill 2009b, p. 94). Gill points out that the increasing sexualisation of culture and a focus on sex generally constituted a means of release and relief after the sexual austerity imposed due to the AIDS epidemic in the 1980s. In addition, with reference to Goldman, Heath, and Smith (1991), Gill contends that changes in the strategy of advertisers in the 1990s were an answer to '"sign fatigue", to viewer scepticism, and also to the impact of feminism on lifestyles and attitudes' (2008, p. 39). This shift in advertising trends formed part of a reconstitution of the sexualised woman figure in adverts from passive terms to agentic, sexually voracious representations with feminist undercurrents of empowerment, liberation, and independence. In other words, the objectification of women in advertisements, which had been challenged by feminists, shifted to a self-objectification, giving the objectified woman a voice which sought to 'reassure' women viewers that this was in fact not demeaning but empowering. However, such 'depictions of women as active sexual subjects may be even more damaging than more traditional objectifying representations in that they seem to similarly exacerbate women's body dissatisfaction whilst also leading more strongly to self-objectification' (Malson et al. 2011, p. 97). Such 'active', rather than passive, sexual objectification of women has implications for advertising texts. As Michelle Lazar has noted, '[u]nlike advertising in earlier periods, which depicted women in obviously demeaning and sexist ways and made feminist critique of patriarchal capitalism a relatively straightforward affair, critique of postfeminist advertising is less clear-cut' (2007,

p. 160). As a result of self-objectification it becomes more difficult to call the advertising industry to task for sexist imagery.

Advertisers are much indebted to the simultaneously simplified yet contradictory manifestations of gender and gender relations that is so characteristic of postfeminism. Highlighting just one of the ten characteristics[2] of the postfeminist advert, as devised by Gill, it is advertiser's *attempts to re-eroticize gender difference,* or in other words, a return to genetic determinism that perhaps suits the needs of advertisers most. The 'repolarisation of gender identities is particularly evident in the dominance of an aggressive but allegedly ironic "gender war" rhetoric, which pervades all aspects of media culture, from *advertising copy* to radio quizzes' (Ging 2009, p. 53; emphasis added). From questionable scientific studies, to popular self-help psychology books, to light-hearted commentaries on the relations between women and men, Ging points out that the trend since the mid-to-late 1990s has been to rely on an appeal to biodeterministic and essentialist sentiments that position women and men as opposites, and as inevitably thinking, talking, and acting at cross-purposes.

Given the complexity of how the contemporary cultural context creates and frames gender discourses, coupled with the fact of continuing significant inequality between the sexes, it is untenable to claim that postfeminism merely represents a harmless rejection or even misunderstanding of feminism. Rather, it is a phenomenon that demands careful feminist critique in the face of persisting universal and material women's rights issues such as domestic violence, rape and sexual assault, gender-based violence in conflict, economic dependency, and the gender pay and pension gap, as well as minimal cultural visibility and voice afforded to women in the fields of media and entertainment. Although advertising continues to exhibit a strong postfeminist sensibility, responses to these issues have been gathering more and more voices over the past five years or so, thanks to a resurgent feminist movement. In fact, any considerations of postfeminism must acknowledge that such rhetoric has not gone unchecked. There is reason to be confident that a cultural, discursive shift is well underway, which is centred around shining a light on postfeminism and on advertising's representational treatment of the sexes. In addition to continued feminist media critique of advertising, there is currently a new wave of feminism and feminist activism. Cochrane (2013) believes that a socially and politically conscious and intersectional feminist movement has commenced. The fourth wave of feminism is outward looking in its social and political consciousness, and the media and advertising's representation of women and men, masculinity and femininity is once again firmly on the agenda.

Situating Advertisers as Cultural Intermediaries and Considering the Social Attitudes of Those Creating Media Texts

Against the backdrop that advertising's representations of gender continue to be problematic, controversial, and contested, there is far less investigation into the working practices and processes that contribute to the creation of these representations. This is significant given that such practices and processes are enacted by individual practitioners in agencies and organisations that are tasked with designing and executing media products that portray the sexes. Clearly, therefore, it is crucial to garner an insight into the people and procedures that influence how society and its members understand gender. Consequently, it is important to consider the prevailing theories concerning the influential nature of the creative and cultural industries (CCIs), as well as considering the social attitudes of the people who create media texts and why they might be significant with respect to stereotypical portrayals of the sexes in advertisements.

From the mid-1990s various academics (Nixon 1996; Mort 1996; McFall 2002; Negus 2002; Cronin 2004) sought to critique advertising in ways that moved beyond simply an examination of text and content, and instead to also account for *how* that content is produced and how creators of cultural content can be understood. In conceptualising advertisers in contemporary society as 'cultural intermediaries', theoretical and academic discussions draw on the relationship between economic structures and the cultural sphere. Such writers conceive of the lines becoming ever more blurred between the two, which some explain through the concept of 'reflexive accumulation' or 'reflexive modernity'

(Lash and Urry concept 1994; Beck et al. 1994, p. 91; cited in Nixon 2003). This idea refers to the motivation to consume being driven by increasingly informed and conscious choices, with the advertising industry at the heart of 'reflexive accumulation' because of its role in acting as cultural intermediary by using culture as a selling point. This process entails embedding goods and services with cultural references, and therefore mining the cultural landscape for specific tropes and discourses with which to adhere in order to market and advertise certain brands and products. Consequently, this involved a strategy shift in advertising that resulted in the 'emotional selling point' (ESP), which is image and lifestyle based with a focus on the consumer, overtake the 'unique selling point' (USP), with a focus on the product. Academic attention afforded to the emergence and centrality of both the ESP and cultural texts to the processes of advertising production, as explored by Nixon (1996), and Mort (1996), suggested that the industry was somehow employing a new and novel approach. As such, these authors, who were employing a practice-based perspective, sought to give due regard to what they considered was the increasing overlap between economy and culture.

McFall (2002), however, posits that this misrepresents the contemporary advertising practitioner as somehow treading new ground by straddling the economic and cultural spheres. She questions the validity of claiming contemporary advertising practitioners as 'new' cultural intermediaries, where this term is understood as bridging supposed gaps between the domains of the economy and culture. She challenges this on two fronts. Firstly, she demonstrates that the earliest advertising practices dating back to 1800 were already bound up in the artistic worlds of art and literature, thereby showing established links between the two spheres over the more-than-200-year existence of the industry. Secondly, McFall suggests that there are grounds for discarding the term 'intermediary' altogether when one considers that culture already permeates everything—social, political, and economic knowledge and experiences. The treatment of modern advertising practitioners as somehow being distinct from their predecessors in their understanding and employment, or deployment, of cultural currency for the benefit of the industry fails to recognise, per McFall, the existing historical evidence, thereby suggesting that this is not a new phenomenon. Thus, she maintains, the role of the advertising practitioner could not be positioned as cultural intermediary, since culture is, and has been, omnipresent in everything.

The problematic position concerning the notion of cultural intermediary as lacking validity is circumvented by Keith Negus' discussion of same. He believes that '[t]he central strength of the notion of cultural intermediaries is that it places an emphasis on those workers who come in-between creative artists and consumers (or, more generally, production and consumption)' (2002, p. 503). In this sense, 'intermediary' is understood in the sense that production is not simply a one-way process to consumption. It is cyclical, and both the operations of production and consumption inform each other in a mutually influencing way. The cultural intermediary, for example, embodied in the advertising practitioner, is the vehicle for this exchange. Negus talks about the 'reciprocal inter-relationship of what are often thought of as discrete 'cultural' and 'economic' practices' (Negus 2002, p. 504). He does, however, take issue with the narrow application of the term 'cultural intermediary' as including only those working in the industries commonly understood as 'cultural', such as advertising and the media. In his view, and echoing McFall, culture permeates society to a much greater extent than simply through the operations of those creative industries that are thought to trade in symbolic production. It must be considered, he argues, that other professions and occupations also act as intermediaries for cultural exchange. He gives examples of trade unionists, priests, and scientists, in addition to 'the suits' in the creative industries who may act as cultural intermediaries and who include senior managers, senior corporate executives, business analysts, and accountants. For instance, he notes, there is often longevity of the accountant figure in the creative cultural firm, resulting in these individuals sometimes becoming highly influential actors.

Negus' case for an extended definition of 'cultural intermediary' that bears with it an implicit understanding of its powerful role in shaping and influencing the consumer-citizen is especially relevant here given that many advertising students who take up work in the advertising industry will not be directly involved in creating adverts. In fact, the breakdown by department in creative, digital, and media advertising agencies as documented by the 2017 census by the Institute of Advertising Practitioners in Ireland (IAPI) (Institute of Advertising Practitioners in Ireland 2017) reveals that the creative roles account for between 17% and 19% of all positions, whereas the executive functions make up 33–35% of agency staff, meaning that the majority of students who graduate will fulfil roles that are not in the creative department. While this present study places an emphasis on the creative role in advertising practice for reasons already stated, the many students who go on to occupy roles on the executive side can still be framed as being influential to the process of mediating between culture and economy, between production and consumption, and can possess a lot of influence in, for instance, negotiating with client companies, choosing specific clients or brands with which to work, formulating a project brief, and challenging or reinforcing a particular brand vision or ethos. Hence, whether advertising students end up engaged in creative work that directly involves the design of advertising campaigns or whether they represent the account handlers or strategic planners of future practice, all such workers can be perceived to be a 'cultural intermediary'.

In elucidating on the concept, Cronin (2004) offers a helpful understanding of the cultural intermediary as one who is central to establishing society's markers for what constitutes 'success'. There has been a cultural shift, she argues, from judging people on the work we do to instead determining our 'success' by how we choose to spend the proceeds of the work we do. Therefore, the cultural intermediaries who set the parameters for what those proceeds should be spent on represent the judges of contemporary society. Or, at least, they construct the grading system that the general public uses to mark one's peers and contemporaries, bearing in mind that cultural intermediaries are also the general public, in that they are intimately bound up with both the work they are involved in producing—for example, in creating advertisements—and in the business of also being consumers themselves. In a cyclical process, similar to that posited by Negus, Cronin observes that 'in the process of producing advertising campaigns, practitioners draw on their own experience as viewers of advertisements and as consumers of products' (2004, p. 353). Likewise, Nixon urges those with an interest in interrogating advertising texts and the industry's practices to pay attention to practitioners themselves given that—what he calls—*informal cultures* 'set limits upon and provide resources for the performance of the creative executive' (2003, p. 35), which is to say that although advertisers utilise information gathered on consumer markets through such tools as focus groups and surveys, they often also rely on their 'gut', as well as their colleagues 'knowledge' of what appeals to different market segments. Consequently, assumptions made about distinct male and female markets may reflect the gendered identities and understandings of advertising practitioners. Crucially, the concept of 'cultural intermediary', as useful for positioning advertisers in this work, is inextricably tied to the phenomenon of 'informal cultures' as identified by Nixon (2003), and which relates to the fact that advertisers are heavily influenced by, and draw on their own subjective and gendered worldviews, the opinions and attitudes of their peers, and the gendered cultures operating in their agencies in order to guide creative decision-making pertaining to campaign design.

So, what is known about the subjective identities and worldviews of those working in the CCIs? Studies by Taylor and O'Brien (2017); Oakley, Laurison, O'Brien, and Friedman (2017); Hesmondhalgh (2017); Friedman, O'Brien, and Laurison (2017); and Saha (2013) shed some light on this. Indeed, in the light of controversies such as #oscarssowhite and #gamergate, which represented explosive reactions and counter-reactions to the White, male dominance of the film and gaming industries, O'Brien, Allen, Friedman, and Saha (2017) make the case for academics formulating research questions that foreground an explicit concern for how the culture industries reproduce and replicate social inequalities within their own industries. This is especially pressing given the nature of creative work in constructing and offering gendered, raced, and classed interpretations and depictions of social groups. As such, positioning and understanding creative workers as 'taste-makers' and 'cultural intermediaries', who come between the realms of production and consumption, offers the opportunity to highlight how content creators, as individual, are tied up with reworking persistent stereotypes with regard to media representations of various categories.

Likewise, in his chapter in *The Media and Class* (2017), Hesmondhalgh traces the various considerations media production analysis (MPA) might incorporate in future in order to address the underexplored issue of problematic depictions of social class in the media, particularly with a regard to media production practices and practitioners. On the issue of the misrepresentation and underrepresentation of the working class in the media,

Hesmondhalgh notes that it often mirrors sexist and stereotypical content. In what he calls the 'class asymmetry explanation', Hesmondhalgh refers to the fact that the media industries are mostly populated by middle-class people, who are tasked with constructing representations of working-class life. However, in order to articulate an in-depth understanding of the misrepresentation of the working class in the media, analyses must 'go beyond the class asymmetry explanation' (2017, p. 24). What is needed is more than just mapping the socio-economic backgrounds of those who populate the media industries, and how organisational cultures and working practices might be implicated in the replication of certain tropes with regard to how the working class is portrayed in the media. It is also imperative to 'consider *how the subjective experience of class shapes production*' (p. 22; emphasis in original)—something that has rarely been undertaken in any comprehensive manner. Furthermore, focus must be given to, as Hesmondhalgh notes, the capitalistic commercial pressures that come to bear on the media industries, some to a greater extent than others depending on the medium in question. Commercial considerations may impact on media practitioners given that the nature of for-profit-media content may lend itself to cheap-to-produce, easy, stereotypical, one-dimensional portrayals of social classes simply because it does not involve employing talented scriptwriters, directors, and copywriters. The same, arguably, may be said of representations of the sexes in advertising design and creation. Applying Bourdieu's concept of 'habitus', which describes our lifelong cultivated tastes, character, and expertise as connected to our ability (or not) to tap into 'cultural capital', Hesmondhalgh offers 'habitus' as 'a way of understanding and *explaining* the very different practices, tastes and values of different classes' (p. 30; emphasis in original). This comes to bear on the processes that shape how middle-class media producers 'choose' to represent the working class, though Hesmondhalgh points out that applying Bourdieu's class-based structural ideas to explain such phenomena must not be at the expense of exploring individual responsibility and divergence from expectations.

A focus on individual attitudes is at the centre of Taylor and O'Brien's (2017) study, which surveyed almost 2500 creative workers' attitudes about supposed meritocracy in the CCIs. The authors offer a stark assessment of the progress that needs to be made in order for the gap to close between what creative workers 'know' to be true about inequalities in the creative industries and what they 'believe' to be true. In other words, despite extensive media attention given to, and social discourse in recent years concerning the sharper focus on social issues pertaining to representations, visibility, and harassment in the cultural and media industries with regard to minority ethnic groups and women, creative workers appear to be lacking in self-reflexivity about the attitudes they hold about inequalities and barriers to advancement in the sector being at odds with that reality. The authors offer a counter-argument to Richard Florida's (2002) contested conception of the creative class as a dynamic, progressive, and open-minded group of people. The findings of their study, conversely, reveal that creative workers are not any more fair-minded or liberal than the general population, and in fact exhibit neoliberal-influenced attitudes about succeeding on merit and talent alone, despite being aware of the structural barriers and inequalities that persist in the industries in which they work. In fact, regardless of the socio-economic background, sex, or race of their survey respondents, 'almost everyone believes that hard work, talent, and ambition are essential to getting ahead, while class, gender, ethnicity, and coming from a wealthy family are not' (Taylor and O'Brien 2017, p. 17). They did, however, find that White, affluent males were most likely to harbour that belief.

Similarly, in a robust critique of Richard Florida's thesis regarding the 'creative class', Peck (2005) unpacks some assumptions made by Florida about the kinds of people that creatives supposedly embody. Primarily, it is the conceit that creatives crave a tolerant and open societal environment in which to live and work that Peck rejects. His issue with Florida's conceptualisation of the creative class tallies with Taylor and O'Brien's (2017) contention that symbolically constructing creative types as possessing a supposed higher regard for social justice, equality, and diversity than the wider general population is not borne out in the facts. In other words, CCI workers cluster among the middle and upper classes tend to be male, and White, and harbour more traditional, and sometimes discriminatory, assumptions about gender and class than is immediately apparent. The precarity and insecurity of much creative work, which is, to Peck's assessment, embraced by such workers, serves to delegitimise the existence of trade unions and the importance of a political underpinning of labour. This depoliticisation of the creative class is suggestive that their outward expression of adhering to principles of equality and fairness is more lip service and a reflection of wanting to self-present as liberal and progressive than to do with any socially and politically engaged concern for injustice, marginalisation, and oppression. Thus, contrary to the reality of the CCIs being populated by relatively elite and privileged people, the impression that persists is very different—which is to say that the myth of the creative sector as populated by people from all walks of life does not align with the statistics.

While Oakley et al. (2017) found that women are, in fact, well represented in the advertising and marketing sector in London compared with other creative industries, with a percentage of 45.6% across the UK according to figures obtained from data collected by the Labour Force Survey quarterly report (2013–2015), BAME (Black, Asian and minority ethnic people) accounted for just 6.8% of those working in the advertising and marketing field. In addition, just over 30% of those populating the advertising and marketing field are from a privileged background (far higher than the national UK labour force coming from an elite background totalling 13.7%). Simply put, whether male or female, those working in advertising are predominantly from upper and middle classes—something that is significant given the fact that the average earnings in the industry are far above the national UK average salary and resulting in a disproportional spread of higher incomes in the CCIs going to workers already from well-off backgrounds.

The issue of race, as regards the social attitudes of those creating media texts, is likewise important to consider. Saha's (2013) work echoes O'Brien et al. (2017) in acknowledging that, although 'symbol creators' and creative workers may often be acutely aware of the politics of representation and are deeply uncomfortable with their role in perpetuating a White, male, middle-class status quo, they often feel they cannot resist playing their part in constructing women, gay, and BAME groups as 'Other'. Saha's interrogation into the temptation and tendency to capitulate to racial and ethnic 'other'-producing representations and portrayals is the focus of her case study of the play *Curry Tales* by the British theatre company Rasa, founded by Rani Moorthy, a South Asian actress and writer. She investigates the processes and decision-making tensions that ethnic-minority and diasporic writers, directors, and producers must traverse in creating cultural content loaded with symbolic meaning about one's community. Indeed, the nuanced and subversive content of the play itself is at odds with the promotional and marketing materials that conversely were suggestive of stereotypical tropes connected to Asian women.

While not charging Rasa with cynicism as regards manipulating and commodifying a White understanding of 'Asianness' simply in order to promote ticket sales, Saha does suggest that the express and conscious decision to promote the production through imagery that was counter to the narratives woven through the play can be explained by reference to a number of considerations. For example, Rasa seems to have well understood that appealing to as wide an audience as possible necessitated pandering, in a sense, to an expected version of Asianness. In this instance, it is embodied in the image that appears in the advertising material of the Asian woman cooking curry. The justification for adopting this approach on the part of the play's creators is in the contention that getting people in through the door, in some respect under a false pretence, is paramount. Once people are in attendance at the theatre, there is at least some chance that they will read the play in the ways intended—which is to say, in its emphasis on defying rather than perpetuating stereotypes. However, argues Saha, this is a problematic assumption to make, not least because those who would have seen the advertisements for the play would far outnumber those who attended the play, and also because the audiences' readings are difficult to quantify and interpret. In other words, the question of whether the play's audience fully and consciously understand that the stereotypical tropes used in the marketing materials in ways that play with racial stereotypes are not borne out in the play's content remains unanswered. In addition to getting people to see the play, Saha notes that the 'blame' for the Orientalist (and perhaps sexist) marketing strategy employed for *Curry Tales* cannot be placed solely on Rasa but is partly explained through a political economy lens when considering the need to 'sell' the play and satisfy their funders, the Arts Council England, which is to say that commercial pressures and also the pressure to deliver something that is expected hinder the creation of symbolic content that resists and challenges perceived assumptions about a particular social group. This is likely echoed too in the advertising industry.

In addition to social class and race, the gendered attitudes of cultural workers are also a central consideration. Acknowledging that little attention has been paid to the workers and working conditions of those in the CCIs, Conor, Gill, and Taylor (2015) contextualise such work in terms of its precariousness and insecurity supposedly mitigated by the personal rewards begot from creative employment. Echoing Taylor and O'Brien's (2017) critique of Florida's (2002), albeit now revised, contention of creative work as characterised by meritocracy, a rejection of conventional work practices and hierarchies, and a preference for working alongside people from varied backgrounds, Conor et al. likewise note that such an assumption about creative workers' supposed respect for diversity is at odds with the inequalities that persist in the culture industries. Women, they contend, 'are consistently faring worse than men. This is true in *advertising*, the arts, architecture, computer games development, design, film, radio and television' (Conor et al. 2015, p. 6; emphasis added). Indeed, non-traditional working practices, which extend to recruitment in the CCIs, serve to marginalise women further, given that a word-of-mouth system of recommendation for open posts favour men who have connections with other men already embedded in the industry. In other words, the relative lack of women across the CCIs is only perpetuated by a networking approach to hiring, which sees men propose other males for vacant positions. This reality is obscured by a culture of individual self-promotion that accompanies such work and an assertion that passion alone and a will to 'Do What You Love' (Conor et al. 2015, p. 2) is all that is required to succeed in the creative space. On that basis, if women are not securing creative work, it is a negative reflection on their desire and drive to be involved in these industries. This emphasis on self-promotion and constructing a 'brand' for oneself is more contentious for women than men, given the mythic recognition of the creative worker as being male. Nevertheless, the tension inherent for women self-presenting as a creative type is effectively denied by the acceptance of the CCIs as representing a field that differs from more traditional, male-dominated prestigious art forms in that 'the capacity for creative work is assumed to be widespread, extending to (raced, classed, gendered) categories of people who were traditionally excluded from "high culture". This, of course, is one basis for myths of equality and diversity in the CCI' (Conor et al. 2015, p. 5).

Therefore, investigating and analysing the people who work in the creative industries, their subjective identities and worldviews, and the organisational cultures and working practices that operate is vital in the quest to get to the heart of what ails these fields and how change might be brought about.

Encoding Gender in Media Texts: Organisational Considerations and Implications for Advertising Students

In addition to considering the social attitudes of cultural workers at the level of the individual, it is also important to interrogate the organisational logics in which they are embedded and how these might be tied to the persistence of stereotypes and the process of encoding gender in media texts. However, the processes that facilitate the encoding of gender in media texts remain a mystified phenomenon. Nevertheless, it is clear that media production is characterised by 'complexities and tensions' (van Zoonen 1994, p. 43), which should be given due consideration, as should the 'personal, organizational and commercial' (1994, p. 46) factors, such as prevailing social discourses, professional codes of conduct, or the chain of command one's decisions—creative or otherwise—must pass through. This is to say that there are micro-/meso-/and macro-determinants shaping the nature of media content. At the level of micro-/individual producers of media texts, feminist media work on production has converged on accounts of women's experience in the field. This work has crucially shined a spotlight on a number of important issues, such as the dearth of women in specific types of roles in media organisations,[3] as well as cultural factors that prove immensely challenging for women media professionals. These factors reflect wider societal attitudes to women, and especially to women working in, heretofore, male-dominated fields. A further challenge women have traditionally had to face in media work is sexist treatment by their male colleagues—sometimes strikingly overt, but often couched in more engrained and endemic displays of gender bias and discrimination. Such considerations must account for the point at which the experience of gender at the individual level converges with organisational components.

Organisational considerations are central to understanding media production, since cultural workers go through a 'process of adaptation' which is 'brought about not by repressive force but by a subtle process of rewards and punishment' (van Zoonen 1994, p. 56). For instance, as Windels and Mallia (2015) note, female advertising creatives are held back from advancing in their careers as a result of organisational cultures that reward traditional masculine styles of work and workplace behaviour. In practice, workers are socialised into agency cultures through a system of 'organisational learning' that is upheld by 'collective social actions in a community of practice' (p. 3). Such learning necessitates being 'able to "read" the situation and act in ways that are valued by other members of the community… Members must learn how to talk and act in the manner of full participants' (Windels and Mallia 2015, p. 7). Since what are valued in the male-dominated 'community' of advertising creative departments are typically masculine characteristics, it consequently proves more challenging for women creatives to 'learn' and therefore succeed and progress. In applying situated learning theory to the career progression of female creative advertisers, the pressure to conform to normative male-defined actions, behaviours, and communication styles also affects women's work identity (Windels and Mallia 2015, p. 9; referencing Salminen-Karlsson 2006, pp. 34–35). This not only impacts creative women's ability to fit in with their male peers, but can result in a fragmented work persona that may have a negative consequence on their moving from lesser positions to more powerful ones.

Crucially, such theories around socialisation and organisational learning have been utilised by Windels and Mallia in ways that allow for the link to be made between the educational and professional spheres. Particularly, they set out four different phases of assimilation into creative department's 'communities of practice'. Beginning with 'pre-peripheral experiences' (2015, p. 13), advertising students are on the cusp of becoming members of the 'community' of professional creatives. However this is a phase of membership that is based on assumptions of what it may be like to take up work as part of a creative team. Such assumptions are not informed by an awareness of the gendered dynamics, organisational environment, and gender norms that form the backdrop of much advertising creative work. Rather, as Windels and Mallia find, students are 'positive about their pre-peripheral experiences in school… (which) "didn't feel like a boys' club"' (2015, p. 14). However, despite students' somewhat misplaced optimism about creative work, the pre-peripheral phase sees students start to 'identify as community members' (p. 14) and to formulate a burgeoning professional identity. Once the advertising student takes up work in the industry, the other three phases of assimilation are enacted: the 'peripheral' level of membership, at which point practitioners learn the ways of the agency, which, as discussed, is heavily determined by gender. Next is the stage of 'progressing from the periphery' (p. 18), which is populated by creatives who are progressing up the professional ladder and have successfully demonstrated an adherence to agency codes and rules. And, finally, the level of 'reaching the centre' (p. 21) entails being a full member of the community.

The dearth of women at the 'centre' of advertising creative departments tallies with Windels and Mallia's assertion that '[b]ecause of gender, many informants did not feel they were recognized as competent members of the community' (2015, p. 16). Van Zoonen (1994) also contended, over 20 years previously, that it is critically important to examine issues of 'professional socialization' and 'shared set(s) of professional values'. She found, for instance, that, despite the existence of feminist-oriented modules in journalism education in the 1980s, the wider 'message that students were given was (that) feminism – even moderately defined – and professional journalism were at odds with each other and this message was reinforced by the experience during internship' (1994, p. 57). For the most part, female journalists tended to shed their feminist values when they transitioned into their professional lives as a consequence of the decidedly unfeminist organisational cultures into which they had entered. Further, as van Zoonen notes, '[a]lready at the level of education … the process of adjusting to professional norms tends to reaffirm a conservative status quo' (1994, p. 57), meaning that students are less likely to enact feminist positions in practice than hypothetically or ideally.

Louise North's (2010, 2015) research into the need and subsequent establishment of gender units in journalism educational modules sounds a somewhat more optimistic tone than van Zoonen. She considers the positive impact that can result on students preparing for a career in mass communication from having specific modules on gender issues during the course of their education. Indeed, although researching in the area of journalistic practices and journalism education, both North's (2010, 2015) and Oakham's (2006) work raises interesting issues regarding the socialisation of 'trainees' or students, as well as educational reluctance to centre gender within instructional courses or modules. In the absence of literature that deals specifically with advertising education and the issue of gender, and also considering the fact that many advertising courses are positioned within journalism and mass communication (JMC) schools,[4] thereby meaning that students of advertising and students of journalism may share modules, both authors are here referenced on the basis that their work allows parallels to be drawn between advertising education and journalism education.

Oakham (2006) examines the socialisation of new/trainee journalists and the role of the trainer in the process of embedding certain working practices in students. Changes in journalistic practices and associated pressures have resulted in a shift in the self-perception of the role— currently more accurately perceived as one that straddles between performing a role that is socially meaningful and understanding journalism work as producing a 'commodity'. In a more diluted sense, there are perhaps parallels here with advertising students, specifically with regard to the belief that journalism is a vocation and therefore difficult to 'teach' echoing discourses of the innateness of 'creativity' and creative skills needed for advertising work. Oakham notes that 'trainers make the distinction between what they can teach and what they cannot teach. The "it" factor often becomes the difference' (2006, p. 191). In this way, the notion of instructing and training a new generation of journalists is an ideologically loaded one that is mirrored with advertising educators. For starters, educators, trainers, and lecturers 'play a key role in the socialisation of the new entrant' (Oakham 2006, p. 183) and yet 'trainers appear to be unclear whether their role is to perpetuate existing norms and practices or to be the implementers of change and innovation' (Oakham 2006, p. 184). In a revealing quote by one educator that Oakham interviewed, the participant comments on the 'traditional approach' to journalism training, which is more aligned with the innate view of journalistic practice: 'This tradition could be said to be sexist, patriarchal and anti-intellectual. Then there is what I call the credential approach … It is underpinned by notions of incremental skill-building' (Oakham 2006, p. 191). This trainer admits: 'Yes, we are trying to create journalists in our own image' (Oakham 2006, p. 191). As such, Oakham notes that such a perspective of mentor-mentee relationship is at odds with emphasising the need for students to be self-reliant self-starters adequately equipped to push for change.

In respect of the distinct lack of gender issues embedded in journalism education, North (2010) believes that to omit gender as a central issue of concern, whether as a consideration for gendered practices of journalism work, gendered work cultures, and/or the gendered content being produced by journalists, is to do a disservice to journalism students. It is imperative, North suggests, that educators raise the issue of women working in newsrooms and the unique gender challenges faced so that they may be 'much better prepared and able to challenge inequity or at least be aware that it is a structural problem rather than an individual failing' (2015, p. 177). This squares precisely with Mallia (2008), who appeals to advertising educators to be open with students about the bias in favour of male creatives working in the industry. Sounding a positive, but cautious note, North suggests that '[g]radual change can take place in news organizations if its workers are more informed' (2015, p. 182)—something that could be claimed for advertising agencies also. However, as she intimates, the biggest barrier to shaping more gender-sensitive and gender-aware students remains the relative paucity of academics with the requisite enthusiasm, knowledge, and motivation to provide a critique and challenge to the industry.

Whatever the link between education and practice, O'Brien et al. (2017) are critical of the CCIs' industry-wide and organisational responses to inequality, which has largely been one of devising policies that aim at increasing the diversity of its employees. This, the authors assert, is too simplistic. The mere presence of more women and minority ethnic groups of people creating cultural content will not necessarily result in representations and portrayals in media that are less stereotypical and one-dimensional. This is because a proportionally better mix of cultural workers that deviate from the ubiquitous White, middle-class, male does not, on its own, wash away the systemic and institutionally embedded power structures that determine production, representation, and consumption. Indeed, in the vein of Roland Barthes' conceptualisation of 'myth' as resulting in the naturalising of contemporary realities—be that the gendered order, or essentialised assumptions concerning race, or the supposed inevitability of class inequalities—such taken-for-grantedness about the way the world is structured through patriarchal, neoliberal capitalist systems are not easily overturned by creative workers—no matter how 'enlightened', aware, or concerned they may be about their own role in reproducing and legitimising social, political, and economic hierarchies. Black et al. (2017) likewise offer a critique of the discourses that circulate around women's empowerment in the media industries and the sentiments summed up by the inspired attempts of Sheryl Sandberg's *Leaning In* to promote cultural change in organisations. The authors, in reference to the media industries of journalism, advertising, and public relations, express dismay at the tone and themes that typified a series of lecture talks on the subject of women's careers in media and communication. In particular, they took issue with how the female speakers replicate binary and stereotypically gendered assumptions about the differential 'strengths' of the sexes. In addition, the speakers' contention that, on an individual basis, women's grit and determination, talents and skills, and having the right attitude can ensure success elides the experiential reality of masculine workplaces, which need to be culturally dismantled for meaningful change to occur with respect to women's career progression, development, and advancement in these industries.

Gendered Working Cultures in Advertising and the Creative Role

The experiential reality of masculine workplaces has been highlighted by empirical research providing insights into gendered advertising working practices and cultures, and gendered identities and approaches to creative work. Nixon (2003), Gregory (2009), Cronin (2004), Alvesson (1998), Nixon and Crewe (2004), and Windels and Mallia (2015), among others, have greatly advanced understanding in this sphere. In particular, their scholarly work identifies explicitly and implicitly hypermasculine working practices that thrive in the organisational cultures present in advertising agencies. Consequently, these authors offer an interesting perspective on the gendered cultures that must be navigated by practitioners working, producing, and creating advertisements in the industry. In particular, the role of the creative in advertising production, and how and why there are gendered understandings and assumptions about creative work are prioritised because of the central role of the creative in thinking up and executing advertising content (Soar 2000).

Hesmondhalgh and Baker (2015), in exploring the issue of cultural production and sex-role segregation, identify a particular challenge for women in media and cultural work. This relates, they argue, to how stereotypes have led to and reaffirm assumptions about the natural capacities of women and men as they pertain to cultural work. Such assumptions can belie the gains made by women or men in certain segregated industries and/or roles. The negative social impact of specific roles in cultural work tending towards an either/or between women and men is such that 'work segregation by sex both draws upon, and in turn contributes to, social "stereotypes" which limit women and men's freedom and recognition – reinforcing the problem of gendered occupational segregation' (Hesmondhalgh and Baker 2015, p. 25). They highlight the dearth of academic inquiry into sex segregation in the cultural industries, mentioning Nixon's 2003 study on creative advertising practitioners as an exception, and suggest that both in training and in practice, cultural work and role differentiation within the cultural sphere need to be formulated as gender neutral. However, the reality of working in the advertising industry is far from gender neutral and instead has been found to be highly and aggressively gendered, and one skewed towards masculine norms and a masculine ethos. This shapes and influences practices and decisions made in advertising work (Windels and Lee 2012), which is significant for the fact that

> [i]n an industry such as advertising, where half the workforce is female and many products advertised are aimed at female consumers, women are still unable to alter the prevailing ethos or the types of advertisements created.

This illustrates just how powerful and resistant to change male cultures are. (Gregory 2009, p. 338)

Alongside sexist attitudes and essentialist assumptions of advertising work, the unique working practices that operate in the advertising industry have proved worthy of careful examination and critique. Creative industries such as advertising may be viewed, as has already been discussed, as progressive, modern, exciting, fast paced, and adapting to changes in society, especially when compared with the more formalised, 'stuffy', perceived conservative nature of other industries, such as banking and finance. However, the reality is much less so, and in fact, 'old productivist ideas of work persist within the so-called "creative economy"' (Nixon and Crewe 2004, p. 132). This, coupled with an imposed informality, leads to untypical work practices that seem to not only tolerate but promote hypermasculine behaviours. Boisterous interactions, showing-off, and mockery spill over into sexist banter with both male and female colleagues. Throughout Nixon's 2003 UK study with advertising practitioners, he notes that 'practices that would have been seen as unprofessional in other occupations were condoned within this area of creative employment' (Nixon and Crewe 2004, pp. 134–135). Consistent with Nixon's study that the supposed non-conformity of the work undertaken in the advertising industry is reflected through casual dress and untypical work practices and behaviours, Cronin's research also finds that this perception actually masks the very traditional patriarchal structures, gendered work practices, and entrenched attitudes regarding gender, class, and race prevalent in the advertising field. She recalls that:

> [o]ne female Senior Creative commented that all the advertising agencies she had worked in had been very conservative in their employment practices, reproducing a white, heterosexual, male organisation: *I think we're really insular … I think we're xenophobic, I think we're homophobic. There are twenty-two teams in this Creative department and there are 4 women. It's a boys' club. (Senior Creative 1).* (Cronin 2004, p. 353)

Allowances made for degrading, sexist, and inappropriate behaviours are justified on the basis that the nature of creative work presupposes a need for uncensored self-expression. This means that *any* form of self-expression is beyond reproach, and 'rules'—for instance, conventional codes with regard to appropriate workplace interaction between the sexes and adherence to even a semblance of political correctness—are seen as stifling. The upshot of this can contribute to a difficult working environment for women. Furthermore, the encroachment of women into those work spaces, especially those who challenge sexist behaviours, is often met with resentment for seeking to overturn the status quo. Distinctly gendered ideas of work, labour roles, and identity abound, and because of the looser, more informal structures of the creative industries, male workers often seek to reassert gendered hierarchies by way of compensation (Nixon and Crewe 2004). Alvesson (1998) posits a similar point and suggests that male advertisers might find it useful to have women in the office in more junior roles because it reaffirms men's superior status to be surrounded by subordinate women. In other words, the production of symbolic labour is problematic for men, given that it is not tangible, 'manly' work, such as working with one's hands. Therefore, the presence of women in lower-ranking roles acts as an antidote to men's anxiety about their involvement in advertising work.

Common among those working in advertising are instances of an exaggerated masculinity as found in the excessive use of drugs and alcohol and through anti-social and sometimes violent behaviours at agency events and industry award shows (Nixon 2003; Nixon and Crewe 2004). Gregory (2009), echoing this, euphemistically refers to the homosociability prevalent in the advertising industry as the 'locker room'. She charges this reality with maintaining and reinforcing entrenched gendered relations in the workforce, which negatively impact on women and discriminate in favour of men. The locker room mentality accounts for extremely low levels of representation of women at managerial and decision-making level, and as such, career progression is an issue for women in the industry. Male homosociability is constructed as

> formal and informal communication, socializing and socialization, such as male networking, male bonding and joking. It may include teasing each other sexually and the sexualization of female colleagues. Male homosociability is both planned and spontaneous and occurs in official and unofficial meetings, in hallways, at lunch and in toilets at work. (Gregory 2009, p. 131)

This type of hegemonic masculinity, present in the advertising industry, is firmly embedded within the organisational cultures of individual agencies. Perhaps more significant, according to Gregory, than the presence of men who fit the mould—that is, who conform to the narrow, reductive, and restrictive characteristics of hegemonic masculinity—are the greater numbers of men who may not fit the profile but who desire to, and who continuously attempt to, adapt to the agency's masculinist norms. This thereby maintains the hegemonic, privileged nature of a particular form of masculinity, or way of being/doing maleness within advertising work. The significance of this lies in the fact that if the advertising industry tends towards the hypermasculine, then women are excluded from even trying to reach the mark, and therefore have less scope to make an influential impact. Locker room culture, as explored by Gregory, freezes women colleagues out. Men use the locker room 'facilities', which include frank, open discussions with other men, as a way to gain validation from their peers. This also results in affirmation or self-validation of their gendered, subjective, work identities. Furthermore, locker room culture manifests in masculinised displays of physicality, much like those in evidence among Nixon's research participants. These include men defining and claiming space through utilisation of bodily strength, such as playing sports, bravado regarding the use of alcohol and drugs, virility pertaining to sexuality and sexual relations with women, and sporting activities as both social and professional events. In these instances, the consequences for women practitioners shift from overt harassment to subtly being squeezed out of promotional opportunities (Gregory 2009).

All of this is significant given that creative advertising roles remain heavily male dominated on a global scale (Grow and Deng 2015)—a situation especially worthy of consideration given that these roles occupy ideologically strategic positions in the industry and given that persistent normative understandings of creative suitability to advertising work impact on the gendered division of labour. Examining how practitioners perceive of the creative process is also relevant, since such understandings have an influence on how they construct their own subjective, gendered identities. Furthermore, even while acknowledging the influential nature of other roles and functions within advertising work, as well as the control client companies have over the direction of campaign briefs, the creative role retains the capacity to shape and drive the approach, tone, and content of specific ad campaigns. For this reason, and as previously stated, the creative function is here given analytic priority over other industry roles. Soar's (2000) empirical research, which investigates ideology and meaning in advertising, focuses on how advertising creatives perceive the process of creativity. Although he does not consider the gendering of that process, his work is useful because he draws on cultural production theories that take seriously the creative as a central player:

> [T]he ad creative invents a story where none existed before. *This is why the creative is possibly the most important actor, ideologically speaking, in the production of ads.* Offering up concepts as if by magic, the ad creative's work is then reified through the routines of the agency around him. (Soar 2000, p. 421; emphasis added)

Soar's position permits a consideration of how advertiser's attitudes can shape the content of advertisements, and therefore it opens up the potential for practitioners to change predominant advertising tropes. Indeed, Soar posits that we can think of advertisements as 'the contrived and somewhat reflective communications of an obscure elite' (Soar 2000, pp. 423–424), such that 'creatives draw on their experience as consumers at least as much as any acumen they accumulate through their lives on the job' (Soar 2000, p. 427). Furthermore, they not only rely on their own tastes and interests to govern their creative decisions concerning ad production, but crucially seek the advice, opinion, and approval of colleagues. This testifies to the impact that a dearth of female creative colleagues with whom to consult can have on advertising campaign design and conceptualisation.

The relative lack of female creative advertising practitioners can be explained via a number of factors—not least the working practices and hostile gendered cultures of agencies. Koppman (2016) offers an interesting analysis of the impact of cultural capital and, what is called, *cultural omnivorousness* (referring to eclectic and diverse cultural tastes) in being a determining factor in the likelihood to apply for and obtain a creative position in the advertising industry. Of specific relevance for the discussion here is her finding that gatekeepers to those prestigious creative roles indicate that they are on the lookout for prospective colleagues that exhibit a 'shared … way of consuming culture, rather than specific shared interests. Two-thirds of my informants with experience hiring creative employees described how shared cultural omnivorousness … influenced their evaluation of potential creative skill' (Koppman 2016, p. 302). Although the focus of Koppman's article was on how middle-class socialisation promotes a diversity and eclecticism of cultural interests that benefits those from this social group in progressing in the creative roles in the ad industry, despite not necessarily being any more creative than members of any other class, and was therefore not on sex segregation in the advertising industry, or, in particular, on the disproportionately high numbers of men in creative positions as opposed to women, Koppman finds that women are not any less likely than men to obtain creative positions as a result of displaying cultural omnivorousness. Nevertheless, her finding that an ability to 'fit in' with the type of personalities that already populate the creative department—people who, according to Koppman, self-identify as 'interesting' and 'different'—may have a bearing on women who come before mostly male creative gatekeepers with a whole different set of cultural reference points and ways for engaging and consuming cultural content.

In a broader sense, Averell (2016), who formerly worked in the advertising industry and is now an independent researcher, conducted a qualitative review of women's experiences in the ad industry and carried out 20 interviews with female advertising practitioners. Primarily, Averell was interested in interrogating the masculine cultures embedded in advertising agencies, investigating if, and how, they affect women working in the industry. She found that women were keenly aware that their acceptance into the agency culture was conditional on adopting and adapting to the prevailing 'bro' culture; this echoes Koppman's (2016) discussion of the importance of 'fitting in' with other creatives and Windels and Mallia's (2015) findings about the impact of gender on 'situated learning' in creative advertising departments. This culture, much like Gregory's (2009) articulation of 'the locker room' in advertising working practices, is characterised by its laddish and immature sensibility—something reinforced by influential practitioners, in particular male CEOs, and creative directors. Averell also found that the women interviewed were likely to feel that they were merely there to support their male colleagues, a feeling especially prevalent where men dominated in the creative roles. As female colleagues they often found themselves humouring and pandering to the egos of the men around them. In essence, the findings of the research reveal that female advertisers perceive themselves as tangential—or 'on the periphery' (Windels and Mallia 2015)—to agency life and as perennial outsiders, skirting around the edges of advertising practice.

The gendered sphere of advertising work and its internalisation of postfeminist iterations of naturalised gender differences are revealed in the industry's tendency to reinforce biologically deterministic notions about women's unsuitability for creative work. The controversial remarks of British advertising executive Neil French at a conference in 2005 attest to this type of attitude: 'women don't make it to the top because they don't deserve to … they wimp out and go suckle something' (cited in Mallia 2008, p. 5). Mallia notes that, because of the uproar and backlash against French's comments, attention is being paid to the issue of women creatives in advertising. However, despite industry debates on the issue, she suggests that a significant research gap remains in '[a]cademic literature (which) is essentially void on the issue of gender bias in creative employment' (Mallia 2008, p. 6). One reason broadly posited to explain why women leave the industry relates to work practices and the valorisation of typical masculine styles of working on creative campaigns. In a comment, telling for its exasperated tone, Mallia quotes Tess Alps, chairman of PHD media in London: 'Men create the standards by which ads are judged and then go around handing out awards to each other' (Mallia 2008, p. 12). This chagrin is echoed by Mallia in her assertion that exposing such prejudice is absolutely paramount, especially with regard to future practitioners:

> Why does it matter? It profoundly impacts advertising education. Students need to know. They need to make an informed decision about embarking on a career where the potential for making it to the top is 80% less if they're female. Should we bother to teach women creative work? (Mallia 2008, p. 13)

This question of whether the 'creative boys' club begins in the classroom was posed by Windels, Lee, and Yeh in their 2010 study of 91 advertising students in a US university. Proportionally, this comprised 47 women and 44 men, in a context where, nationally, 64.9% of students undertaking JMC programmes—in which advertising is positioned—are women. They set out to find out if 'students have already developed gendered expectations about the creative department while still in college and to understand whether it affects their decision-making' (2010, p. 17). Their survey consisted of two elements: firstly, students were asked to respond to the question of whether they perceived creative positions to be male dominated or not and, secondly, to select, out of three candidates,[5] from a detailed CV who they deemed most competent to fulfil a role as a creative director. The researchers hypothesised that the male candidate would be selected more often than the female, with alternating justifications that either education was more important to suitability to the role or experience was more pertinent. On the first question, 80.2% of students correctly believed that creative positions in the industry are male dominated, with slightly more men providing that response than women, and likewise more creative students than non-creative students holding that view. However, in response to the second question concerning creative competence for the role of creative director, students' understandings of the actual dominance of men in these roles in the industry did not impact their selection choice. That is to say, there was no discernible gender divide concerning the selected candidate, with most students seeming 'to prefer the more educated candidate to the more experienced candidate' (p. 21). In their discussion of the findings, the authors credit the educators with probable equal treatment of male and female students, resulting in their knowledge that creative positions are skewed in favour of men not impacting on their understanding of creative competence. They tentatively conclude that it appears the 'creative boys club' does not begin in the educational setting. However, they add a note of caution—being that theirs was a small-scale study of one university, and that the results could be indicative of a particularly egalitarian approach within that advertising programme.

Ethical Considerations for Advertising Practitioners and Students

Windels et al.'s (2010) study and subsequent inference that the creative boy's club dominating the advertising industry does not begin in the classroom stands as an anomaly amidst the dearth of academic investigation into the area of advertising education, in general, and gender and advertising education specifically. Furthermore, there is little agreement in advertising research about the need to engage with issues of stereotyping and ethical concerns at all at the educational level (Khang et al. 2016; Banning and Schweitzer 2007; Drumwright and Murphy 2004, 2009; James et al. 1994). Nevertheless, several important research studies have been carried out on these topics.

In considering ethics in conjunction with advertising practice, there are two spheres in which ethical questions play out: the professional sphere (in terms of adherence to legal codes governing advertising content) and the realm of the personal (referring to wider, social understandings of ethical and moral considerations). In the first instance, professional codes of standards set out guidelines or manuals—usually self-regulated by the industry—to which advertisers should abide in order to comply. However, without a wider commitment by advertising practitioners to contemplate ethical dilemmas raised by advertising practice, a reliance on a 'what is legal is moral' foundation to govern decision-making culminates in practices that do not account for a plethora of such concerns raised by the work of advertising (Drumwright and Murphy 2004). Indeed, the Code of Standards as laid down by the ASAI (Advertising Standards Authority of Ireland) does not refer to the specifically ethical challenges of advertising practice. While the rules call on advertisers to 'respect the dignity of all persons … (and) respect the principle of the equality of men and women' (ASAI 2016), the code more expressly and consistently references the imperative to not cause 'offence' rather than an appeal to what is socially, morally, and ethically desirable. As such, where issues of an 'ethical' nature are discussed here, it refers to a broader concept that accounts for 'what ought to be done, not just with what legally must be done' (Cunningham 1999, p. 500; cited in Drumwright and Murphy 2004, p. 7). In other words, references to ethics, and particularly to the ethical stances of this study's research participants, encompass discourses about the social effects of advertising and its content.

Indeed, Drumwright and Murphy's (2004) research study, which involved in-depth interviews with advertising practitioners, looks at ethical considerations among advertising practitioners. Although it does not specifically refer to advertisers' engagement with considerations of representing gender roles and norms in particular ways, the study does hold relevance here in terms of what it reveals around advertisers' likelihood to even acknowledge issues that represent an ethical dimension. In positioning the research, the authors note that 'we know little about how advertising practitioners react to ethical issues when they arise' (2004, p. 7). The findings of the study suggest that, ethically speaking, participants fell into one of three categories, exhibiting the following characteristics: moral myopia, moral muteness, or moral imagination. Moral myopia is recognisable by a sort of blindness to moral considerations, which 'affects an individual's perception of an ethical dilemma' (Drumwright and Murphy 2004, p. 11). Consequently, as the authors note, it proves especially challenging for these types of practitioners to make ethical decisions. The authors identify six categories of moral myopia, which represent how practitioners justify and understand their disregard for ethical implications of advertising and their actions. These include the supposition that *consumers are smart* and would easily recognise and disregard problematic advertising content. Drumwright and Murphy point out that it is an unusual position to take given that advertising is supposed to be adept at convincing consumers to buy into the message of the advertisement. Secondly, those practitioners with moral myopia displayed a tendency to *pass the buck*, in which responsibility is displaced to society, such that the advertiser makes a claim to be merely mirroring social relations that already exist, whether problematic or not. Responsibility is also shifted to the client company that commissioned the campaign. There was also the defence that *what is legal is moral*, and therefore anything within the remit of legislation and codes of practice was acceptable. Participants of their study also invoked the *first amendment* article, which raises the issue of their right to free speech, freedom from censorship, and freedom of creative expression. Drumwright and Murphy also identify the phenomenon of *going native* and the *ostrich syndrome*, which involve, respectively, wholesale adherence to the client company's brand ethos, without regard or room for ethical consider-ations, and also sticking one's head in the sand and effectively ignoring obvious moral issues.

Moral muteness, on the other hand, is characterised by the recognition of ethical issues. However, despite such acknowledgement, the individual remains silent on them. There are four categories of moral muteness. *Compartmentalisation* involves the ability to effectively leave one's con-science at the office door when going to work and picking it up again when one leaves work. It is aided by the enjoyable aspects of the work. Indeed, '[c]reativity was viewed by our informants as a chief virtue' of advertising work (Drumwright and Murphy 2004, p. 14). Then there was the sentiment that *the client is always right* and the advertising prac-titioner could not and would not challenge the client company on its desired direction. Additionally, practitioners exhibiting moral muteness believe that *ethics is bad for business*. For example, '[o]ne particularly strong disincentive was that ethics was viewed as a conservative con-straint, a sentence to blandness in advertising messages' (Drumwright and Murphy 2004, p. 15). Finally, there was the fear of opening up *Pandora's Box* if one began to let moral and ethical considerations take its place in work practices and decisions.

The third and final category of advertising practitioner showed a moral imagination. These are referred to as 'seeing, talking' advertising practi-tioners. They appreciate ethical concerns and make nuanced decisions and choices guided by these concerns. Taking into account all three cat-egories of advertising practitioner and their relationship to ethics, it was found that organisational culture, above all else, played a key role in terms of into which of the categories people were likely to fall. Drumwright and Murphy's recognition that the findings of their study hold profound implications for educators therefore has relevance to this present work. They believe that 'educators should expose and sensitize students to ethi-cal questions and dilemmas that they are likely to encounter as practitio-ners' (2004, p. 21). In addition, '[t]o combat moral muteness and moral myopia, students must also understand the issues of organizational cul-ture and climate that encourage ethical behaviour' (2004, p. 21). It is also incumbent on educators to empower students to challenge advertising practices, and should take place, they argue, in the beginning phases of an advertising student's training.

Tuncay Zayer and Coleman's (2015) study on ethics and 'advertising professionals' perceptions of the impact of gender portrayals on men and women' (p. 264) is similarly innovative in bringing together the two research components of gender and advertising practice. They note that much academic critique of advertising sets out to expose its social impact, while not accounting for ethical concerns at the individual level of the advertising practitioner. They acknowledge that

> professionals perceptions[6] occur within the context of broader institutional forces and are based largely on assumptions professionals hold about gender and vulnerability in society. (p. 264)

Using Drumwright and Murphy's studies as templates—particularly as they related to explorations of practitioners and ethics—their research participants were asked to comment on the extent to which they felt men and women were differentially affected by gender portrayals in advertising. Mirroring the three categories identified by Drumwright and Murphy (2004), the authors uncovered four such categories from the analysis of their data. Firstly, there were *silent professionals*, which lines up with Drumwright and Murphy's category 'moral myopia', characterised by a moral blindness. Then there were those who fell into the *Men are from Mars, Women are from Venus* category. 'These informants clearly not only draw from discourses of gender and vulnerability in society but they also rely on the taken-for-granted notions of gender prevalent in their institutions' (p. 268). Tuncay Zayer and Coleman argue that, although it is somewhat desirable that advertisers would demonstrate recognition of feminist-related concerns about portrayals of women in advertising, these practitioners were thought to be buying into a discourse that posits women as susceptible to social pressures, while men are not. The third category identified refers to those professionals who *Talk the Talk* and who 'demonstrate awareness that advertising images may negatively affect both male and female audiences' (2015, p. 269). However, similar to 'moral muteness', they do not follow their convictions, citing organisational, career progression, or client company's constraints on what they can or cannot and will or will not do. Finally, those who *Walk the Walk* align with Drumwright and Murphy's conception of having a 'moral imagination'. These practitioners 'expressed a moral responsibility in making ethical advertising choices' (p. 270).

Once again, organisational cultures and working practices are thought to dictate practitioner categorisation, as are personal views held with respect to confused understandings of gender, sexuality, and sex. The authors expand on this: 'we find in our study that some ad professionals adhere to institutional norms and shared understandings in their agencies that promote hegemonic masculine discourses, particularly as regulation with regard to gender portrayals in advertising is lacking' (p. 271). In addition, they argue that '[h]istorical discourses of vulnerability … have not only dichotomized gender and positioned women as particularly vulnerable (Coleman 2012) but also reinforced conceptualizations of men as immune and women as susceptible to the influence of advertising' (p. 272). On an optimistic note, their findings revealed that some advertising practitioners were mindful of their role in potentially perpetuating unhelpful gendered imagery.

As an update to their 2004 study Drumwright and Murphy (2009) extended their scope to include academic, as well as industry-wide, perspectives on advertising ethics. In positioning the research, they note that '[w]hile advertising ethics has been recognized for some time as a mainstream topic (Hyman, Tansley, and Clark 1994), research is thin and inconclusive in many important areas' (2009, p. 85). However, they point to the fact that there are difficulties in getting advertising practitioners to buy into advertising research that relates to its ethical concerns, perhaps because of an anti-intellectual bias. A quote from their study by an industry leader is telling:

> I think that having academics give recommendations on how to conduct business in the real world is a waste of time … I think there is a big disconnect between how the academic world sees the world and how the world really is. (Drumwright and Murphy 2009, p. 99)

In terms of how advertising academics and educators position ethics on their courses, it ranged from important to perfunctory. The dilemma for educators is such that '[o]ur responsibility is to teach students that they do have a choice in how to communicate with people' (Drumwright and Murphy 2009, p. 92). Yet, '[b]ecause we're churning out professionals to be effective in this business, we don't want to be, in a sense, planting tremendous doubts about the efficacy about what we're doing' (Drumwright and Murphy 2009, p. 93)—thereby echoing the dilemma faced by the journalism trainers in Oakham's (2006) research. Furthermore, it is seen that there is a challenge in encouraging students to apply critical skills without 'turn(ing) out people who will only take on idealistic clients' (Drumwright and Murphy 2009, p. 93). In addition, it was recognised that there is a problematic conflation of law and ethics in undergraduate modules, and furthermore that, with limited resources and time, the focus is often on practice-oriented modules rather than on exploring the theoretical implications of advertising, such as ethics. Therefore, ideally, a 'systematic approach to incorporating ethics into the curriculum would be expected to involve more than part of one course' (Drumwright and Murphy 2009, p. 93). It was concluded that, as per their 2004 study, organisational culture was the key to 'mitigating the barriers to ethical decision-making and encouraging ethical sensitivity' (Drumwright and Murphy 2009, p. 99).

Expanding on the understanding of ethics in the professional and educational sphere, a 1994 study by James, Pratt, and Smith explored practitioner and student perspectives on ethics, which were found to be markedly divergent: '[w]hen compared with students, practitioners are significantly less likely to agree that [a]dvertising agencies' practices, for the most part are based on high professional standards' (James et al. 1994, p. 79). This aligns with Windels and Mallia's (2015) discussion of advertising student's hypothetical 'knowledge' of advertising practice during their 'pre-peripheral' phase being one of optimistic idealism. James et al. conclude that students place a greater emphasis on the importance of ethics to advertising work. However they tentatively suggest, similar to van Zoonen (1994), that following the transition from student into professional life, working practices and the reality of working at an advertising agency curb students' more idealised regard for ethics. The challenge to respond in ethically informed ways to advertising work has resulted in the establishment of advertising standards and codes. These codes usually comprise a rule book of sorts, devised by industry representatives, and to which advertisers adhere, on a self-regulated, voluntary basis. This response has proved divisive, with some arguing that 'such codes may not improve the professionalism and practice of advertising ... (while) [s]upporters, on the other hand, contend that the rationale for such codes is to help the industry distinguish what precisely is wrong from what is right' (James et al. 1994, p. 72). Whatever one's position on that point, James et al. contend that through conscious engagement with regard to ethical considerations, practitioners can pre-empt challenges and act appropriately. Furthermore, they maintain that 'to help prepare advertising practitioners to act in socially responsible ways, educators should stress ethics in the classroom' (1994, p. 80), a point echoed by Drumwright and Murphy a decade later.

The three spheres discussed in this chapter—the representation of the sexes in adverts, gendered advertising practices, and advertising education—inform the other in mutually influencing ways such that the problematic gender content of adverts may result because of the persistence of organisational and agency practices and environments that are hypermasculine and disinclined towards portraying the sexes in ways that are not stereotypical. Additionally, as advertising students begin their progression into professional practice, they become socialised into such practices and 'learn' approaches to advertising work that are valued by their peers and superiors and that are therefore advantageous to their career advancement. Despite the lack of empirical evidence that it would be effective, it is at this juncture—during their years of education and training—that concerted effort could be made in producing a future cohort of practitioners that question and resist such socialisation that results in the perpetuation of stereotypical and sexist advertising content. It is, therefore, of central importance to examine how students of advertising view issues of gender, generally, and what their attitudes are towards representations of gender in advertising, especially those of a postfeminist bent. In addition, an important follow-on concern centres on the extent to which representations of and discourses on gender are currently a consideration during the course of advertising training.

Notes

1. This is something that, arguably, has gained even more momentum since the publication of Tasker and Negra's book in 2007, as evidenced, for example, in the threat to reproductive rights currently playing out in the US.
2. The other nine characteristics include appeasement of women's anger, use of more edgy/authentic looking models, shift from sex objects to desiring sexual subjects, focus on being and pleasing ourselves, articulation of femininity in adverts, eroticisation of male bodies, development of queer chic, use of gender reversals in ads, and revenge themes.
3. See the European Institute for Gender Equality (EIGE) 2013 report 'Advancing Gender Equality in Decision-Making in Media Organisations', which gives an EU overview of the hierarchical and sectoral segregation of women's participation in media organisations. For instance, the study found that women account for less than one-third of all top-level decision-making positions in surveyed media organisations across the EU member states.
4. However, this is not the case in Ireland, where the BA and MSc courses in advertising taken as case studies for this research are both positioned within the business discipline.
5. Of the three candidates, two were men (one was deemed unqualified, while the other was deemed qualified, alternately in terms of education and then in terms of experience) and one was a woman (she was deemed qualified, alternately in terms of education and then in terms of experience).
6. That is, perceptions of how vulnerable or impervious men and women were to representations of gender in advertising imagery.

References

Alvesson, M. (1998). Gender Relations and Identity at Work: A Case Study of Masculinities and Femininities in an Advertising Agency. *Human Relations, 51*(8), 969–1005.

ASAI Code 7th Edition. (2016). Retrieved from http://www.asai.ie/asaicode/

Averell, M. (2016). Bro Culture in Ad Agencies and the Impact on Women. Blog post printed on the website *The Insight Inn* on November 2, 2016. Retrieved from https://theinsightinn.com/2016/11/02/bro-culture-in-ad-agencies-and-the-impact-on-women/

Banning, S. A., & Schweitzer, J. C. (2007). What Advertising Educators Think About Advertising Education. *Journal of Advertising Education, 11*(2), 10–20.

Barthel, D. (1992). When Men Put on Appearances: Advertising and the Social Construction of Masculinity. In *Men, Masculinity and the Media*. Newbury Park: Sage.

Beynon, D. (2002). *Masculinities and Culture*. Maidenhead: Open University Press.

Black, S., Estrada, C., de la Fuente, M. C., Orozco, A., Trabazo, A., de la Vega, S., & Gutsche Jr, R. E. (2017). "Nobody Really Wants to Be Called Bossy or Domineering": Feminist Critique of Media "Industry Speak". *Journalism Practice*, 1–17. https://doi.org/10.1080/17512786.2017.1399812.

Cochrane, K. (2013). *All the Rebel Women: The Rise of the Fourth Wave of Feminism*. London: Guardian Shorts.

Coleman, C. A. (2012). Construction of Consumer Vulnerability by Gender and Ethics of Empowerment. In C. C. Otnes & L. Tuncay Zayer (Eds.), *Gender, Culture, and Consumer Behavior*. New York: Routledge.

Connell, R. W. (1987). *Gender and Power*. Sydney: Allen and Unwin.

Connell, R. W. (1990). An Iron Man: The Body and Some Contradictions of Hegemonic Masculinity. In M. Messner & D. Sabo (Eds.), *Sport, Men and the Gender Order*. Champaign: Human Kinetics Books.

Conor, B., Gill, R., & Taylor, S. (2015). Introduction: Gender and Creative Labour. In B. Conor, R. Gill, & S. Taylor (Eds.), *Gender and Creative Labour* (pp. 1–23). Chichester: Wiley-Blackwell.

Coy, M., & Garner, M. (2012). Definitions, Discourses and Dilemmas: Policy and Academic Engagement with the Sexualisation of Popular Culture. *Gender and Education, 24*(3), 285–301.

Craig, S. (1992). *Men, Masculinity and the Media*. Newbury Park: Sage.

Cronin, A. M. (2004). Regimes of Mediation: Advertising Practitioners as Cultural Intermediaries? *Consumption Markets & Culture, 7*(4), 349–369.

Cunningham, P. H. (1999). Ethics of Advertising. In J. P. Jones (Ed.), *The Advertising Business* (pp. 499–513). Thousand Oaks: Sage.

Drumwright, M. E., & Murphy, P. E. (2004). How Advertising Practitioners View Ethics: Moral Muteness, Moral Myopia, and Moral Imagination. *Journal of Advertising, 33*(2), 7–24.

Drumwright, M. E., & Murphy, P. E. (2009). The Current State of Advertising Ethics: Industry and Academic Perspectives. *Journal of Advertising, 38*(1), 83–108.

European Institute for Gender Equality. (2013). *Advancing Gender Equality in Decision-Making in Media Organisations.* Retrieved from http://eige.europa.eu/sites/default/files/documents/MH3113742ENC-Women-and-Media-Report-EIGE.pdf

Faludi, S. (1992). *Backlash: The Undeclared War Against Feminism.* London: Vintage.

Fejes, F. J. (1992). Masculinity as Fact: A Review of Empirical Mass Communication Research on Masculinity. In S. Craig (Ed.), *Men, Masculinity, and the Media.* London: Sage.

Florida, R. (2002). *The Rise of the Creative Class: And How It's Transforming Work, Leisure, Community, and Everyday Life.* New York: Basic Books.

Friedan, B. (1963). *The Feminine Mystique.* New York: W.W. Norton and.

Friedman, S., O'Brien, D., & Laurison, D. (2017). 'Like Skydiving Without a Parachute': How Class Shapes Occupational Trajectories in British Acting. *Sociology, 51*(5), 992–1010.

Gauntlett, D. (2002). *Media, Gender and Identity: An Introduction.* London: Routledge.

Gill, R. (2007). *Gender and the Media.* Oxford: Polity Press.

Gill, R. (2008). Empowerment/Sexism: Figuring Female Sexual Agency in Contemporary Advertising. *Feminism & Psychology, 18*(1), 35–60.

Gill, R. (2009a). Beyond the 'Sexualization of Culture' Thesis: An Intersectional Analysis of 'Sixpacks', 'Midriffs' and 'Hot Lesbians' in Advertising. *Sexualities, 12*(2), 137–160.

Gill, R. (2009b). Supersexualise Me! Advertising and "The Midriffs". In *Mainstreaming Sex: The Sexualization of Western Culture.* London: I.B. Tauris.

Gill, R. (2016). Post-Postfeminism?: New Feminist Visibilities in Postfeminist Times. *Feminist Media Studies, 16*(4), 610–630.

Gill, R. (2017). The Affective, Cultural and Psychic Life of Postfeminism: A Postfeminist Sensibility 10 Years On. *European Journal of Cultural Studies, 20*(6), 606–626.

Ging, D. (2005). A "Manual on Masculinity"? The Consumption and Use of Mediated Images of Masculinity Among Teenage Boys in Ireland. *Irish Journal of Sociology, 14*(2), 29–52.

Ging, D. (2009). All-Consuming Images: New Gender Formations in Post-Celtic-Tiger Ireland. In D. Ging, M. Cronin, & P. Kirby (Eds.), *Transforming Ireland: Challenges, critiques, resources.* Manchester: Manchester University Press.

Ging, D., & Flynn, R. (2008). *Background Paper on the Stereotyping of Women in Advertising in the Irish Media*, 1–91 [unpublished].

Goffman, E. (1979). *Gender Advertisements*. London: Macmillan.

Goldman, R., Heath, D., & Smith, S. L. (1991). Commodity Feminism. *Critical Studies in Mass Communication, 8*(3), 333–351.

Gregory, M. R. (2009). Inside the Locker Room: Male Homosociability in the Advertising Industry. *Gender, Work and Organization, 16*(3), 323–347.

Grow, J., & Deng, T. (2015). Tokens in A Man's World: Women in Creative Advertising Departments. *Media Report to Women, 43*(1), 6–11 & 21–23.

Hanke, R. (1998). Theorizing Masculinity With/In the Media. *Communication Theory, 8*(2), 183–201.

Hesmondhalgh, D. (2017). The Media's Failure to Represent the Working Class: Explanations from Media Production and Beyond. In J. Deery & A. Press (Eds.), *The Media and Class*. New York: Routledge.

Hesmondhalgh, D., & Baker, S. (2015). Sex, Gender and Work Segregation in the Cultural Industries. In B. Conor, R. Gill, & S. Taylor (Eds.), *Gender and Creative Labour* (pp. 23–36). Chichester: Wiley-Blackwell.

Hochschild, A. (1989). *The Second Shift: Working Families and the Revolution at Home*. Penguin.

Institute of Advertising Practitioners in Ireland. (2017). *IAPI Census*. Retrieved from http://census.iapi.ie/industry.html

James, E., Pratt, C., & Smith, T. (1994). Advertising Ethics: Practitioner and Student Perspectives. *Journal of Mass Media Ethics, 9*(2), 69–83.

Khang, H., Han, S., Shin, S., Jung, A., & Kim, J. (2016). A Retrospective on the State of International Advertising Research in Advertising, Communication, and Marketing Journals: 1963–2014. *International Journal of Advertising: The Review of Marketing Communications, 35*(3), 540–568.

Kilbourne, J. (1979). *Killing Us Softly: Advertising's Image of Women*. Retrieved from http://www.jeankilbourne.com/videos/

Kilbourne, J. (1999). *Can't Buy My Love: How Advertising Changes the Way We Think and Feel*. New York/London: Touchstone.

Kimmel, M. (1987). *Changing Men: New Directions in Research on Men and Masculinity*. Newbury Park: Sage.

Koppman, S. (2016). Different Like Me: Why Cultural Omnivores Get Creative Jobs. *Administrative Science Quarterly, 61*(2), 291–331.

Lazar, M. M. (2007). Feminist Critical Discourse Analysis: Articulating a Feminist Discourse Praxis. *Critical Discourse Studies, 4*(2), 141–164.

Levy, A. (2006). *Female Chauvinist Pigs: Women and the Rise of Raunch Culture*. London: Pocket.

Mallia, K. E. (2008). New Century, Same Story: Women Scarce When Adweek Ranks "Best Spots." *Journal of Advertising Education, 12*(1), 5–14.

Malson, H., Halliwell, E., Tischner, I., & Rudolfsdottir, A. (2011). Post-Feminist Advertising Laid Bare: Young Women's Talk About the Sexually Agentic Woman of 'Midriff' Advertising. *Feminism & Psychology, 21*(1), 74–99.

McFall, L. (2002). What About the Old Cultural Intermediaries? An Historical Review of Advertising Producers. *Cultural Studies, 16*(4), 532–552.

McRobbie, A. (2004). Post-Feminism and Popular Culture. *Feminist Media Studies, 4*(3), 255–264.

McRobbie, A. (2007). Top Girls? Young Women and the Post-Feminist Contract. *Cultural Studies, 21*(4–5), 718–737.

Mort, F. (1996). *Cultures of Consumption: Masculinities and Social Space in Late Twentieth-Century Britain*. London: Routledge.

Negus, K. (2002). The Work of Cultural Intermediaries and the Enduring Distance Between Production and Consumption. *Cultural Studies, 16*(4), 501–515.

Nixon, S. (1996). *Hard Looks: Masculinities, Spectatorship and Contemporary Consumption*. London: UCL Press.

Nixon, S. (1997). Advertising Executives as Modern Men: Masculinity and the UK Advertising Industry in the 1980s. In M. Nava, A. Blake, I. MacRury, & B. Richards (Eds.), *Buy This Book: Studies in Advertising and Consumption* (pp. 103–119). London: Routledge.

Nixon, S. (2003). *Advertising Cultures: Gender, Commerce, Creativity*. London: Sage.

Nixon, S., & Crewe, B. (2004). Pleasure at Work? Gender, Consumption and Work-Based Identities in the Creative Industries. *Consumption Markets & Culture, 7*(2), 129–147.

North, L. (2010). The Gender "Problem" in Australian Journalism Education. *Australian Journalism Review, 32*(2), 103–115.

North, L. (2015). The Currency of Gender: Student and Institutional Responses to the First Gender Unit in an Australian Journalism Program. *Journalism & Mass Communication Educator, 70*(2), 174–186.

O'Brien, D., Allen, K., Friedman, S., & Saha, A. (2017). Producing and Consuming Inequality: A Cultural Sociology of the Cultural Industries. *Cultural Sociology, 11*(3), 271–282.

Oakham, M. (2006). In Our Own Image? The Socialisation of Journalism's New Recruits. *Australian Journalism Review, 28*(1), 183–197.

Oakley, K., Laurison, D., O'Brien, D., & Friedman, S. (2017). Cultural Capital: Arts Graduates, Spatial Inequality, and London's Impact on Cultural Labor Markets. *American Behavioral Scientist, 61*(12), 1510–1531.

Peck, J. (2005). Struggling with the Creative Class. *International Journal of Urban and Regional Research, 29*(4), 740–770.

Pfeil, F. (1995). *White Guys: Studies in Postmodern Domination and Difference.* London: Verso.

Pollay, R. W. (1986). The Distorted Mirror : Reflections on the Unintended Consequences of Advertising. *Journal of Marketing, 50*(April), 18–37.

Rivers, N. (2017). *Postfeminism(s) and the Arrival of the Fourth Wave.* Cham: Palgrave Macmillan.

Saha, A. (2013). 'Curry Tales': The Production of 'Race' and Ethnicity in the Cultural Industries. *Ethnicities, 13*(6), 818–837.

Salminen-Karlsson, M. (2006). Situating Gender in Situated Learning. *Scandinavian Journal of Management, 22*, 31–48.

Savran, D. (1998). *Taking It Like a Man: White Masculinity, Masochism, and Contemporary American Culture.* Princeton: Princeton University Press.

Sedgwick, E. K. (1995). Gosh, Boy George, You Must Be Awfully Secure in Your Masculinity! In M. Berger, B. Wallis, & S. Watson (Eds.), *Constructing Masculinity.* New York: Routledge.

Soar, M. (2000). Encoding Advertisements: Ideology and Meaning in Advertising Production. *Mass Communication and Society, 3*(4), 415–437.

Tasker, Y., & Negra, D. (2007). *Interrogating Postfeminism: Gender and the Politics of Popular Culture.* Durham: Duke University Press.

Taylor, M. & O'Brien, D. (2017). 'Culture Is a Meritocracy': Why Creative Workers' Attitudes May Reinforce Social Inequality. *Sociological Research Online, 22*(4), 1–21.

Toynbee, P. (1987, November). The incredible, shrinking New Man. *The Guardian.* Retrieved from http://www.theguardian.com/century/1980-1989/Story/0,,110228,00.html

Tuncay Zayer, L., & Coleman, C. A. (2015). Advertising Professionals' Perceptions of the Impact of Gender Portrayals on Men and Women: A Question of Ethics? *Journal of Advertising, 44*(3), 264–275.

van Zoonen, L. (1994). *Feminist Media Studies.* London: Sage.

Vokey, M., Tefft, B., & Tysiaczny, C. (2013). An Analysis of Hyper-Masculinity in Magazine Advertisements. *Sex Roles, 68*(9–10), 562–576.

Whelehan, I. (2000). *Overloaded: Popular Culture and the Future of Feminism.* London: Women's Press.

Williamson, J. (1978). *Decoding Advertisements: Ideology and Meaning in Advertising*. London: Marion Boyars Publishers Ltd.

Windels, K., & Lee, W.-N. (2012). The Construction of Gender and Creativity in Advertising Creative Departments. *Gender in Management: An International Journal, 27*(8), 502–519.

Windels, K., & Mallia, K. L. (2015). How Being Female Impacts Learning and Career Growth in Advertising Creative Departments. *Employee Relations: The International Journal, 37*(1), 122–140.

Windels, K., Lee, W.-N., & Yeh, Y.-H. (2010). Does the Creative Boys' Club Begin in the Classroom? *Journal of Advertising Education, 14*(2), 15–24.

Zaitchik, M. C., & Mosher, D. L. (1993). Criminal Justice Implications of the Macho Personality Constellation. *Criminal Justice and Behavior, 20*, 227–239. https://doi.org/10.1177/0093854893020003001.

3

We're Just Different (But Equal): Unpacking Students' Gendered Views

In exploring, among other issues, whether and the degree to which characteristics of postfeminism retain influence on constructions and understandings of gender, and relationships between the sexes, it is worth reiterating why such an examination matters. It is important because both the polarisation of the sexes' narrative and the very narrow markers of success that had come to characterise postfeminist discussions regarding women's equality need to be contested (Tasker and Negra 2007). The postfeminist discourse is perhaps most dangerous for the simultaneous, albeit counter-intuitive contentions that men and women are fundamentally different, and that the fight for equality has been won, leading to complacency and acceptance of the current status of women in contemporary society. It is incumbent upon those invested in achieving women's rights and equality between the sexes to interrogate the cultural aspects of society that work against achieving a true valuing and respect of both women and men. Cultural manifestations of sex-based inequality are, at the same time, more difficult to recognise, articulate, challenge and overturn. Bearing this contention in mind, this chapter seeks to deconstruct and understand attitudes held by advertising students to gender, gender roles, and feminism and their position as to whether equality has been

© The Author(s) 2019
A. O'Driscoll, *Learning to Sell Sex(ism)*,
https://doi.org/10.1007/978-3-319-94280-3_3

achieved, in addition to exploring the ways in which they talk about women and men and relations between the sexes.

As mentioned, feminism has re-emerged as a cultural, social, and political movement and talking point. Feminist voices are growing louder, and are intent on drawing attention to various forms of gender inequality: cultural and otherwise. Nevertheless, the increased awareness of feminism and gender equality issues has not been seen, for the most part, to translate among the participants of this study into a 'felt' and convincing concern for women and girls as facing continued oppression. This chapter outlines how salient attitudes to women and men work to construct a gender discourse that is androcentric and thereby, in the main, unsympathetic and lacking in empathy for women.

Gender: Roles, Attributes, and Behaviours

It was imperative to ascertain whether and if students tend towards a belief in naturalised differences between women and men, or if they are critical of reductive assumptions of supposed distinct male and female traits and characteristics, since to (mis)understand gender as innate and biological is to uphold the 'sex/gender system'. As conceptualised by Rubin (1975), the sex/gender system operates in the service of patriarchy in how it arranges society according to biological functioning and reproductive capacities. It thereby defines separate genders and attendant gender roles to females and males accordingly, which are imposed through a process of socialisation and cultural expectations. The implications of the sex/gender system are felt in cases where women and men transgress those gender boundaries and are accordingly sanctioned—socially, and otherwise. While this patriarchal system is reductive to both men's and women's freedoms to live full and diverse emotional, creative, and intellectual lives, women's confinement for so long to the domestic sphere, the lack of value afforded to women's voices, not to mention the violence meted out to women and girls on an endemic scale globally, highlights how the female sex is persistently more disadvantaged than men within the confines of how gender operates. Consequently, as a starting point, it was deemed central to this project to explore student understandings of the concept of gender, and gender essentialism, since these positions could then be compared with attitudes to more specific issues concerning representations of gender in advertisements, as discussed in the next chapter.

Gender Essentialism

Students were asked on the questionnaire to indicate where they believe the source of the differences between men and women lies; which is to say, do they subscribe to a biologically deterministic view of sex-based difference, or do they believe that socialisation plays a role in this regard (see Table 3.1)?

For the most part, those who answer that differences between women and men are 'natural' did not respond further on the question; only 21% of female respondents and 32% of male respondents who answer in that vein expanded on their answer. In one such answer, a 19-year-old 1st-year female student added that 'Even male and female animals act differently, it's not something society teaches', while a 22-year-old 3rd-year male student responded that 'I think men and women are naturally different, testosterone levels etc. Look at a group of men hanging out compared to women hanging out.' Somewhat similarly, a 22-year-old 3rd-year female student said that 'men and women are different and always will be, but should still be treated the same'.

On the contrary, 93% of female respondents and 54% of male respondents who answer that gender differences are learned did expand on their

Table 3.1 Questionnaire question—*Please tick. Do you think ...? A. Men and women exhibit naturally different characteristics because of their biological make-up. B. Gender differences are learned. Explain/further comments*

	Male respondents (%)	Female respondents (%)
Natural differences due to biological make-up	46	36
Gender differences are learned	24	27
Both nature and nurture	25	29
Did not answer the question/left blank	5	8

answers and sought to explain their understanding and elaborate on why they took that position. Many of these answers were insightful and well considered:

> Little girls are bought dolls and boys are bought cars. We learn how to behave, what is "socially acceptable". (Female student, 2nd year, age 18)

> No one is born misogynistic. (Male student, 1st year, age 18)

Thoughtful answers were provided also by those students who sought to explain how both nature and nurture play a role:

> Both, naturally we are different but you don't see many males wearing dresses and make up due to how many people see what it is to be a man. (Male student, 4th year, age 22)

Looking at some of those sex-disaggregated percentages outlined in Table 3.1—that more male students than female students believe differences between the sexes to be biologically determined (46%:36%), and that far more female students than male students clarified *why* they thought gender is socially imposed (93%:54%)—both of these discrepancies are significant and could be explained by the fact that women have had to internalise and reflect more on gender and its socialisation and attendant expectations and roles. Men, arguably, have not been so confined by their gender and are, far more so than women, considered the 'universal' human being, or as being genderless. While less than half of questionnaire respondents subscribe to the view that differences between the sexes are natural and biological, the survey[1] results (see Table 3.2) revealed a considerably higher percentage demonstrating an understanding of gender that is aligned to a biological conceptualisation. This may have been due to the age of the respondents, since survey participants were first-year students in the first semester of their degree course, or indeed the open phrasing of the question may have prompted such responses.

While there were lots of references to 'sex', 'male', 'female', 'sexual orientation', and 'reproductive parts', there were only a few nuanced and

Table 3.2 Survey question—*What does the term 'gender' mean to you?*

	All students (both male and female) (%)
Biological understanding[a]	65
Social constructionist understanding[b]	28
Too ambiguous/vague to code or left blank	7

[a]This category includes answers that broadly align to an essentialist understanding of gender, and reference such words/terms as 'male', 'female', 'sex', 'sexuality', 'sexual orientation', and 'reproductive/genital parts'
[b]This category includes answers that are more nuanced and make some reference to gender as concerned with socialisation, or as a 'cultural construction', and/or make an attempt to explain gender as 'identity', or as allowing one to 'identify' in a certain way

more accurate[2] understandings of gender as referring to cultural constructions, or as being associated with biological sex but also as distinct from it. There was one ambiguous, but potentially quite brilliant and insightful answer provided by one student, who said: Gender doesn't mean anything. Nevertheless, the survey results indicate that the majority of students do not have a grasp on the difference between biological sex and gender.

Across the 12-student interviews, it was possible to probe deeper into students' generalised attitudes to gender. While there is a strong awareness of the different societal expectations pertaining to women and men in terms of roles and behaviours, as well as declarations about the divergent spheres of gendered recreational interests, there are variations regarding whether and the degree to which students question essentialist assumptions about the sexes. Students sometimes outright refute assumptions made about men and women based on biology, and provide examples to contradict that narrative, or they align themselves with a naturalised gender differences discourse and exhibit essentialist beliefs. However, such delineations were not always clear cut, and more often than not, there was evidence of contradictory opinions held by students, revealed by simultaneously expressing sentiments which reject biologically determined differences between the sexes while also buying into long-established and embedded notions of appropriate masculinity and femininity. There was similarly little, to no, critical awareness of the implications for meaningful and genuine equality between the sexes of assumptions that position women and men as fundamentally and innately different.

Fiona quite clearly was coming from a biological determinist or essentialist perspective regarding men and women and natural difference. There were numerous examples of this during the interview exchange that broadly fit into traditional gender-role notions of women's aptitude for the domestic realm and for childcare, with men positioned as adept at manual tasks and having heightened sexual appetites. In discussing her hypothetical future husband/partner, their children and allocation of certain tasks, she said: 'Well… naturally enough if I had kids I would want to stay at home with them.' Because she seems to feel neither anguished nor find the idea of strictly defined gender roles worrisome or problematic, she was able to express, with certainty, how and why men and women are naturally different. This surety was grounded in her belief that equality has been achieved for women in Irish society: 'we're just so equal here'.

Demonstrating less clear-cut gender essentialist sentiments, Paul expresses the view that he has not had to think about gender in any specific sense because of having a feminist, 'bread-winning' mother and a 'chilled-out' father. Consequently, he says, he did not grow up with traditional, restrictive versions of what it is to be a man, or likewise what is appropriate for women. One consequence of this is his tendency to be friends, indiscriminately, with both women and men, based on interests and not on expectations or experience regarding their gender. He does not subscribe to a view of the sexes fulfilling certain roles, of being different in any significant way, or that certain stereotypes are true or accurate. For instance, he disputes the notion that women are more organised than men, or that men are physically stronger than women. However, immediately following that exchange, he contradicts his 'gender-blind' viewpoint when talking about making decisions concerned with designing and planning an advertising campaign:

> I suppose I am saying like I don't really think (in a) biased (way) but I guess … whenever I am thinking of something it always has to a very beautiful woman or something … I think actually truthfully I would find it weird if I saw a woman opening a door for a man or something like that, I would think that was a bit out of the ordinary.

In the main, the interviews reveal that students understood gender roles and expectations to be socially imposed and thereby reductive. However, when the conversations turned from the abstract, intellectual level to the specific and personal, contradictions started to emerge. In other words, when speaking about experience with friends, their girlfriends, and their boyfriends, they mostly subscribe to the view that men and women have different interests and there was a natural degree of segregation between them. More specifically, there was evidence of a clear sex/gender differences discourse that culminates in a 'different-but-equal' narrative, which is cultivated around a sense of men and women 'complementing' each other:

> He (female student's boyfriend) just hangs around with the lads and I give him that space. And like saying that, I'd go shopping with the girls and he wouldn't necessarily tag along but like yeah, I suppose there are different spheres but you can kind of compromise as well. (Colette)

Of course, while it is not objectionable or necessarily 'sexist' that the experience of students is one of male and female friends and intimate partners having different, and often typical gendered, interests depending on their sex, it is significant that this is not critiqued or questioned to a greater degree.

Drilling down further into attitudes to gender, an inventory was taken of the kinds of traits, attributes, and characteristics that students assign to men and women. Although students were asked to identify 'stereo(typical)' characteristics, the degree of similarity, consistency, and high frequency of certain keywords and terms associated with male persons, and a separate set of similar terms for females points to widespread and long-standing established associations pertaining to the sexes, regardless of whether they can be considered to be typical or stereotypical. That is to say, that in a society in which true equality between the sexes has been achieved, the following question would not make sense, or at least would not elicit such dichotomously differentiated answers with respect to supposed male and female attributes. The five most commonly used words in connection with male characteristics are detailed in Table 3.3.

Table 3.3 Questionnaire question—*What key words describe (stereo)typical _male_ characteristics?*

Male respondents	Female respondents
Strong	Strong
Tall	Big
Macho	Handsome
Muscular	Masculine
Dominant	Tall

Table 3.4 Questionnaire question—*What key words describe (stereo)typical _female_ characteristics?*

Male respondents	Female respondents
Big (i.e. 'boobs', 'bum/ass', eyes, hair)	Skinny
Caring	Emotional
Kind	Beautiful
Emotional	Pretty
Hair (i.e. blonde, big, straight)	Gentle

Outside of physical traits, direct references to personality characteristics were coded for whether they could be considered broadly 'positive' or 'negative'.[3] While this required a judgement call, it was a useful exercise and highlighted that, where negative words were used to describe stereotypical male traits, both women and men most frequently made reference to characteristics connected to a cold, individualistic emotional suppression, such as 'emotionless', 'selfish', 'arrogant', 'insensitive', and 'egotistical'. Where positive words were used to describe stereotypical male traits, both women and men used words that made reference to an active assertiveness, such as 'independent', 'authoritative', 'leaders', 'brave', 'active', 'funny', and 'confident'. Such positive words tend to refer to traits that are self-empowering or are connected with asserting dominance or power over others.

Such associations with being male are starkly contrasted with those characteristics connected with being female. The five most commonly used words in connection with female characteristics are detailed in Table 3.4.

Again, apart from physical traits, direct references to personality characteristics were coded for whether they could be considered broadly 'positive' or 'negative'. Where negative words were used to describe stereotypical female traits, both women and men most frequently made reference to characteristics connected to emotional, physical, and intellectual weakness, such as 'passive', 'self-conscious', 'dependent', 'fragile', 'weak', and 'irrational'. Where positive words were used to describe stereotypical female traits, both women and men used words that made reference to an emotional generosity and warmth, such as 'caring', 'kind', 'loving', and 'thoughtful'. Interestingly, the male answers offered a far broader range, scope, and frequency of positive words connected with women and typical female traits, with words such as 'fun', 'playful', and 'smart' not present in the female answers—suggesting perhaps an affection for women on the part of the young men not mirrored among the female students concerning their own sex. Overall, however, where positive words are used, they tend to be references to characteristics that benefit others, with little reference to self-empowering traits such as intelligence, intellect, and creativity. The majority of answers to these two questions align broadly to the traditional realms of caring (the domestic and private spheres) reserved for women alongside traits of fragility and vulnerability, with men more often associated with the public realm in terms of being connected to concepts of leadership and courage, with attendant characteristics of strength. This speaks to the longevity of patriarchal-imposed distinct private-public roles for women and men.

Understanding of Feminism

While attitudes to feminism were less central to the study's considerations, it was important to garner a sense of this among students, particularly in establishing if the latest upsurge of feminist activism has made an impact on student attitudes. Consequently, students were asked to articulate their understanding of what feminism means (see Table 3.5).

The majority of both male and female respondents demonstrated an accurate understanding of feminism, although a significantly higher proportion of female answers than male responses were unambiguous. Antagonistic and contradictory answers by male respondents include such sentiments as feminists take things too seriously/like to complain, that equality is already achieved, feminism is 'bullshit', feminism is too aggressive, feminism elevates women above men, and that feminists' want

Table 3.5 Questionnaire question—*What does the term 'feminism' mean for you?*

	Male (%)	Female (%)
Understood[a]	58	86
Antagonistic[b]	18	2
Contradictory[c]	9	4
Too ambiguous/vague to code or left blank	15	8

[a]The category of 'understood' means that answers exhibit a broadly accurate, articulate understanding of the core tenet of feminism being about equality and the struggle/fight to bring about equality for women
[b]The category of 'antagonistic' means that answers demonstrate an antagonistic or negative view of feminists/feminism
[c]The category of 'contradictory' covers answers that express an understanding of the core tenet of feminism being about equality, but which qualify that understanding with a contradictory statement

too much and are guilty of double standards. Only one female respondent answered in a way that was antagonistic towards feminism, believing that feminists take things too seriously. The two women that demonstrated contradictory opinions about feminism suggest that feminists take things too seriously, and that feminism elevates women above men. While, broadly, students took a position on feminism that showed an understanding of it being concerned with the struggle or fight to bring about equality for women, socially, politically, and economically, the greater numbers of men than women who make qualifying or hostile statements is significant, and serves to undermine the legitimacy of feminist concerns in the eyes of this study's male cohort. A more favourable response in support of feminism is seen in the survey responses (see Table 3.6).

While very few in number, answers in the vein of antagonistic include feminists patronise women, feminism elevates women above men, feminists like to complain, and equality has already been achieved. The contradictory position suggests that feminism elevates women above men and that feminists are extremists. There is a strong understanding and articulation of feminism as fighting for and the promotion of equality between women and men. So, how do understandings of feminism translate to perceptions of its continued relevance and personal identification with it (as a concept, as a movement, as an identity label)? Students were asked whether they thought feminism retains relevance in contemporary society (see Table 3.7).

Table 3.6 Survey question—*What is a feminist?*

	All students (both male and female) (%)
Understood[a]	88
Antagonistic[b]	7
Contradictory[c]	3
Too ambiguous/vague to code or left blank	2

[a]The category of 'understood' means that answers exhibit a broadly accurate, articulate understanding of the core tenet of feminism being about equality and the struggle/fight to bring about equality for women
[b]The category of 'antagonistic' means that answers demonstrate an antagonistic or negative view of feminists/feminism
[c]The category of 'contradictory' covers answers that express an understanding of the core tenet of feminism being about equality, but which qualify that understanding with a contradictory statement

Table 3.7 Questionnaire question—*Do you think feminism is still relevant in today's society?*

	Male respondents (%)	Female respondents (%)
Yes	75	86
No	14	6
Too ambiguous/vague to code or left blank	11	8

While the majority of respondents confirm the continued relevance of feminism, there were varying justifications for this. Just over half of male respondents who agree that feminism is still relevant expanded on their answer and offered further insight. The most common reasons for answering in this vein came with a caveat: that feminists were alienating people and/or detracting from the issues, or answers made reference to the need to address certain issues, and that things were improving but are not quite there. Those who did not believe feminism remains relevant were a relatively low figure. There is a degree of confusion that contemporary feminism is about insulting men, about going too far, of wanting women to be seen as better than men, or of being too controversial or hypocritical. For those that deny its continued relevance, there is not a lot of expansion on their position. Two of those respondents made reference to the hypocrisy of feminists as their reason for its irrelevance, while one answer posited that 'Celebrities posing naked etc. have devalued the cause'. While this may be interpreted as 'slut-shaming', this comment perhaps represents an astute critique of a postfeminist/third-wave feminist sexualisation of culture, and its associated contention that female self-sexual objectification is empowering.

The vast majority of female respondents believe that feminism remains relevant, and 20 of these 45 respondents expand on their answer and offer further insight. They include references to the prevalence and visibility of cultural feminists such as Beyoncé, or Emma Watson, and the dominance of feminist discussions and conversations. They raise these examples to demonstrate that it is now okay to be feminist and to proclaim one's feminism. However, there was little indication of reflection on why they think feminism remains relevant in terms of issues to be addressed. That is to say that the focus was on feminism as a 'label' or identity, rather than as an issue-based political and social movement. However, several answers did turn the focus to such concerns as pay gaps, or women presented as objects in advertising and the media, or that feminism remains more pertinent elsewhere/outside Western world. In addition to collated responses to whether students believe feminism to be relevant, they were also asked if they personally identify as feminist (see Table 3.8).

There is a fairly even split between respondents who answer 'yes'/'no'/ and a variation of 'kind of' to whether they consider themselves to be feminist or not. Those that answer 'yes' mostly do not elaborate. The 'no' respondents justify their answer in terms of being put off by the radical

Table 3.8 Survey question—*Are you a feminist?*

	All students (both male and female) (%)
Yes	49
No	33
'Not feminist, but ...'[a]	9
Do not know	5
Too ambiguous/vague to code or left blank	4

[a]'Not feminist but ...' relates to answers where participants respond broadly that while they support the principle of equality between the sexes, they would not support or identify as 'feminist'

or supposedly militant elements or perceptions of feminism, or prefer to identify as an 'egalitarian', with answers such as 'No, these days feminists are more "anti-male" than "pro-equality"', typifying this response. It is an interesting breakdown of yes/no self-identified feminists given that the majority (i.e. 88%) of survey respondents showed they accurately understood the core tenet of feminism being about equality between women and men. Therefore, this points to some cultural hang-ups about aligning oneself with the feminist movement, as well as disconnect between recognising that feminism promotes equality without a corresponding personal imperative or need to support that tenet.

Gender Equality

How and whether student's attitudes to gender, gender roles, and feminism fit with their view as to whether equality has been achieved was examined (see Table 3.9).

Across both male and female respondents' answers, which are broadly comparative, the majority of both sexes respond that equality has not been achieved. Answers justify this by pointing to the wage gap and issues of employment, or they raise the continued objectification of women. Other answers make reference to structural barriers to equality (e.g. maternity leave policies), and attitudinal issues (e.g. that women are considered inferior to men). Only a few students referenced rape or rape culture,[4] with—very surprisingly—no explicit reference to levels of violence against women. On-the-fence answers tend to say that here has been massive progress, that equality has been mostly achieved but that

Table 3.9 Questionnaire question—*Do you think equality between men and women has been achieved in Western society?*

	Male respondents (%)	Female respondents (%)
Yes	29	33
No	64	57
Yes *and* no/ambivalent	5	6
Too ambiguous/vague to code or left blank	2	4

there is a little way to go, or some tweaking still needed. Those that say 'yes' to this question make reference to the changing roles of women in society. They assert that women have the same opportunities as men, with a few illustrative examples used to back up their points that society and employment operate on a meritocratic basis and therefore gender is no longer of relevance. It is significant that the proportion of men and women who do not believe that gender equality has been achieved is considerably lower than the figures indicating that feminism remains relevant. One would expect these percentages to align and to be broadly similar. That is to say, that while three quarters of male respondents and over 80% of women answered that feminism remains relevant, these figures were notably lower among those who do not believe that equality between the sexes has been achieved. If students subscribe to the continued need for feminism, they do not appear to be making the link as to why. Again, this indicates an emotional and intellectual disconnect with what feminist campaigns are trying to achieve.

In the interview exchanges, students demonstrated that they are mostly operating under the illusion that equality between the sexes has been achieved. Common narratives include that things are improving or getting there, that it is changing, or that it is a generational issue, meaning that for younger generations' issues of sexism are not a problem. There was also the assertion that other countries and cultures remain problematic, accompanied by a distinct lack of concern for the status of women in Irish society. There was only really one outlier, Des, who expresses a belief that equality between the sexes remains a long way off:

> I guess it's like we're so over that kind of stage you know … I think at this stage we all kind of blend, like our generation blend. (Della)

> Obviously our generation it's different. Like, we've grown up in a different way to our parents or whatever but I guess yeah maybe like with our generation kind of it will completely change or whatever. (Cat)

This investigation into attitudes to gender, gender roles, and attributes, which is mostly predicated on questionnaire and survey data, indicates that students lack a clear understanding of the concept of gender and how it is socially constructed and operationalised in the patriarchal society in which they have grown up. Consequently they do not possess adequate intellectual and emotional tools to question more deeply embedded assumptions surrounding social expectations, and what constitutes real and true equality between the sexes. This absence of a framework to categorically reject reductive gender notions is not without its implications. Indeed, from a radical feminist perspective, in striving for equality and an end to women's oppression, the feminist movement must seek to strive towards a complete dismantlement of the concept of gender, and its associated restrictive and reductive gender roles. Therefore, given that a significant cohort of students express views and opinions that align themselves to a naturalised gender differences discourse and by so doing serve to reinforce gender and gender roles as something innate and biological, such worldviews and beliefs represent a backslide away from achieving an elevation of women and an equality with men.

In interrogating student's understandings of gender, it is important to consider Judith Butler, whose gender theorisations since the 1990s have been massively influential. Butler (1990) took issue with how gender had, up to that point, been conceptualised. She notes that 'the presumption of a binary gender system implicitly retains the belief in a mimetic relation of gender to sex whereby gender mirrors sex or is otherwise rejected by it' (Butler 1990, p. 6). In other words, she takes issue with the assumption—both contested and accepted—that 'man'-masculinity maps onto male bodies, and that 'woman'-femininity maps onto female bodies. Indeed, Butler also questions the naturalness and inevitability of two sex classes, thereby suggesting that sex may be culturally constructed and imposed by persistent scientific and medical discourses. Most notably, Butler opened up a new way to understand how gender was enacted, such that our gender is 'performed' through repetitive practices and acts. By incorporating a greater variety of non-conforming performative aspects linked to one's gender identity, we destabilise the gender binary of masculine and feminine. It is in this space that the binary and its associated imposition of heterosexuality may be subverted. Furthermore, Butler contends that understanding gender to be socially constructed risks giving too much credit to social processes, and therefore represents a shifting from biological determinism to cultural determinism. However, her insightful and challenging contributions to feminist understandings of sex and gender have been challenged by some critical feminists (e.g. Grant 1993; Hekman 1999; Kotthoff and Wodak 1997, as referenced in Lazar 2007, p. 150). For instance, referring to Butler's postmodernist reconfiguring of gender as performative, Lazar (2007) points out that there are limitations within the 'gender-as-performance' approach, since this allows for too much agency on behalf of 'subjects' to resist gender norms and overemphasises the capacity for individuals to enact and produce competing and alternative gender categories, without due regard for material reality or how gender ideology is operationalised in patriarchal society. While of course there is subversion and rejection of gender expectations, the longevity of patriarchy is testament to the effectiveness of the sex/gender binary hierarchical system 'imposed' on and subscribed to by the majority of women and men. Instead, understanding gender from a social constructionist perspective and situating its perpetuation within a 'doing gender' approach maintains that any questioning of a gender binary must give due regard to how the two genders of man-masculine and woman-feminine are positioned in hierarchical relation to one another, with masculinity enjoying superior status to femininity. In other words, '*doing gender* in interactions means creating hierarchical differences between groups of people' (Lazar 2007, p. 150; emphasis added). In a radical feminist understanding of gender, a non-patriarchal society would not be one which opens up room for more 'genders'. Instead, gender would not exist, since any such expression of what we understand to be masculine or feminine behaviours (or a deviation from the two) would not have the same function in upholding patriarchal norms.

Understanding the 'function' of gender and its nature in service of patriarchy is paramount in order to enable a rejection of gender roles and stereotypes—something the students surveyed demonstrated they were not adept at. Rather, their tendency to hold gender essentialist views merits very careful consideration. Therefore, the question is posed: why do students—although not all—take up a gender essentialist view? Arguably it is because, as Whelehan suggests (2000), it is not known what the world would look like if a gender revolution was successfully staged, and patriarchy and male dominance overthrown. Therefore, it is much more comfortable to fall back on biodeterminist and essentialist arguments about 'the way things should be' and how men and women are naturally different. Indeed, asserting that students' analytic inability to interrogate the concept of gender and that their skewing towards a natural gender difference narrative both actively work against the struggle to end women's oppression is compounded by the finding that, although students demonstrate mostly favourable attitudes to feminism, a significant proportion of approximately one-third of all 107 questionnaire respondents express the view that gender equality has been achieved in Western society. As hooks (1984) has argued, the 'feminist movement to end sexist oppression actively engages participants in revolutionary struggle. Struggle is rarely safe or pleasurable' (p. 28). As a consequence, it is understandable that most people not only shy away from such a movement but deny the aims which are its foundation.

Bourdieu (2001) theorises the mass denial of masculine domination over women somewhat differently. He refers to the fact that people are implicated in their own subordination because of a seemingly blind acceptance of the natural order of things. He calls this the *paradox of doxa* and identifies masculine domination 'as the prime example of this paradoxical submission, an effect of what I call symbolic violence, a gentle violence, imperceptible and invisible even to its victims' (p. 1). Gender essentialist beliefs have the effect of leading people to believe that things are as they should be. Writing more than 30 years earlier, Millett posits that women's subordination to the dominant position of men was explicable in terms of 'acceptance of a value system which is not biological' (Millett 1970, p. 37). At a time when feminist academics and writers, among other disciplines, were seeking answers as to the true meaning of 'gender' and an understanding of whether and what were the genuine and innate differences between men and women, Millett acknowledged that definitive answers to such questions might never be reached. Nevertheless, as she astutely points out, '[w]hatever the "real" differences between the sexes may be, we are not likely to know them until the sexes are treated differently, that is alike. And this is very far from being the case at present' (Millett 1970, p. 39). While the gap representing the differential ways that the sexes were treated in Millett's time has narrowed, it has not closed altogether, and therefore, those answers remain elusive. The true extent of sex-based difference remains difficult to grasp also because of the continued operation of patriarchy, which Millett conceptualised as being harder to eradicate than the class system because of its assumed naturalness.

Women and Girls as the Problematic and Burdensome Sex: 'He Jokes About All the Girls Who Get Dolled Up to Go to the Match'

Emerging from conversations about women and men was a strong sense that women represent a set of problems to be fixed, that their experience of being in the world is not easy or joyful, but rather is burdensome. The converse of this is a sense that the male experience is aspirational and relatable—a view that is identified here as androcentric. In other words, students tend to talk about femininity and masculinity in ways that privilege the male experience and denigrate traditionally associated female traits and interests. In an exchange with Damien, he expresses horror at the idea of a remake of *Ghostbusters* with an all-female cast:

> I was just showing my outrage really like I just had visions of them turning Ghostbusters into some sort of a chick flick or rom-com. I was like "no you can't do that" … if I'm going to see a film with an all-female cast it's just I would expect a certain genre of film that I'm not necessarily into you know, so romantic comedy or something like that. It's just that was the immediate thing that struck me is like "no this is going to turn into some bloody love story" or something like that.

This comment is indicative of a marginalisation of women from the 'universal' or the mainstream, such that it is assumed that remaking a classic like *Ghostbusters* with four women reprising the main roles violates the sanctity of men's central position in symbolic spaces. This is echoed in the, albeit muted, backlash to the BBC's announcement that the next *Doctor Who* will be played by a woman: actress Jodie Whittaker. Indeed the issue of appropriate femininity was further discussed by Damien, who talked about 'aggressiveness' and assertiveness not being attractive or acceptable on women. He recounts working on designing an advertising campaign, which was premised on developing an idea for a ready meal for two. He and his male classmate devised a campaign that would show a finicky male partner criticising the way his girlfriend makes his cup of tea, and the advert goes on to show the male protagonist being critical of the artwork of one of his young students in class, and other such scenarios. The advert was conceived to culminate in the girlfriend serving him his dinner in the evening. Fully expecting her partner to find fault, she is waiting for the complaint, but he merely shrugs and asks 'what?' This represents the height of compliment. Damien expresses surprise that the art director of the agency at which he was interning thought that the advert, as it had been conceived, might cause offence. In his defence, Damien explains: For the ad to work, someone has to give someone their dinner. Man or woman it doesn't matter, I just thought the male came off (better) as the difficult, nasty person rather than the woman.

He went on to say that his 'intent wasn't to be sexist'. But he qualifies that by saying:

an audience could really, really hate a woman that's really nasty ... I just think men can get away with it a bit better ... Mary Lou MacDonald[5] – I just don't like that woman. To me she just comes off really rigid and nasty but she's no different than any other lads, it's just I would see her being that little bit more unbearable, and I don't know, it might be the fact that she's a woman and I just don't see woman in that bossy kind-of, always giving out ... She always seems to be trying a lot harder than the lads do ... My reaction to her is different, and it probably is my outlook on what I probably feel women's roles should be in society and it's obviously not right, but I just don't really see women having that nasty streak in them. And when I do see it, it just kind of turns me off them.

This points to the double standard pertaining to appropriate male and female behaviours, with a female politician far more scrutinised and harshly judged than her male colleagues for similar behaviours. When pushed on this, Damien explains that he thinks of women as 'motherly figures' and therefore does not like to see characteristics displayed by women that do not conform to those notions. Despite awareness that this is maybe unfair, Damien sticks to this view point. Kevin also clearly exhibits internalisation of a gender differences discourse, and a sense of not being able to relate to women or women's experiences. He constructed women as foreign and separate entities to that with which he is familiar. The only way to 'know' women and the female market is through market research, he attests. Kevin differentiates women as high maintenance and appearance oriented and also positions girls as being 'a bit more of a pain' to be out socialising with.

The survey results expanded on this sense of women tied to inherent pressures or constraints on them. Students were asked to expand on what they thought were society's expectations of women (see Table 3.10).

While the phrasing of the question may have been somewhat loaded, it is nevertheless revealing that cultural expectations referenced in the responses mostly cluster around motherhood and domesticity. One quote exemplifies the typical response: 'Women are seen as sex objects or mothers. The expectations of women are to be sexy or be a mother.' Coming from young adults, this is extremely significant and attests the longevity of associations of women with either being saintly and motherly, or sexual and 'sexy' for male gratification, thereby denying women complex and multidimensional existences.

While the concept of domesticity is analysed in detail in the next chapter, the issue of women as domestic and emotional labourers came up in several interview exchanges. This concerns the view that assumes women to be better at the social and emotional side of work or otherwise. Emotional energy for women was expended in a number of ways. These included the onus on women to embrace or fit an ideal of femininity,

Table 3.10 Survey question—*What kinds of expectations of women are there, typically, in our culture?*

	All students (both male and female) (%)
Reference to domesticity/care-giving/marriage/ motherhood/working mothers	46
Reference to physical appearance/looking 'beautiful', beauty standards	14
Refer to *both* domestic and appearance	10
Other/variety of answers	25
Too ambiguous/vague to code or left blank	5

deciding to reject that ideal altogether, or in alternately negotiating and navigating the terms of that idealised version of femininity. In addition, opinions were expressed that position women as gatekeepers of order and of not letting men and boys get out of hand, such that men and boys have a tendency to a boisterous, fun-loving, and irresponsible side:

> I think generally women are, women do seem to be better at that like I mean I don't know I think they can hide when they're in a bad mood or something like that, men can't really do that. (Paul)

> In primary school ... the girls would have a problem with something being thrown around the classroom, they would automatically see the danger of it whereas the only thing that would be going through one of the guys heads being of that age is 'he hit me, I'm going to throw the ball back at him', and also it seems to maintain that idea from going from a mixed school in primary to all lads school in secondary school that seemed to just keep us in a sort of arrested development. (Nick)

Beauty and the Tyranny of Perfection

In terms of physical appearance, the concept of 'beauty'—both prompted and unprompted—appeared repeatedly in exchanges with student interview participants. Whether curvy or skinny, unrealistic and unachievable, or realistic and attainable, it remains crucially important for women to believe themselves to be beautiful and to be perceived as such. Certainly, there is growing awareness of the unattainability of normative beauty standards. However, this has led to the sense that such pressures are no longer so problematic, with the burden shifted onto women to be impervious to oppressive social expectations given that they are now 'armed' with the knowledge of the 'falsity' of representations of femininity and beauty. Therefore, within this discourse of beauty, there is a shift towards self-surveillance, and women negotiating their way—on an individualistic basis—through the quagmire of severely restrictive notions of appropriate female appearance and conforming to standards of physical attractiveness. Interestingly, several of the young women interviewed came out in defence of 'skinny'. They express resentment that the pressure to be curvy now seems to have eclipsed the pressure to be skinny. Whatever the ideal of the day, social pressure to be beautiful prevails and is acknowledged by almost all 12 interviewees. However, it is notable that several of the male interviewees lacked awareness of how their own views add to that social pressure. For instance, Paul recounts his experience of seeing his girlfriend constantly struggle with accepting her physical appearance and recognises that cruel comments and jibes by men and boys about how women look add to that. Having acknowledged that, however, he admits that the default woman he designs an advertisement around has to be beautiful. Kevin, meanwhile, expresses distaste at women wearing too much make-up, thereby unconsciously adding to social expectations that often set women up to fail, such that there is a pressure on women to be beautiful and attractive, but if there are visible signs of her working to achieve that, they are pilloried for it. 'Beauty', for the most part, remains a primarily female concern. Students express an understanding that men have avoided this because of differential male-female media portrayals and social standards and expectations.[6] There was also a sense that men lack the vanity that goes hand in hand with a preoccupation with physical appearance:

> Most of them (women) would be a lot more conscious of their hair shampoo, like what does it do for them, does it make it shiny does it make it soft, whereas most guys they just say a €2 bottle of Tesco shampoo or something will do me fine as long as it cleans my hair. (Kevin)

In a lengthy exchange on the issues of the female body, image, and beauty, Fiona understands 'beautiful' to be something that women can 'transform' into by consuming various products and through undertaking certain practices such as making physical changes to one's appearance by using make-up or dyeing one's hair. Although she talks about women benefitting from more 'realistic goals of what women should look like', she makes the distinction that if women are fat or unattractive, they should not be told that they are beautiful. Presumably since this would require too great a suspension of disbelief, such women should be encouraged to 'believe' they are beautiful:

If I was doing the Dove (advertising campaign) I would have said like 'believe you're beautiful' not like 'you are beautiful' because people are going to be like "no I'm not", but if you say 'believe' it's something like it would be like "maybe I am", like it would give you kind of hope or belief inside that maybe you are.

This leaves the work of having to feel attractive as a fat and/or 'unattractive' woman squarely on the individual woman rather than a reconfiguring of what, as a society, we might think is attractive about women. By contrast, she notes that 'I think when a man is good looking he is genuinely good looking and women do look … like, most women are gorgeous without make up but women's beauty is artificial beauty'. Echoing this somewhat, Gillian identifies an apparent tension inherent in the presence of 'real' and regular-looking women featuring more prominently in advertising and the media. This reality, she suggests, does not satisfy the aspirational aspect that women require and look for in the presence of supermodels used to advertise products. In other words, women do not want to be regular or 'real', they want to aim to look like a supermodel.

This perception of the centrality of issues of beauty to women's lives is played out in a wider context that is tied to a kind of tyranny of having to be perfect. This relates to how women have internalised ideas that they need to be and look perfect. This narrative of 'perfection' occurred in general exchanges that touch on the societal pressure on women to look or to be a certain way. The social pressure for women to look perfect has an impact on their innate confidence in abilities that are not connected to their appearance. While there were some comments that social pressure to look a certain way is affecting men, for the most part that is not the consensus. Della identifies a shift in desired body type from skinny to curvy and laments that naturally skinny women are being accused of starving themselves. She expresses frustration at not being able to win at the game, and that the goalposts of what constitute the perfect female body keep shifting. She suggests that 'I think women really struggle with their looks in that way 'cos it's always kind of … they're basing themselves on a photo-shopped person and I think that really sucks'. She does not, however, include herself in that struggle. Likewise, Cat thinks that she escaped such social pressure to look attractive and be appearance oriented for a bit longer than slightly younger women and teenagers. While she admits to enjoying clothes and make-up, she would not subscribe to the view that 'beauty' equals 'empowerment' and notes that 'I feel like there's other ways of being empowering'. Advertising, as well as popular cultural media figures such as Kim Kardashian, adds to the notion, as Cat believes, that women's value is in their attractiveness.

Feelings of (Dis)Empowerment

Sharply connected to the concept of beauty and to the tyranny of having to be and look perfect, issues pertaining to feelings of empowerment, and indeed disempowerment, emerged. Disempowerment for women was expressed in ways that appeared to manifest through self-objectification, sexual expectations and sexual harassment, oppressive beauty regimes (expressed as being annoying and oppressive), and a lack of confidence, in college and in work environments/contexts. Empowerment for women, on the other hand, was available through having more 'achievable' beauty standards. For example, several of the female interviewees express the potential for empowerment as a sort of 'negotiated' exercise or process, through buying into beauty pressures just enough to feel good and conform, but not too much for it to feel oppressive. In addition, they clearly gain confidence through their academic achievements, as evidenced in expressions of enthusiasm for the degree course and enjoyment with various aspects connected to advertising work, such as the creativity it allows. It is noteworthy that none of the young women explicitly expressed feeling personally disempowered. However, in a long exchange with Colette about her experience of being groped in a nightclub, issues of disempowerment and lack of control were clearly surfacing:

> I was wearing like a reasonable length dress, it was mid-thigh and I was just walking up to the bar and some fella who was just sitting there, he randomly slapped me on my ass as I was walking by, and like I didn't … like, nothing I did suggested that that's what I wanted or that's what I was interested in or that made me feel good about myself which it didn't, I was actually quite annoyed … And I don't know, it's unwelcome at times, especially

unwelcome because I have a boyfriend, so I wouldn't have any interest like that and I'm kind of thinking, 'What have I done to kind of show that I'm interested?' and in a lot of cases it's nothing.

She went on to make the correlation between that incident and such issues as shaming women for their sexuality, the prevalence of rape culture, and expectations for women to be available and beautiful, while simultaneously being mocked for being vain. She feels distinctly frustrated with a discourse that sets women up to fail; they're damned if they do and damned if they don't. She spoke of double standards between what is acceptable for young men and women, and how this leads to her feeling backed into a corner with very little recourse to exercise personal agency:

I actually got really annoyed about something I saw on Facebook last night. A few guys in the class actually 'liked' it. It was a picture and it was all girls sitting in a room getting ready, putting on make-up and whatever and the caption was, 'Let's spend extra long getting ready for the men we're going to ignore this evening.' And they 'liked' that. Obviously I'm not going to fall out with them over it. But it did annoy me, that it's saying they (the girls) get ready and just because they look nice they have to give the men loads of attention and if they don't it's like you're a bit mean or something.

This exchange with Colette demonstrates that she has given a great deal of thought to this issue. She recognises the unfairness of such expectations on women to be readily available for men, both in a sexual capacity and in terms of men expecting women's time and attention. However, apart from this conversation, the female students interviewed did not personally identify with feeling, in any sense, disempowered.

Damien spoke at length about his thoughts and experiences with prostitution in Dublin, and the disempowerment women face through sexual violence and working in prostitution. He explains how he had changed his perspective after coming into contact with some organisations that work with prostituted women. Before this he felt clearly that, while trafficked women could be considered victims, women in prostitution were there through their own fault. However, after exposure to people who work with and support women to leave prostitution, he now believes otherwise and is sympathetic to all women working in prostitution. The use of women who work as prostitutes was regarded in his circles of friends as a very casual occurrence, accompanied by jokes about how the friends in question 'can afford it'. While he says that he has not and would not pay for sex because he is in a committed relationship and that it is a bit 'impersonal', he recounts visiting a brothel with a friend a number of years ago and watching his friend pick out a woman from the line-up and go upstairs with her. The conversation afterwards, he explains, was a fascination with the different ethnicities and body shapes on offer and what sex would be like with the women. He expresses dismay that, in trying to educate his friends, he has found them resistant to changing their views, especially his best friend. Significantly, he reveals that this particular friend of his who has regularly paid for sex holds very entrenched views about traditional gender roles:

> He says he wants the traditional woman, you know. He wants to have kids, and she stays at home, and it's just like 'you're not gonna get that these days', it's hard to find you know, things are changing, and he's like 'that's kind of what I want'. He is of the, I suppose, old-fashioned kind of mind; he wants to be the one working.

Such an attitude reflects long-entrenched 'virgin-whore' dichotomies, which construct women as one-dimensional beings who exist in service of men. However, Damien says, this is not necessarily representative of his experience of heterosexual, committed couples and he sees a lot of sharing of care responsibilities and of 'strong' women and stay-at-home dads but admits that, if he had children, staying at home with the kids would not be the life for him. As such, Damien both simultaneously recognises the ways in which women can be, and indeed are disempowered through both prostitution and a social pressure to sacrifice their career and working lives to stay at home and care for children, but seems unwilling to be part of a solution to overturn that reality. In general terms, there was little-to-no expression of male disempowerment, except when conversations shifted to representations of men and masculinity in advertising texts, which is discussed in the next chapter. Rather, male empowerment was expressed through their ability to flex creative muscles, through developing a professional expertise, and the sense of insight and knowledge garnered from the undergraduate and postgraduate training environment.

'I Am Different'

Running alongside an ability by the young women interviewed to identify areas of potential disempowerment for women, without a corresponding association of those feelings personally, was a narrative of 'I am different'. This was not present in the male student interview exchanges. This involved women expressing themselves in ways that differentiated and distanced themselves from other young women. Consequently a sense of solidarity with other women appeared to be largely absent. It is suggested that this individualised experience manifests from an internalisation of a neoliberal self-empowerment discourse. Perhaps, also, a lack of female representations that chime with their own opinions and experiences represents another reason for this distancing. Della, who came across as very driven and motivated, recounts how she was drawn to the high pressure, the deadlines, and the large workload involved in working in the advertising industry. She talks about being ambitious to reach a high, managerial level, and is very aware of women not being in dominant positions in the advertising industry. She sees herself as a corrective to that, and expresses frustration at fellow female classmates who lack confidence to progress:

> Some girls they're just like, "Oh no I couldn't do that, I can't do that, that's just not ... that's too much" and stuff. And like it makes me want to scream and go "Yes you can!"

Meanwhile, Colette, somewhat contradictory to her earlier expressions of disappointment that women are judged on how they look and what they wear, also seems to reinforce that judgement:

> When I'm on a night out, and I see like, I don't know, a girl with a tiny dress on, and I actually turn round to my friends and say, 'If I ever come out in a dress that short, just kill me.'

She also endorses her boyfriend making fun of women who dress up when attending football games:

> He jokes about all the girls who get dolled up to go to the match sort of thing, and then there's a pub they all go to afterwards and like 'the session mots[7] are here, dolled up to the nines'.

This distancing tactic employed by some of the young women interviewed works to inadvertently reinforce notions of women as high maintenance and as a burden, and works against a value for women and their full and diverse lived experiences. Women's collusion in their own oppression as explored by Bourdieu (2001), and as previously discussed in this chapter, may also be explained by considering McRobbie's (2007) concept of the 'sexual contract'. By this, McRobbie is referring to the conditional advancement of women, and is based on the understanding that women are compelled to fit uncomplainingly into existing structures, rather than seek any fundamental changes to the established gender order. It is used to quell the upheaval caused by feminist demands and campaigns. As a consequence of the 'sexual contract', women's visibility is tolerated, but it is sharply mitigated through codes and conventions of appropriate dress, beauty standards, and use of voice. Appearance especially needs to be carefully negotiated by women in environments where they are taught not to antagonise, or threaten, the position of men. This negotiation becomes manifest in a 'postfeminist masquerade', which incorporates a hyperfeminine style of dressing, expressly and consciously invoked so as not to stray over into the gender-deviant realm of masculine dressing. In addition, it is a style often adopted by successful and powerful heterosexual women in order to remain attractive to men, since ambition and power are deemed to be turn-offs in women, as referenced in the many on-screen examples of demanding, difficult women who destroy men's confidence and emasculate them through their superior intellectual, economic, and professional prowess. While this 'hyperfemininity' was not in evidence with the female students of this study, the extent to which physical attractiveness remains integral to her worth and social value and capital is without question.

The 'sexual contract' and the conditionality of women's equality are firmly embedded within an individualisation of women's experiences.

Meritocratic practices are assumed to be in operation, which denies inequalities and injustices predicated on biases, prohibitive maternity leave policies, gender pay gaps, and sex-role segregation in the labour force, for example. This results in the presumption that women, and indeed men, who find themselves socially or economically disadvantaged only have themselves to blame for not taking full advantage of the opportunities open to them. This kind of discourse divests those oppressed, marginalised, and subjugated groups in our society of the chance to recognise and call to account the structural injustices that work against them. Indeed, both neoliberalism and the after-effects of 1990s New Feminism could be held to account for this individualisation, such as in evidence among the female student participants of this study.

The 'New Feminism' that emerged in the 1990s, alongside the third wave of feminism—which itself was characterised by a focus on issues of race, representation, and queer theory—is often viewed as particularly problematic for its tendency to overstate the gains made by feminists for women in contemporary, especially Western, society. Indeed, New Feminism went hand in hand with the 1990s-postfeminist trend of rejecting the notion of women as victims. This may explain why female students simultaneously distance themselves from other women and from feelings of disempowerment. However, this vehement rejection of the victimised woman was never fully proffered with a corresponding recognition that women are often made victims and vulnerable by patriarchal factors in society, since such elements are presumed to no longer exist. Rather, somewhat counter-intuitively, it is coupled with the resurrection of postfeminist-driven offensive and sexist humour. In addition, this strain of feminism has been criticised for its propensity to remain at the level of the individual woman. Its appeal was that women could achieve self-empowerment through making certain choices, such as how one chooses to conduct one's personal and romantic relationships, spend one's money, or opting to remain long-term single and childless (Whelehan 2000). In other words, third-wave New Feminism has been critiqued for its lack of collective consciousness. If women are focused solely on their own subjective experiences and situations, it did not leave the feminist movement in a healthy position in terms of its ability to pose a serious challenge to patriarchal structures and institutions. This individualised conceptualisation of empowerment is something in evidence among female participants of this study. Besides New Feminism and an influential postfeminist culture, a wider context of neoliberalism has served, over the preceding 20 years or so, to make it more difficult for women's continued oppression to be framed in a coherent and collective sense. This is because '[t]he neoliberal view of the individual is as a self-governing, independent entity, engaging endlessly in self-examination and improvement' (Moran and Lee 2013, p. 374). Personal enhancement is achieved through increased consumer consumption, and thereby dispenses the need for an examination of how structural and systemic factors work to disempower people along sex/gender, class, and racial lines.

Despite the disheartening picture painted in this analysis, in the past number of years, a new strain of feminism has been emerging. This is now widely recognised as the fourth wave of feminism, which differs from New Feminism in its outward-looking social and political consciousness, although aspects of third-wave feminism and notions of empowerment through sexual objectification have been retained. There are indications, however, as evidenced by this upsurge of feminist activism, that postfeminism may be loosening its grip. Nevertheless, although commenting almost two decades ago, Whelehan (2000) makes a compelling point about equality between the sexes that is worth reiterating. She warned that attempts to make meaningful and long-lasting gains for women and to remedy the subjugated status of women in society can only be effective if there is an accompanied abandonment of reductive gender norms. Despite feminist victories won and rightly celebrated, if this is not achieved and if the concept of gender continues to exert heavy influence, it is debatable how much progress is being made.

Indeed, it is yet to be seen whether some of the beliefs that underpin the transgender movement have stalled and reversed the progress made in extricating gender norms from a supposedly natural association with biological sex. Some of the discussions around transgenderism and the associated transactivism appear to assert that natal male transwomen may have been born with a 'female brain' or 'female essence'—often seen to manifest through an interest in conventionally feminine interests—and that natal female transmen, conversely, exhibit an interest in masculine pursuits, which is suggestive of possessing a 'male essence' or 'male brain'. As argued by Brunskell-Evans (2018), '[i]n contrast to enabling freedom, by insisting gender is inherent rather than a social construct, the gendered intelligence offered by transgender doctrine … endorses the very gendered norms of "masculinity" and "femininity" it is purported to revolutionize' (p. 42). This thereby 'reinforces the myth that "men" and "women" are different species of human being … with different desires, different needs, different aptitudes, and different minds' (Murray 2017, p. 7; quoted in Brunskell-Evans 2018, p. 46). In other words, such a reconfiguring of 'gender' as innate and of 'sex' as socially constructed asserts, albeit unwittingly but no less surely, that the gendered concepts of femininity and masculinity relate firmly and differentially to women and men, respectively, even if 'women' and 'men' no longer refer to sex-based categories but ones to which individuals can self-identify as belonging.

Such a contention risks reinforcing gender stereotypes, and potentially aligns the transgender movement with the neurosexist contention that we have 'male' or 'female' brains—something debunked by critical scientific evidence. Cordelia Fine, in her book *Delusions of Gender: How Our Minds, Society, and Neurosexism Create Difference* (2010), offers a robust rejoinder to arguments and 'evidence' that insist differences between the sexes are innate and biological. Instead, she makes the convincing case for sex differences that can be explained, in part, by culturally and socially imposed gender stereotypes (Fine 2010). Nevertheless, despite such arguments, there remains widespread inconsistent usage of the terms 'sex' and 'gender', where they are often conflated and used interchangeably. This has arguably further served to undo the work done by radical feminism's insistence that the notion of gender should be rejected altogether, since it would free both sexes from its constraining implications. This blurring of 'gender' and 'sex' is echoed in student's tendency to take up viewpoints that are aligned to a belief in gender essentialism and therefore suggests that future professional decisions to represent the sexes in adverts in ways that do not rely on gendered notions of masculinity and femininity are unlikely to materialise.

The Tomboy: 'Men Are Always Willing to Give It a Go, You Know. And with a Tomboy… They're Always Willing to Give It a Go'

Reductive gender norms apparent among study participants that construct women and girls as the problematic sex conversely serve to laud the 'tomboy' as the apparent ideal. This trope of the 'tomboy' was only referenced by Damien and Nick, but it is given life and has the space to emerge because of an individualised 'I am different' discourse among the women and girls, which sees the young women interviewed, with the exception of Fiona, dissociate from their female peers, particularly those who may be understood to be feminine and 'girly'. In addition, discursively constructing males as easy-going and low maintenance supports a more general approval of women and girls deemed to be 'tomboys'. Talking about hearing anecdotal stories about working in nightclubs, Nick says:

> The women's bathrooms are a lot worse than any male ones, that's just something I've heard from people working in the industry. All of them will tell you the same things, 'cos women are the ones doing up their makeup and things like that in the bathroom whereas men just go to the bathroom and walk out. In nightclubs, that's why there are no queues for the men's bathrooms.

While that reality might be largely true, it does suggest a perception that, whereas with women a trip to the bathroom is arduous, and involves doing themselves up—reinforcing notions of women as vain and high maintenance—men on the other hand just go to the toilet and leave, with no fuss. Nick goes on to say that having lived with girls, he has not noticed any major differentiation, with some of the girls very 'easy-going' and some of the guys very 'uptight'. However, even this innocuous comment reveals an expectation that the reverse to be mostly true. He expresses a belief that differences between women and men manifest more depending on personality type rather than sex/gender, but he does concede that there are distinct spheres of recreational interests between the sexes. In relation to going to an all-boys school, Nick paints a picture of an environment characterised by freedom and rebelliousness, and banter and fun, and being able to say well-meaning but vulgar things without fear of offending. However, in discussing what might have been different if he had attended a mixed-sex high school, he describes girls as more sensible, responsible, and mature, and thus positions them as something akin to killjoys. He predicts, for instance, that throwing a football around in class would not happen in a mixed-sex class. The impact of going to an all-boys secondary school, he believes, was to keep them in a state of 'arrested development', which would have been avoided if girls were present. That is to say, girls are understood to be a calming and 'civilising' influence.

While the sexes may exhibit distinct characteristics from a young age as a result of both 'nature and nurture', according to Nick, it is clear that a higher value is placed on supposedly masculine skills, traits, and interests. Explaining that, as a kid, he was 'allowed to try an awful lot of things I shouldn't have been able to try', such as dancing, Nick thus implicitly understands that for a boy to express attraction to typically feminine or girly hobbies was far less accepted and encouraged than the reverse. He expands on this by acknowledging that for a girl to be into boyish hobbies like martial arts might lead to her being labelled a 'tomboy'. However, on whether this should be construed as an insult, or not, he says:

[I]t depends on how it's said as opposed to the actual term and where it's coming from, like if it's coming from a group of girls calling you a tomboy it's … or if it's close friends in school calling you a tomboy that could be bad but if it comes from, like my close friend referring to his little sister as a tomboy, that's just 'she has interests similar to ours, good on her'.

This is an interesting assessment from Nick. since it suggests that he thinks the term 'tomboy' applied to a girl by other girls would imply a certain degree of bullying or meanness, whereas the label represents a compliment if used by boys—a kind of endorsement of the girl for showing an interest in 'their' hobbies. Arguably this statement draws on gendered notions of female bitchiness and male camaraderie.

Damien, in talking about gender differences, appears to denigrate attributes and interests most commonly associated with girls and femininity.

He observes that the interests and hobbies of his mixed-sex group of friends manifest along traditional gender lines, with his female friends spending their leisure time 'having a glass of wine, (and) talking about kittens', while his male friends meet up to watch UFC (Ultimate Fighting Championship) together. Obviously this comment is tongue-in-cheek, but he does go on to articulate an awareness of the role that socialisation plays in instilling in girls and women a lifelong preoccupation with and insecurity about their appearance. It is this early and sustained social value placed on female attractiveness that can be blamed for 'how non-tomboys are developed'. Furthermore, in the same vein of the discussion with Nick concerning gendered hobbies for boys and girls, Damien likewise maintains that boys are more heavily socially penalised for associating with girly or 'feminine' diversions, while consequently girls enjoy far more social approval when they take up boys or 'masculine' pastimes. This is because girls who are understood to be tomboys are seen as 'strong', whereas a boy playing with 'girls toys' would be made fun of for being a 'sissy' or 'gay', something deemed to be an insult. This notion of tomboy-girls as 'strong' is in contrast to how he perceives many girls and women as reticent to throw themselves into new situations, and instead to respond to challenges by complaining: 'Men are always willing to give it a go, you know. And that's with a tomboy, they're always willing to give it a go, sort of thing.' Damien is obviously exasperated and annoyed by this perceived introversion and shrinking away from new situations by women:

> I do strength-and-conditioning classes in the morning on Tuesday's and Thursday's and, it's just, you see when new girls come in, it's just kind of eh, it's always a rigmarole, whereas new lads come in, they get straight in, they'll do the exercises, whether they can do it or not, they'll get tired, they'll stop, they'll have a break but girls… (puts on a whining voice) 'I can't do iiitttttt', and they complain a lot more and I think, kind of, the tomboy, and the strength thing is just seen more as getting on with things, you know.

While these exchanges suggest that Damien conceives of men and masculinity as favourable, he demonstrates an understanding that gender norms and a lack of encouragement of girls can lead to a certain passivity by women. Nevertheless, such an acknowledgement seems to only extend to an intellectual recognition of the negative effects of gender socialisation on females, since when the topic of working mothers or assertive female politicians is raised, he expresses discomfort with both. Similarly, Nick talks in ways that suggest women can learn from men's example and that they need to be more like men. In an exchange about encouraging and convincing two female housemates to join him and male friends on a ski holiday, he suggests that because the young women thought of themselves as 'fragile' and that those activities were not for them, they had not given it a go. He intimates that what was needed was for the girls to be taken in hand by their male friends and initiated into the ways of taking on a 'cool' pastime. As such, girls are not cool on their own terms, but only on male-defined terms. While this is somewhat patronising and condescending, he is perhaps right in his assertion that without the example of other young women undertaking adventurous activities in as large numbers as young men, that there persists a sense of such things as not being for them.

The 'tomboy' motif is one that is well-established. In an article on the subject, Peterson (2014) lays out its history through an exploration of Hollywood Cool Girls, from the actress Clara Bow who came to prominence in the 1920s through to Jennifer Lawrence in the contemporary period. Peterson deconstructs the appeal of Lawrence and the sentiment that she's 'just like us', but comes to the conclusion that

> no, she's not like us. She's like a perfect character out of a book. Specifically, a book by Gillian Flynn called *Gone Girl* ... in which a main character describes a very particular yet familiar archetype: "Men always say that as the defining compliment, don't they? She's a cool girl. Being the Cool Girl means I am a hot, brilliant, funny woman who adores football, poker, dirty jokes, and burping ... Cool Girls are above all hot. Hot and understanding. Cool Girls never get angry; they only smile in a chagrined, loving manner and let their men do whatever they want." (Peterson 2014)

Peterson's deconstruction of the tomboy narrative contains echoes of both Gill's 'affective life' of postfeminism (2017) and also McRobbie's 'sexual contract', which results in a self-imposed silence on women in relation to grievances they have, since to point out injustices, inequalities, and double standards is to, purportedly, victimise oneself and to demonstrate that one is not adept enough at navigating a world that expects a certain feistiness from women in exchange for enjoying the benefits of sexual equality. Similarly, Peterson notes that 'cool girls' or tomboys do not complain or protest or whine or make a fuss; rather, she is 'fun … never nag(s), or stay(s) home watching rom-coms; she never complain(s) or (is) scared or shy' (2014). This distinction between women who are 'fun' and who don't 'nag' and those who are 'scared' or 'shy' was in evidence in the ways that both Nick and Damien discussed tomboys as being like them, as opposed to more typically feminine girls, who were discursively constructed as akin to being bores or drags. Although it's preferable that women, in practice and in terms of perceptions, are associated with such traits as being fearless and brave and light-hearted, this archetype of the cool girl/tomboy is not a simple celebration of women who display these characteristics. Rather, the portrayals of tomboys that populate popular films, novels, and pop songs serve a more complicated and concerning purpose. Her role of being easy-going and accommodating, both in general terms and towards the men in her life, is reflective of a tacit agreement that—in the wake of massive shifts in the gender order—she must suppress any further demands or unease with the status of women and relations between the sexes. This, Peterson argues, represents a way for men and women to move forward in a markedly altered gender climate by mitigating societal unease that women 'once emancipated, would become … castrating bitches' (2014). In other words, women would be afforded a degree of equality with men as long as they did not make any further demands. Consequently, instead of posing a threat to the masculine order, the tomboy/cool girl soothes men's worries about having to relinquish more power by her happy-go-lucky and carefree demeanour. Although it is acceptable that women could be lively and spirited, if her passions extend to feminist change, she begins to pose a threat to this precarious arrangement. It is a delicate balancing act, since 'to be "cool" is to tread a fine line between something different, something almost masculine, but never anything *too* masculine, or assertive, or independent' (Peterson 2014). Thus, women's increased presence in previously male-dominated spheres and spaces is permitted on the proviso that they cheerfully fit into, rather than overhaul, those male structures.

Furthermore, not only does the tomboy-type not pose a threat to or challenge men's status, she makes it easy for men to like her by maintaining an attractive appearance and not making demands: whether emotional or otherwise. Above all, as Peterson tells us, the Cool Girl is beautiful. Crucially, however, she does not care if she is beautiful, which is what makes her so appealing and therefore 'beautiful'. This very clearly butts against the 'beauty' narrative that is so apparent among interview participants in this study, but also echoes the sentiments that women cannot win. If they try to look beautiful they are labelled self-conscious and vain. But, if they eschew such standards, they are picked on and ridiculed, as confirmed by Paul in his admission that men and boys can be 'pretty harsh towards girls who they consider ugly and stuff like that'.

Considerations of Gender in the Curriculum and in the Classroom

While it is not possible to ascertain if the educational gendered cultures in which these students are embedded feed the themes and strands discussed heretofore in this chapter, it is likely that these discourses are internalised by students through wider social and mediated gendered interactions. However, gender has clearly been considered and discussed at the institutional and curriculum level. With 92% of questionnaire respondents indicating that they have learnt about gender in their modules, this implies that they are conscious of having had discussions based around the subject throughout the course of their studies. At the undergraduate, BA level there are over 40 modules offered during the four-year degree course. In order to ascertain the extent to which 'gender' and other associated concepts are formally and specifically embedded into the design of the course, searches were conducted for the following keywords across all 47 module descriptors and outlines: *gender, women, men, represent* (representation/s), femini* (femininity, feminist, feminism), masculin* (masculinity, masculine), stereotyp* (stereotypes, stereotyping), sex* (sexist,* *sexism, sexualisation),* and *ethic* (ethics, ethical).* This investigation revealed that while there were no references to *men, femini*, masculin*, stereotyp*,* or *sex** present in the online detailed module descriptors, there were three references to 'gender'; in the reading list of two modules, and also in the description of another module, which deals with self-concept, gender, and body image. There was one reference to 'women' and one reference to 'representation', and references to 'ethic*' across six different modules, ranging from general ethical considerations concerned with children and vulnerable groups to mostly ethical issues in connection with research and advertising practice. On the whole, there does appear to be a good effort made at undergraduate level to deliver to students critical, sociologically, and theoretically based modules throughout the course of the four years that aim to offer a counter-narrative to the less critical and more practical modules offered on advertising and marketing strategies and practices. However, there is very little specific mention of gender and no references to stereotyping. While needing to be mindful of areas of interest and experience by lecturers and the possibility that a concern with issues related to gender are not accounted within those spheres of expertise, the lack of inclusion of gender could, and arguably should, be formalised and made explicit in the module designs and descriptions. At master's level, only a very general course overview is provided online, with no module descriptors on either the creative or the executive stream. Some theoretical modules are covered in the first semester on consumer behaviour, advertising research, and marketing communications. Beyond that, modules are mostly practical and practice based. There is no indication or mention of a focus on critical thinking, ethical issues, or gender or diversity outlined in the course content.

Observing Gender in Action: First-Year, Undergraduate Students Discuss Gender and Related Issues

An invitation was extended by a lecturer to sit in on several classes in which students were discussing gender, feminism, and sexism in the media and advertising. This component of the data collection was very valuable in terms of bearing witness to the contributions offered by students with respect to the various issues raised. The students in this group were playful, rowdy, and boisterous. Students were encouraged to think about how gender has been conceptualised in the media and what kinds of images denote and signify gender and/or biological sex, and to consider how women have been systematically annihilated by the media, through a lack of visibility and a trivialising of women. The content also covered issues of gazing and power dynamics. Throughout class time, students were afforded an opportunity for open exchange and dialogue, and they were asked for reactions and opinions. For instance, in commenting on an image of a woman in a short skirt,[8] some students expressed attitudes that strayed into discourses of shaming women who are sexually active and victim-blaming women who are sexually assaulted. Responses to this image ranged from a female student saying 'if a girl wears that, she can't expect men not to look at her'. Another female student asks 'why shouldn't she wear that?', while a male classmate suggests 'she's not someone you'd bring home to your mother'. Conflating the class discussion of social judgement and sexual double standards with assumptions of the inevitability of sexual harassment and assault if dressed in a short skirt, a young man in the class posits the view that girls as well as men think that a girl in a 'belly top ... (is) asking for it'. This notion of 'asking for it' quite clearly references rape and veers into victim-blaming territory. However, there were some more nuanced responses to the image and to some of the in-class commentary, with one girl proffering the most complex and considered reaction to the image in suggesting that 'it's not men or women [who attach these labels to women], it's society and the media'.

There was also a quite hostile exchange in the class following a screening of the trailer for the 2010 Jean Kilbourne documentary *Killing Us Softly 4: Advertising's Image of Women*. In reaction to the clip, a male student reacts in a somewhat defensive manner. While he allows that Kilbourne 'has a point', he takes issue with feminists claiming that media and advertising images can cause violence against women. He makes reference to contemporary conversations happening around the issue of rape on US university campuses, and says that the link between imagery and violence has been repeatedly proven to be untrue. Moreover, he says that men are more often victims of violence than women. A female student then chimes in to say that she had seen a video of a woman who had formerly been a feminist but had stopped being so because she became aware of the lack of support for male victims of violence. At which point, another male student makes a comment on the prevalence of male rape in prison, seeming to bring up this example to prove that violence and sexual assault is more an issue for men than women. The students, or at least those who were most vocal, reach a consensus that there is little connection between violent acts and advertising images.

Coy and Garner (2012), in fact, do draw contextual links between sexualised culture, of which advertising imagery contributes massively (Gill 2007, 2008, 2009a, b), and violence against women and girls, in creating what they term a 'conducive context'. If the message is repeatedly sent that girls and women are responsible for the sexual conduct of both sexes, this bears with it an assumption of women and girls as emotional and moral labourers for both women and men, echoing the discussion with Nick about girls being more mature and responsible, and keeping boys in check. Both sexes are taught, within this context, that girls must be sexually available in order to be considered sexually attractive, yet paradoxically are derided for being sexually active. Accompanying the double standard, there is often victim-blaming in instances of sexual assault and rape—a narrative that emerged in this class discussion. Such an exchange as witnessed in this class demonstrates, at a minimum, a fundamental misrepresentation and misunderstanding of the problem of violence against men, and the lack of understanding or recognition of the prevalence of violence against women. It also indicates an unawareness of how sexualised imagery in advertising and the conflation of sexual and violent tropes in adverts can feed wider discourses of women as sexual objects. The potent consequence of objectification, as Kilbourne (1979, 1999) has pointed out, is that violence is more readily enacted on another human being who has been consistently objectified and thereby dehumanised. However, there appears to be reluctance on the part of some of the students in the class to acknowledge how the persistent objectification of women is connected to violence against women and girls. Indeed, in another exchange during a class in a later week, a male student defiantly asks if the lecture content will cover the topic of violence against men, or is it all 'rape culture and shit'. This exchange prompts a female student to ask 'aren't men also cropped in advertising?' Some students were demonstrably defensive to too much attention being paid to women, whether that is in discussions of violence against women or depictions of women, and also appear to be conscious of a supposed misandry.[9] As a result of this interruption, other classmates echo and express a concern for men.

This observational component of the study offered a compelling snapshot of some attitudes and opinions that were on the more antagonistic end of the scale being voiced and given expression. More generally, in order for the educational space to start thinking about how to engage advertising students with a critique of gender, one area that could, and indeed should, be tackled—given the attitudes and confused understanding of students to issues of gender—is that related to gender essentialism. Hearn and Hein (2015), whose research is focused on marketing and consumer research (MCR), are critical of the depoliticisation of any references to gender theory within the body of MCR. They note that

> examples of gender essentialisation based on ... biology emerged in studies of hormonal differences linked to consumer behaviour ... Despite widespread critique of this work, including the conflation of sex and gender, or the reduction of gender based on biology, psychology or fixed identity ... its persistence and high academic ranking highlights that marketing scholars continue to be particularly interested in understanding fundamental differences between men and women and perhaps tacitly assume that these differences define gender. (Hearn and Hein 2015, p. 5)

The authors are also critical of marketing research that consistently ignores the operation of gendered systems of power. Such research agendas and priorities undoubtedly impact, influence, and come to bear on advertising education, and it is an issue that advertising lecturers and course designer would do well to heed.

Throughout this chapter, and the analysis that underpins the discussions, treading the line between trying to avoid essentialising women and men and pointing to instances where traits and characteristics traditionally and normatively associated with women and girls are denigrated is difficult. Another tension to acknowledge is the obligation within this study to draw attention to, and discuss with students, the issues still faced by women and girls without perpetuating a sense of the female sex as a bundle of problems to address. While admitting to not always being able to avoid sliding into discussions that reinforce rather than refute differences between the sexes, or being able to untangle where the direction of the conversations set by me starts and students' own constructions and understandings of gender begins, the painstaking coding and analysis process has nevertheless enabled an accurate picture to emerge in connection with student attitudes to gender.

This chapter has dealt with a multitude of simultaneously contradictory and competing discourses and narratives that sit (uncomfortably) side by side. For instance, there is at one and the same time an acknowledgement of how socialisation works to silence and ignore women and girls, while also denying that the issue of equality between the sexes is one that still needs to be addressed. There is widespread recognition of social forces that disproportionately lead to women internalising restrictive and reductive pressures to look and act in a certain manner, while actively adding to such issues by virtue of buying into notions of appropriate and desirable versions of femininity: versions that can be often one-dimensional and contradictory. Generally speaking, student attitudes across questionnaire, survey, and interview data align with a gender-different-but-equal discourse. Such a narrative most commonly associates women with notions of domesticity and caring, and as emotional labourers responsible for both sexes. Women and girls are also discursively constructed as self-conscious, high maintenance, lacking in confidence, and not funny or adventurous. Instead they are seen to be anguished over beauty and body-image issues, as evidenced in a belief that women simultaneously need more realistic standards but also 'want' to aspire to supermodel looks. This image of the 'problematic' girl-woman does not extend to the 'tomboy', since she is seen to emulate men. Men, on the other hand, are understood to be cool, easy-going, adventurous, and low maintenance and are associated with strength and confidence. This carefreeness on the part of male students is maintained until they are asked to think about women's and girls' female-based oppression, at which point there is resistance to translate the 'knowledge' of the continued subordination of women and girls into sympathy and empathy, or at its more extreme, there is a refuting that the gender hierarchy still exists.

Although an account of the differential attitudes to issues of gender between male and female students has been provided in this chapter, particular attention was paid to the opinions of the men interviewed. This is because, firstly, and for the most part, their attitudes manifested as a more consistent discourse, and secondly, the male students are far more likely than their female classmates to go on to take up creative roles in the industry, and therefore will hold more influence in driving advertising campaigns. The young women's opinions, on the other hand, proved to be more varied, disparate, silenced, or complicit with male opinions. Reasons proffered for this include such concepts as Bourdieu's *paradox of doxa* and collusion in one's own oppression, as well as McRobbie's 'sexual contract' and the individualised, neoliberal context that currently operates.

Notes

1. The survey was devised by the lecturer on a first-year undergraduate module. The 57 completed surveys were offered for use in this study. It was not possible to disaggregate the data into male/female responses.
2. I am fully aware of the debates concerning the contested notion of innate 'gender identity' in reference to transgenderism and transactivism. Nevertheless, the term 'accurate' here refers to a framing and understanding of gender within a radical feminist tradition. For reasons previously stated, this conceptualisation of gender offers, I believe, the most useful means for interrogating the continued operation of patriarchy.
3. Some characteristics were coded as 'neutral' (i.e. if it was ambiguous, or could be interpreted as either good or bad). Those traits were not included for further consideration.
4. Rape culture refers to a social and cultural climate in which the rape and sexual assault of women is tolerated, normalised, denied, or facilitated as a result of attitudes held about women's supposed culpability in their subjection to sexual violence. Such a culture is certainly aided by prevailing discourses and understandings of men's sexuality, sexual appetites, and subsequent actions as aggressively beyond their control, and women's sexual conduct and actions as accountable for both sexes.
5. Mary Lou MacDonald is an elected Irish politician and President of the Sinn Féin party.

6. However, there are some exceptions to this, which manifest in a concern for men and their body image. This is discussed in detail in Chap. 4.
7. 'Mot' is a Dublin slang word for girls or women, while 'session' in this context refers to a night out of heavy drinking.
8. See here for the image discussed: http://www.huffingtonpost.com/2013/01/18/rosea-lake-vancouver-judgments-skirt-length-photo_n_2504950.html
9. This trend is further discussed in Chap. 4.

References

Bourdieu, P. (2001). *Masculine Domination*. Stanford: Stanford University Press.

Brunskell-Evans, H. (2018). Gendered Mis-Intelligence: The Fabrication of 'The Transgender Child'. In H. Brunskell-Evans & M. Moore (Eds.), *Transgender Children and Young People: Born in Your Own Body*. Newcastle upon Tyne: Cambridge Scholars Publishing.

Butler, J. (1990). *Gender Trouble: Feminism and the Subversion of Identity*. New York: Routledge.

Coy, M., & Garner, M. (2012). Definitions, Discourses and Dilemmas: Policy and Academic Engagement with the Sexualisation of Popular Culture. *Gender and Education, 24*(3), 285–301.

Fine, C. (2010). *Delusions of Gender*. New York: W.W. Norton & Company.

Gill, R. (2007). *Gender and the Media*. Cambridge/Malden: Polity Press.

Gill, R. (2008). Empowerment/Sexism: Figuring Female Sexual Agency in Contemporary Advertising. *Feminism & Psychology, 18*(1), 35–60.

Gill, R. (2009a). Beyond the 'Sexualization of Culture' Thesis: An Intersectional Analysis of 'Sixpacks', 'Midriffs' and 'Hot Lesbians' in Advertising. *Sexualities, 12*(2), 137–160.

Gill, R. (2009b). Supersexualise Me! Advertising and "The Midriffs". In *Mainstreaming Sex: The Sexualization of Western Culture*. London: I.B. Tauris.

Gill, R. (2017). The Affective, Cultural and Psychic Life of Postfeminism: A Postfeminist Sensibility 10 Years On. *European Journal of Cultural Studies, 20*(6), 606–626.

Hearn, J., & Hein, W. (2015). Reframing Gender and Feminist Knowledge Construction in Marketing and Consumer Research: Missing Feminisms and the Case of Men and Masculinities. *Journal of Marketing Management, 31*(15–16), 1626–1651.

hooks, b. (1984). Feminism: A Movement to End Sexist Oppression. In *Feminist Theory: From Margin to Centre*. Boston: South End Press.

Kilbourne, J. (1979). *Killing Us Softly: Advertising's Image of Women*. Retrieved from http://www.jeankilbourne.com/videos/

Kilbourne, J. (1999). *Can't Buy My Love: How Advertising Changes the Way We Think and Feel*. New York/London: Touchstone.

McRobbie, A. (2007). Top Girls? Young Women and the Post-Feminist Contract. *Cultural Studies, 21*(4–5), 718–737.

Millett, K. (1970). *Sexual Politics*. Urbana: University of Illinois Press.

Moran, C., & Lee, C. (2013). Selling Genital Cosmetic Surgery to Healthy Women: A Multimodal Discourse Analysis of Australian Surgical Websites. *Critical Discourse Studies, 10*(4), 373–391.

Peterson, A. H. (2014, February). Jennifer Lawrence and the History of Cool Girls. *BuzzFeed*. Retrieved from https://www.buzzfeed.com/annehelen-petersen/jennifer-lawrence-and-the-history-of-cool-girls?utm_term=.kt3z1Y5bxV#.cr54xgE31o

Rubin, G. (1975). The Traffic in Women: Notes on the "Political Economy" of Sex. In R. R. Reiter (Ed.), *Toward an Anthropology of Women*. New York: Monthly Review Press.

Tasker, Y., & Negra, D. (2007). *Interrogating Postfeminism: Gender and the Politics of Popular Culture*. Durham: Duke University Press.

Whelehan, I. (2000). *Overloaded: Popular Culture and the Future of Feminism*. London: Women's Press.

4

The Reverse Stereotype and the Double Standard: Expressions of Concern About Advertising's Treatment of Men

During interviews with students, the most common advertising gender themes of sexualisation and domesticity were explored. It was considered important to get a handle on how students interpreted such imagery and whether they accepted or rejected depictions of women as sex object or housewife/homemaker, and the reasons and justifications underlying their attitudes, since women have far more frequently been reduced to these roles than men in advertising. It was broadly found that most students found the sexualisation and sexual objectification of women in advertising problematic, at some level. However, there was some confusion and misunderstanding about what constitutes sexual objectification. Furthermore, such abstract, hypothetical, or theoretical concerns for reductive depictions of women as sex objects appeared to fall away when the discussion moved onto issues of what could or should be done to address this.[1] Adverts that equate women with the domestic realm proved to be far less contentious for students. Indeed, none of the students interviewed expressed a concern with this ubiquitous trend in advertising. Rather, it was explained and justified on a number of fronts, which is covered in the following chapter.

It is noteworthy that, aside from discussions of women in advertising imagery occupying extreme ends of a spectrum as either '*sex objects*' or

© The Author(s) 2019
A. O'Driscoll, *Learning to Sell Sex(ism)*,
https://doi.org/10.1007/978-3-319-94280-3_4

'*mothers*'—to echo one student answer when asked to declare what are the cultural expectations of women in society—exchanges specifically connected to gender and advertising turned towards a concern for how men are being portrayed in adverts. This marks a departure from the discussions of the preceding chapter, which, when talking about men, in a general sense, lacked much or any sense of anguish or concern. However, when homing in on critiques and examinations of gendered advertising trends, this concern for men and boys becomes present and subsequently tended to result in exchanges with students in which they then pronounce wider issues connected to social pressures on men and boys as areas of concern. Siding with the male position, for the most part, was also found to be the case, particularly among female students, when analysing reactions and interpretations to the Carlsberg advert 'The Crate Escape'—details of which are outlined towards the end of this chapter.

Sexualisation of Women: '*The Female One Is Just Way More Voyeuristic*'

On the questionnaire, students were asked to think about if, whether, and how advertising might affect women and girls, and their view of themselves (see Table 4.1). There was no specific mention, in the phrasing

Table 4.1 Questionnaire question—*A lot of people claim that advertising damages young girls' and women's self-esteem. What do you think about that?*

	Male (%)	Female (%)
Agree	**71**	**82**
References to 'beauty', and/or 'body image', and/or physical appearance, and/or to 'unrealistic'[a] beauty standards	*74*	*74*
Disagree	7	8
Depends[b]	11	8
Too ambiguous/vague to code or left blank	11	2

[a]Includes references to the use of Photoshop and/or air-brushing
[b]'Depends' relates to answers where participants did not respond broadly 'agree' or 'disagree' and instead referred to contextual, circumstantial, and determining factors concerning the question being asked

of the question, to beauty or body-image pressures, or to sexualisation and objectification.

Overall there is an understanding that advertising might damage the self-esteem of women and girls. Although the question does not reference 'beauty' or 'body image' or women's bodies, almost all respondents interpret the question this way, thereby implicitly tying a woman's self-esteem to how she looks. There is extensive critical awareness of 'unrealistic' beauty standards, and of women as victims to that social pressure. However, there is no evidence of any questioning of why beauty should be a marker at all tied to women's confidence. In other words, student responses put forward the view that if women had more achievable and attainable beauty goals such as promoted in the Dove Campaign for Real Beauty, which is offered repeatedly as an example, it would be much better for women and girls. They do not critique why that should be a goal at all. No respondent makes a connection between advertising imagery and women's and girls' self-esteem in terms of rarely being shown in positions of authority or expertise, although one respondent does make a connection with how women are not treated as equals in wider society and that this is reflected in advertising. A small number of respondents suggest that if there are such issues, advertising is not responsible, or further that things have improved to the degree that it is no longer a concern. Students were also asked if the continuing concerns of feminists over the objectification of women in advertising is still justified (see Table 4.2).

While expanded answers were too numerous and diverse to code or categorise systematically, an attempt was made to choose what appeared as the most common and similar type of justification for answering in a particular way. Overall the majority of answers are 'yes', with responses backing the view that objectification of women is a persistent and prevalent trend in advertising and results in negative social implications.

Table 4.2 Questionnaire question—*Traditionally, feminists have been concerned with the objectification of women's bodies in advertising. Do you think this is still an issue? Explain/further comments*

	Male (%)	Female (%)
Yes	80	90
No	18	8
Too ambiguous/vague to code or left blank	2	2

Common reasons for answering in this vein also allude to the 'unrepresentativeness' and 'unrealistic' nature of such images, thereby implying a misunderstanding of 'objectification' in confusing it with images of 'beautiful' women. Other confused notions about what is meant by 'objectification' interpret such feminist concerns as amounting to sex-negativity or body shaming. Objectification, more accurately, should be understood as involving the presentation of a person in decontextualised and dehumanised ways that deny them complexity, subjectivity, and multidimensionality. The term 'sex-negativity', on the other hand, refers to a feminist position taken in respect of sexual activity. In the popular lexicon of feminist debate, sex-negativity stands in contrast to sex-positivity, with the former a term applied to feminists who seek to position sexual behaviour and sexual activities, especially between heterosexual sexual partners, within a wider understanding of patriarchal power relations, and the latter referring to those feminists who maintain that sexual tastes and preferences practised between consenting people should not be within the remit of feminist concerns. Consequently, the finding outlined above suggests that some students are conflating feminist concerns of the continued prevalence of the objectification of women with the popular contention that feminist concerns about sex and presentations of the female body unhelpfully fuel a culture that shames women for their sexual preferences and for displaying their bodies. Somewhat similarly, several other answers suggest that although women may continue to be objectified, this is potentially empowering: 'If a woman or man have worked hard to achieve a certain body and don't mind showing it off ....' This student answer trails off but is reflective of postfeminist sentiments concerning liberation through self-objectification. Some 'yes' answers take a resigned tone, such that respondents believe objectification of women to be inevitable, and that men are also objectified in advertising. Additionally, those respondents answering 'no', although few in number, make reference to advertising having improved to the degree that objectification is no longer an issue. One might have expected that the inclusion of the word 'feminist' in the question may have elicited some pushback responses. However, given that over 80% of both male and female responses agree that sexualisation and objectification of women in advertising remains an issue, this speaks to students' awareness of the

Table 4.3 Questionnaire question—*Do you think men's bodies are objectified and eroticised in contemporary adverts in the same way as women's?*

	Male (%)	Female (%)
Yes	84	52
No	13	46
Too ambiguous/vague to code or left blank	3	2

trend. Students were likewise asked about their understanding and opinion on the objectification and eroticisation of men's bodies in adverts (see Table 4.3).

It is significant that only 3 out of 46 male respondents who answer 'yes' to this question and contend that men's bodies are objectified and eroticised in the same ways as women's bodies sought to offer further insight. These answers include the following: 'Yes. But men being men, there is more of a deal about seeing a woman with little/no clothes on', 'Yes. However, they are not objectified as consistently', and 'Yes. But not nearly as often or with the same repercussions.' None of the male respondents who reply that male bodies are not objectified or eroticised in adverts in the same way as women's expands on their answer. Somewhat similarly, only one female respondent answering 'yes' expands on her answer. She offers the following comment: '*Diet Coke gardener ad*' by way of making her case—thereby suggesting that the existence of this one example of a male body presented in an objectified way is commensurate with the far greater volume of adverts that objectify and eroticise women. Further, only 2 out of 24 women who do not believe that men are objectified in advertising in the same way as women offer something further, namely, 'Not in the same way … But still' and 'not as often'.

The sex-disaggregated data is significant for this question, with a much greater proportion of male respondents believing that men are objectified in advertising in similar ways to women. However, with little expansion on their answers, it is suggested that this points to a lack of conviction, for the most part, in answering in this manner. Nevertheless, during interviews, students proved to be more capable than had been anticipated in identifying differential gendered signifiers in advertising imagery. Much in line with Gill's (2009a, b) research in this area, some students were quick to underscore how various visual cues in the adverts that were being discussed work to position men as sexually, or otherwise, dominant and women as vulnerable and submissive. This meant that, for the most part, students were able to demonstrate, during the interview, a proficiency at decoding gendered content embedded in adverts, meaning that they could adequately and accurately 'read' gender in ads. Of those students who were able to identify concepts of power, dominance, and subordination, not all took a critical stance against restrictive and reductive gender depictions in advertising.

In reading two Nivea adverts for women and men's shower products, which depict the sexes in very different ways, several students were especially good to identify aspects of voyeurism, and the male gaze in the women's adverts versus notions of functionality, authority, and power in Nivea ads for men. Colette very astutely and correctly identifies how something like a shower product is advertised differently to men and women, with women shown using the product in a 'sensual' way. The impact of the 'gaze' on the female figure in the advert is such that the viewer holds power over her. Colette touches on how objectification and sexualisation 'reduce' women, in terms that it represents a reduction to something less than she might otherwise be. She offers a very articulate and nuanced discussion of the pressure for women to succumb to self-sexual objectification, while being very clear that women should not be shamed for showing their bodies or capitalising on their sexuality. However, she expresses disappointment that there are not more diverse representations of women in popular culture. In deconstructing the women's Nivea advert she notes that 'she's not looking, you're doing the looking and you're doing the appraising'. Conversely the man being portrayed is more in control, and as if 'he has the upper hand because he's laughing at some joke that you don't know about'. She offers an interesting analytic deconstruction on why the shower pose of the woman would not work for men:

> I think it would be nearly too submissive or something that we're like… I don't know, I can't even phrase it … it wouldn't work as well, I don't think men would respond to it as well as they would with the other one. I think … if he was to take that pose, it would be kind of submissive and a bit more, like, weaker or something.

She suggests that the reason men are rarely, if ever, depicted in advertising as sensually lathering up is because it reflects wider societal attitudes and expectations for women and men, with the submissiveness of women 'not even noticed because it's so normalised, I think'.

Also comparing the male-female Nivea shower ads, Cat uses the term 'voyeuristic' for the woman and 'functional' for the man. She adds that the woman showering is '*indulgent*' and '*gratuitous*'. The prevalence of sexual tropes in advertising has meant, according to her, an internalisation that goes unchecked because it is so common and ubiquitous. However, echoing Gill (2008), she did point out that she does not agree that men are objectified to the same degree as women and even in cases where they are that:

> it's not like there's the same history of it and you can't kind of claim, like... you know, women there is a history, there is still a need for feminism and it's all this kind of precedent of women being show in a certain way or represented in a certain way that it is still offensive.

However, on discussing further the Nivea adverts, she simultaneously holds the view that she does not find the sex-differentiated representations troubling, problematic, or offensive. She suggests that the same product uses starkly different imagery to depict women and men engaging with it because 'product categories necessitate that you have to advertise them differently'. However, she does say that far more ads should be focused on being entertaining in ways that are not sexist.

More generally, Della is very critical of common motifs in fashion ads and brands which depict women as so often semi-clothed and lying on top of, or clinging to, a man in a needy manner. She talked about being tired and bored with seeing the same objectified tropes in adverts, but demonstrates that she does not have an understanding of how such a prolonged perpetuation could lead to women internalising social pressures to look a certain way. For instance, she expresses exasperation with other young women who are offended and shocked at the unrealistic body sizes of a Topshop mannequin or a Barbie doll, and suggests that it is women in competition with each other that drives this pointless preoccupation more than anything else. Yet, simultaneously, Della was highly critical of fashion advertising for both creating and contributing to a cultural climate that pressures women to have certain body types:

> In ads themselves I have noticed that there is a big difference, like the guys … are always kind of, like, this really cool kind of person, whereas girls kind of look like a sex object basically.

Bernard was also able to deconstruct a Gucci advert in relation to its commentary on wider social gendered relations. This print ad depicts a desert scene in which a woman dressed in a short gold dress kneels at the feet of a shirtless male whose head does not appear in the image. In her crouched pose, she has a hand tentatively on one of his feet while he towers over her in a physically imposing posture. His reading of the advert includes the observation that the woman looks 'scared, alarmed', and that although the male is 'more exposed … he is the dominant partner. She's seeking refuge from him in the Wild West or what appears to be the Wild West. She's a defenceless individual.' Bernard points out that he learned to pick up on the visual clues that offer such a reading of this ad from class discussions about the dominant role of men in advertising imagery. It was clear from several students that Laura Mulvey's concept of the 'male gaze' had been well explained by one or more of their lecturers. To their astute understanding, it offers an explanation for why advertising often portrays the sexes in such ways that confer on men a higher status and power while simultaneously disempowering women. In Mulvey's highly influential 1975 essay 'Visual Pleasure and Narrative Cinema', she employed a psychoanalytic assessment of the contradictory centrality of phallocentrism and the image of the woman to narrative film. She suggests that '[i]n a world ordered by sexual imbalance, pleasure in looking has involved implicit collusion with active/male and passive/female tropes' (Mulvey 1992, p. 27). She coined the term 'the male gaze' to refer to the phenomenon of men looking at women, and women watching themselves being looked at. In Freudian terms, because the image of the woman signifies castration for the male, she must be represented in passive, that is to say, non-threatening, terms. Although Mulvey's articulation of the male gaze is somewhat fatalistic, since it ascribes a problematic voyeurism to all viewers, regardless of whether they are women or men

(Rose 2001), her examination of a gendered visuality is both echoed in other work undertaken in respect to gender and representation (Berger 1972), and influential for scholars drawing on her dyadic concepts of images of passive women and active men:

> Men *act* and women *appear*. Men look at women. Women watch themselves being looked at. This determines not only most relations between men and women but also the relation of women to themselves ... Thus she turns herself into an object. (Berger 1972; cited in Pollock 2007, p. 21)

Berger's assessment of visual culture and of the sustained prevalence of male-active and female-passive motifs is echoed by the student participants of this study over 40 years later in their readings of contemporary advertisements. Through from Goffman (1979), Williamson (1978) to Kilbourne (1999) and Gill (2007, 2008, 2009a, b), this speaks to the longevity of such established notions about femininity and masculinity.

Discussing issues related to the sexualisation and objectification of women's and men's bodies reveals that the female student responses are slightly more nuanced and tend to appreciate the complexity of a shaming/rape culture more than the men interviewed. There was a sense, among both male and female students, that they know what they should say, but do not really internalise those concerns. Sexualisation and objectification appear not to be issues of significance for men: either as victims themselves or in a concern for women and girls. Women's bodies and selves were understood to be objectified and commodified through imagery (e.g. through advertising) and through the activities of culturally powerful figures (e.g. the practices of Miley Cyrus and Kim Kardashian). Not every student interviewed demonstrated an ability to identify sexual patterns and themes in adverts. For instance, Kevin rejects the notion that contemporary advertising has a tendency to objectify women:

> Not at the moment no. I think there's only two ads that spring to mind, as I said the Hunky Dorys and the Club Orange ads, the rest of the ads even tailored towards men they're not really as gender orientated or anything like that. So, just Lynx, Club Orange and Hunky Dorys.

This comment indicates that Kevin does not see what is obvious because of its ubiquity. Nevertheless, even though he dismisses the assessment that sexual objectification of women in advertising remains prevalent, in another discussion, he suggests that adverts that are successful at engaging with men have something in common: 'like, once a guy sees an ad with a macho guy and a girl on his arm and all the money in the world, like, things like that, it does appeal to him, it definitely does'. Consequently, his description of such an advert equates a 'girl' with 'money'—in other words an asset obtained by the 'macho guy'. This effectively objectifies the woman in the advert and strips her of power and agency. Paul, likewise, found it difficult to recognise the pervasiveness of the sexual objectification of women in advertising. He attributes this to his temperament, which is to say that he does not often get distressed or outraged, thus seeming to brush away the concerns of people who draw attention to such content and to imply that different reactions to sexist adverts can be chalked up to an issue of sensitivity.

The sexualisation of culture, in which the objectification of women's bodies in advertising texts is a part, grew out of a contemporary postfeminist gendered landscape. In the past decade or more it has become increasingly prevalent and pronounced, as well as scrutinised and critiqued. Postfeminist discourses of empowerment through self-objectification, individual choice, a repolarisation of the sexes, and of a consumerist narrative constructed around reinvention have provided the catalyst for the proliferation of sexual imagery that is a feature of a sexualised culture (Gill 2008; Coy and Garner 2010). Sexualisation involves 'the extraordinary proliferation of discourses about sex and sexuality across all media forms … as well the increasingly frequent erotic presentation of girls', women's and (to a lesser extent) men's bodies in public spaces' (Gill 2007; cited in Coy and Garner 2012, p. 287). There is, as Coy and Garner recognise, a 'recurrent theme of empowerment through the approving male gaze' (2010, p. 661). This is closely correlated to social pressure for women to be beautiful and sexually attractive to men, with sexual attractiveness understood to mean sexual availability. While conforming to those pressures is constructed as empowering, Coy and Garner make the crucial distinction between genuine empowerment and agency which bears with it the capacity to reject normative associations of femininity and female sexuality, against 'choices' made within a context in which those pressures are normalised and considered inevitable and which bolster the commodification and assimilation of female sexuality into male-defined terms.

Positioning feminism as a lifestyle choice coupled with the postfeminist contention that sexual objectification is empowering has facilitated a 'socio-cultural climate where some young women perceive that a positive self-identity can be built on reclaiming the sexualized portrayals that modern feminism has sought to challenge' (Coy and Garner 2010, p. 658). Similarly, since young people are usually loath to be seen as out of touch or passé, there is therefore much widespread conformity to post-feminist representations of women as sexualised objects. Especially constrained to conform are those women working in the cultural and media industries, says McRobbie, since they are supposed to be adept at keeping their finger on the pulse. To take an example, McRobbie notes that '[a]s a mark of a post-feminist identity young women journalists refuse to condemn the enormous growth of lap dancing clubs despite the opportunities available for them to do so across the media' (2004, p. 259). The findings among participants of this study indicate that the discourse discussed above regarding the supposed power to be harnessed from embracing sexual objectification was not one that was referenced by the female students in this study. However, although they do not subscribe to such a viewpoint, they also somewhat condone objectified representations of women in advertising through their ability to ignore or overlook these depictions, especially when pushed on what action might be taken to eliminate such imagery.

Domesticity of Women: *'I Presume That's Still True That Women Are Doing the "Whatever"'*

Although most students showed themselves to be capable of identifying concerning sexual themes and representations in adverts, they also express opinions that aligned to the view that advertising is now 'post-gender', meaning that some interviewees believe advertising no longer pays attention to gender in any significant or meaningful way. Despite being critical of how the advertising industry portrays women as 'sex objects', Della believes Irish advertising to mostly portray a gender-equal relationship between women and men, with neither taking centre stage. She notes that Irish advertising tends to focus more on both sexes socialising and having fun together. When asked if advertising has become more or less sexualised in recent years, she answers definitively that she does not think advertising has become more sexualised. However, she may be interpreting 'sexualised' as meaning more gendered or with more obvious gender roles in advertising:

> I don't think it's become more sexualised, I think going back to the 1960s and 1970s, ads were very much so genderised. Like, the female was the one at home doing the cleaning.

Nevertheless, although she misunderstands the question concerning the proliferation of sexualised images of women and girls in contemporary culture, this comment indicates a belief that advertising is 'post-gender' and cannot be charged with assigning reductive gender roles to women and men in advertisements. This was echoed by both Fiona and Kevin, who express similar views of advertising as no longer gendered in any significant or meaningful sense:

> I wouldn't think it would be a very big feature in Ireland's advertising because we're just so equal here. I know the pay scales aren't but in regards to perceptions, men and women are equal. (Fiona)

> There is one that comes to mind with SMA,[2] the whole Irish mothers; 'we've seen yous, we've gotten to know yous over the years', and it's just images and clips of I'd say new mothers just with their babies and getting splashed with food or in the supermarket. That'd be the only one that comes to mind that looks like it's toward a specific gender role. (Kevin)

The idea that advertising is post-gender was closely related to lack of acknowledgement that there are defined gender roles evident in adverts, with Kevin's comment implying that women are no longer confined to the housewife and caring role in advertising campaigns. However, that being said, there was simultaneously also a wide recognition of the 'housewife' or the 'busy working mom' trope in ads, albeit with some suggestion that this is changing, with men also shown in domestic product adverts. Accompanied by this recognition is a distinct lack of a sense of unfairness on the part of the students concerned with unequal burden-sharing of domestic and care responsibilities between women and men, with the exception of Des, who feels this role is undervalued and should not be assumed to be reserved automatically for women.

Fiona, for instance, appears to subscribe to opposing and divergent viewpoints about desirable relations between the sexes. On the one hand, in the big, that is to say abstract, picture she understands and describes well the principles of feminism, although she rejects association with feminists she considers to be 'extreme'—a distinction she does not qualify. However, in her imagined future reality, she expresses views that suggest that the notion of both male and female life partners taking on an equal domestic load would not be tenable, since women possess a natural ability for these roles. She fails to understand or recognise how the onus on women to take on the responsibility of the majority of household work upholds inequalities between the sexes. In terms of advertising domestic products, Fiona applauds as progressive the increasingly common depiction of the 'busy working mom' in adverts, as opposed to the stay-at-home housewife:

Back then it was the woman in the house during the day you know at 1 o'clock, the time when women would be at work now and she's cleaning the house and then he comes home and she's like 'oh blah blah you're home' but now it's the woman rushing out to work or how to get things done fast so you can get to work or pick up the kids. The mam is actually busy during the day now, not that it's the woman's role to stay at home ... There has been a big change.

She also added that she sometimes sees 'men actually doing chores in the ads', although she demonstrates that she is well aware that women are the primary target market for domestic products, since 'you wouldn't see an ad for Harpic or Cillitt Bang on Sky Sports News'. Fiona's gender essentialist views are clear here, and impact on both her personal worldview with respect to male and female gender roles, and her reading of adverts that uphold and naturalise the polarisation of the sexes.

Colette, meanwhile, notes that, although adverts for breakfast cereal, for example, would tend to show a mother preparing breakfast for her child while the father goes out to work, there is progression away from those depictions. She talks about an advert for Birds Eye in which there is a male character making dinner for his girlfriend—something that would have been considered highly unusual in advertising in the 1950s. Della similarly raises the issue of changes in advertising, and talks about Fairy Liquid and the fact that they released an advert featuring a man washing the dishes. She raises this example as proof that the trend of domestic products targeting women has changed, and that 'to some extent they're trying to get everyone'. Revealingly, however, she admits that in a class project that involved marketing and advertising a bleach product, although they initially wanted to target both sexes, they ended up predominantly targeting women.

An assumption of equality achieved and gender stereotyping as no longer prevalent was expressed by Kevin: 'I don't see too many ads that say a woman is the mother and therefore she stays at home and does all the shopping and them stereotypical roles', and yet directly following that comment he indicates that a washing-up liquid advert would inevitably be targeted at women/housewives/mothers, since that is the first target market that would spring to mind. He interprets the kind of advert that shows the man as incompetent at housework, or as purposely trying to be bad so he does not have to do such chores again, as humorous. However, where he does find it problematic is because it depicts men as lazy, rather than recognising why such depictions of male incompetence in the home might be problematic in terms of its social impact in continuing to burden women with the responsibility for domestic and care work:

> I think they'd (women watching such an ad) just find it humorous, thinking 'yeah, yeah, yous are all lazy and now we have an ad about yous'. I think they'd take it with a bit of humour and finally it shows what men are really like doing the washing and now 'we've caught yiz rapid'.[3]

Significantly, in widening the potential target market for a washing-up liquid advert, he talks about the single dad, or stay-at-home dads, but does not think about or include the working dad, unlike the implied working mother, who remains the primary target. This serves to undermine the case that both working partners should be distributing domestic work equally.

In terms of the ubiquity of advertisements for household products, Cat's position is that these ads are instantly forgettable, but that—she assumes—for the most part they tend to show women using the products. She suggests that this is probably the case because women, in reality, predominantly do undertake the work of domestic chores in the home, and that if men were shown in such ads, it would be less credible or believable. If she was given a brief to create an advert for a domestic product, she says it is far more likely that she would put a woman, rather than a man, in the ad using the product because of a number of reasons: firstly, that it is simply just true that more women do the cleaning and do the shopping for cleaning products; secondly, as a long-established approach to advertising domestic products, it is deemed to be a safe bet; and thirdly, domestic products represent a boring brief, so the inclination is to do what is quick and easy.

Expressing a similar view, albeit lamenting the continued equating of domesticity with women, Nick suggests that this is because throughout the years market research is telling advertisers that women and 'housewives' are its target market. While he admits that this is probably sexist, he explains that advertisers are caught in a Catch-22 situation. However, he makes allowance for the fact that maybe the market research is shoddy or flawed and works to uphold an assumption that may no longer be true. Arguably, this might indeed be the case, because Nick talks about 'housewives' and 'wives' but does not account for households in which both male and female partners are working. In discussing adverts that show the 'busy working mom', he does point out that it might be progressive in a sense because it alludes to the woman working outside the home, but he concludes that it is ultimately unhelpful in showing women taking on the responsibility of the domestic tasks. He laments this as a continued trend, since it limits women in terms of associating them to the traditional sphere of cooking and cleaning, and it is limiting to men such that it 'perpetrates the negative connotation that men don't clean at all'. In his experience, women do tend to do the cleaning because they have a lower 'tolerance' for the state of the homes they want to live in. Whether this is an intentional device by men, given that they can assume women will cave in and do the cleaning, was not made clear by Nick. However, having indicated that girls are quicker to tidy and clean, he did suggest that living in a mixed-sex student house, they all try to be fair and divide up communal cleaning tasks.

Bernard demonstrates, through the use of one example, how men are shown as incompetent fathers/partners/husbands in the home in adverts. Although, when pressed, he acknowledges the significance of the fact that men are only shown in advertising as idiots in the home and not at the workplace: 'Some advertisers seem to be playing again on the stereotype that … [men do] not do much at home.' He recognises the impact that advertising narratives can have on the lived realities and experiences of male-female relations in the home: 'the advertising industry is feeding on the stereotype and the stereotype is growing from the advertising industry'. Although he demonstrates that he is aware of the double shift that disproportionately affects women, he does not give the impression that he considers this as unjust:

> Now, a lot of females work … outside the family home. They also have to juggle the domestic responsibilities as well, childcare issues, family home so they're doing two jobs at the same time, at least two jobs at the same time.

Yet, having identified that reality for women, he goes on to say that 'there's a stereotype out there maybe that the man isn't pulling his weight, for the want of a better expression'. This notion of men not pulling their weight as a stereotype is not compatible with the idea that women actually do bear an unequal share of domestic and care responsibility. In other words, the language here is important; either men not pulling their weight in the home is a stereotype and therefore is a simplistic view of a more complex reality, or it is an accurate reflection of reality and serves to contribute to women having to do 'two jobs at the same time'. He cancels out one position by inference to the other.

Much like Cat, Gillian does not show much emotional or intellectual investment in the imagery or representation side of advertising, especially in terms of domestic products. While acknowledging that, probably, it is not desirable for adverts to show mostly women using household products, she is fairly unfazed and simply says, of supposed changes in gender roles in the home, 'I think society's definitely moving away from that and advertising kind of needs to catch up a bit with that maybe.' Given that she does not subscribe to a naturalised gender difference point of view and believes that, beyond physiological and physical strength, sex/gender is not a marker for differential capacities and abilities, her lack of investment in the impact of advertising imagery is remarkable.

Again, like Nick, and demonstrating a slightly more in-depth critique than the female students of associations of women to domesticity, Damien refers to class discussions on the problem of the continued representation of women doing most of the domestic work in the home in ads, and notes that the class tended to counter this trend with assertions of change predicated on one example: the 'Barry Scott, Cillit Bang' adverts. However, he correctly asserts that this does not represent significant change, since the Cillit Bang adverts in fact do not show the male 'Barry Scott' character in the ad cleaning a kitchen. Rather, according to Damien, the ad is stereotypically 'male' in being about strength in terms of its allusions to 'power' and 'hard-core' cleaning. Damien comes up with several examples of ads and campaigns that target women and men based on stereotypical assumptions about gender roles, with man as the protector and woman as the carer and nurturer. He admits to being a bit blind and ignorant of such things until they are pointed out in class, but he does give a good account in terms of demonstrating an awareness of the problematic and prevalent depictions of women in the domestic setting in advertising. However, despite an intellectual appreciation for these concerns, they do not appear to extend to his personal life and he notes, as reported in a previous discussion, that he would have no interest in being a stay-at-home dad. In addition, his response to his friend that 'wants the traditional woman' is that 'you're not gonna get that these days', it's hard to find you know, things are changing'. Rather than acknowledging that relations between men and women have been transformed and that equal burden-sharing is the fair and right thing to do, this comment sounds a resigned tone at the changes that have occurred between the sexes. Since women have sought to take the option of exclusive homemaker and caregiver off the table, men have had to move with it.

Across a variety of discussion topics Des represents the outlier position in terms of attitudes to gender, in a general sense, and to advertising imagery. Echoing Cat and Nick, Des suggests that a Catch-22 situation is at play in terms of the fact that cooking and cleaning products are targeted at women because they do those tasks. He also contends that because advertising reflects that, this works to reinforce those roles. However, Des expresses a value in the role of housewife and stay-at-home mothers, a sentiment he extends to teachers also, as doing something socially valuable and not easy, and deplores that these roles are undervalued, denigrated, and downplayed by society. He suggests that, if it made sense for him and his future (hypothetical) family, he would willingly be a stay-at-home dad, and would never automatically expect his wife and the mother of his children to give up her job:

> If the situation ever came along where I had kids and I was on an average job and my wife was on a really good job and the decision was there for me to stay at home and raise the kids, I would have no problem doing that if it was beneficial to all of us.

Nevertheless, despite Des' gender-equal views, the fact remains that women are far more likely to be portrayed in domestic roles in advertising. In a study[4] carried out in 2008, commissioned by the-then Equality Authority, Ging and Flynn found that 'compared with men, women are still overrepresented as homemakers (in advertising) and underrepresented in public and professional life' (2008, p. 5). This study comprised a sample of almost 800 adverts across various Irish media platforms, such as newspaper, magazine, billboards, television, and radio in order to capture the extent to which and the ways in which women, specifically, are stereotyped in advertising in the Irish media. On the whole, the authors note, adverts are seen as using vastly different imagery and tactics to market and advertise very similar products to both sexes. This is something that was clearly in evidence in discussions with students regarding the Nivea shower product ads. Advertisers differentially target women and men by playing on long-established and stereotypical notions of innate characteristics and capacities. For instance, within the sample, there was a strikingly clear gender divide in terms of equating men with activity and women with passivity. This was achieved through such devises as the use of voiceovers, visual depictions of speaking and silence, and body positions. The sexes, much like Gill has asserted (2008), are also sexualised and/or objectified in different ways—often through invoking 'the gaze', or through specific facial expressions, be they serious, serene, or flirtatious, with the authors finding that men are only shown in a flirtatious manner in just 2.1% of the sample compared with 15.5% of women. On the whole, women were found to be objectified more often than men in the sample set of adverts in the study. This finding contradicts some student views that Irish advertising is post-gender and not particularly implicated in perpetuating differentially and sexist representations of the sexes. In addition, where tropes of infantilisation were present, Ging and Flynn found that male characters and bodies that were infantilised conjure notions of immaturity, whereas when women are infantilised there is a sexualised element not present in depictions of men.

Significantly, in the sample of adverts analysed that relate specifically to a cleaning product, it is almost exclusively women shown using it. The one exception found by the authors is an advert for the brand Bounty and its paper towels range. The 'Carry on Cleaning' campaign for Bounty centres around two male characters in drag representing stereotypical, dowdy, and competitive housewives who delight in the efficiency of the product. Thus, although the authors do not say so, this advert does not in fact represent an exception, since the depiction of men in drag serves to tangentially locate women, once again, within the role as homemaker and cleaner—albeit embodied through the male protagonists. Additionally, there were 'no adverts in the television sample which showed men doing routine household chores (cleaning, ironing, washing up)' (Ging and Flynn 2008, p. 44). Furthermore, in addition to visual and physical presence within a domestic setting, when female voiceovers are used in adverts,[5] they are most often used in connection to home and care work.

In adverts that are located in the home, men make up a significant proportion of those individuals present (40%). However, despite the near-equal presence of men and women in domestic settings in adverts, the sexes are either shown engaged in different activities, or when men and women are portrayed doing the same activity, such as cooking, even this is differentially represented. For example, the study found that, whereas men prepare food for themselves, women are not shown as cooking exclusively for their own consumption, but rather, in all situations analysed, women were seen to be cooking for others. This positions cooking as a 'self-empowering' skill for men; where for women, it is in service of others. Thus, this echoes findings discussed earlier concerning students' reflections on (stereo)typical traits of women and men. Analysis of those responses showed that positive traits connected to women benefit other people, whereas for men, the positive traits relate to self-affirmation and self-empowerment.

Aside from undertaking similar activities in the home, such as cooking, there was a distinct gender divide in terms of 'caring' as opposed to 'playing' with children: '5.9% of the women in the sample were depicted as caring for children as compared with 0.7% of men ... 3.1% of men in the sample were depicted in play with children compared with 1.7% of women' (Ging and Flynn 2008, pp. 38–42). Furthermore, no advert in which both men and women were present showed the male character undertaking routine domestic tasks while the woman plays with the children—unlike the reverse, in which the male protagonist in the ad is shown kidding around with his children while the mother-wife-partner character is shown cleaning up or preparing food. This infusion of fun and humour into adverts in which men are present is something Gareth identifies as an integral and inevitable component of male-targetted advertising.[6] Indeed, when men are shown doing domestic tasks, Ging and Flynn posit that resorting to a comic set-up works to 'defeminise' what is assumed to be women's work. This echoes a wider trend of

> young men hanging out in urban spaces, playing pranks on one another, being loud and carefree and generally having a laugh. Women, by contrast, were rarely seen to occupy public space in this way and were rarely portrayed as playing pranks, refusing to be serious or 'breaking the rules'. (Ging and Flynn 2008, p. 39)

The notion of men being fun and easy and taking up visual and physical space in the world, with women confined to more serious, restrictive, and mundane settings and tasks, chimes with the discussions of the previous chapter in terms of constructing women and their experiences as burdensome and men's as free of those chains. However, an awareness of the constraining and reductive nature of connecting women with household duties was completely absent during discussions about the prevalence of women in domestic settings in ads.

Indeed, reverting to a biologically deterministic belief that women *naturally* belong in domestic settings, an assumption that was prevalent before second-wave radical feminists challenged it, Fiona seems to offer evidence of this pre-second-wave position. When talking about the culpability of advertising for overwhelmingly depicting women doing housework, she maintains:

> I think it's nothing to do with advertising. Like I wouldn't trust my Dad to go do the full week's shopping ... It's just one of those gender role things; the woman does the shopping, and the man fixes the doors ... Naturally enough, if I had kids I would want to stay at home with them ... I wouldn't trust a man to go into a shop and pick up the right things.

Such a gender essentialist viewpoint held by a young woman is surprising until considering that her childhood and teenage years coincided with the zenith of postfeminism and its regressive assertion that women and men are fundamentally and inevitably different. In addition, Fiona's comment provides a reminder of how tenuous and unrooted are the psychosocial shifts that occurred in the wake of the second wave. Although the 1980s is noteworthy for such cultural manifestations as the 'new man' with his aptitude for caring, emotional perceptiveness, and housework, in fact it soon became clear that, in the aftermath of work done by second-wave feminists, an utterly and permanently altered gender order had not materialised. Instead, as Hochschild termed it, 'the stalled revolution' (1989) saw women continuing to bear the burden of the double shift. This unequal burden of domestic and care work placed on women remains a central issue for feminists in contemporary campaigns. A 2011 Organisation for Economic Co-operation and Development (OECD) study highlights why, aside from issues of fairness and equality between the sexes, it matters that we have an accurate picture of who does the bulk of unpaid work in the home: 'Since women traditionally do much of the unpaid work, so neglecting to include it underestimates women's contribution to the economy' (Miranda 2011, p. 6). The author found that in none of the 26 OECD countries surveyed was there parity between the sexes in terms of unpaid work in the home:

> Tasks that have traditionally been thought of as "women's work" (e.g. cooking and cleaning) continue to be primarily performed by women. In the countries surveyed, 82% of women prepare meals on an average day, while only 44% of men do. Also the average time spent by women on cooking is four times the time spent by men. (Miranda 2011, p. 25)

Women, on average, were undertaking an additional two-and-a-half hours' work at home than men, per day.

Given that Irish advertising appears to reflect the reality of Irish women's lives as disproportionally burdened by domestic and childcare work, it is remarkable that there is not greater pushback or discontentment in evidence among the female students interviewed. In seeking an explanation, Pat O'Connor is useful for illuminating the conditions specific to Ireland that may shed light on the reluctance of female students interviewed to firmly dismiss the link between women and the private sphere. Although published 20 years ago, O'Connor's following observation is noteworthy: '[i]n Ireland, the social subordination of women was seen, until very recently, as "natural", "inevitable", "what women want". It was reflected in women's allocation to the family arena, where their position was given rhetorical validation' (1998, p. 245). In fact, Ireland's Constitution, first drafted in 1937, retains the home as women's realm:

> The State recognises that that by her life within the home, woman gives to the State a support without which the common good cannot be achieved … The State shall, therefore, endeavour to ensure that mothers shall not be obliged by economic necessity to engage in labour to the neglect of their duties in the home. (Quoted in Hilliard, p. 2016)

While this constitutional provision does not stipulate that women should not enter the professional workforce; nevertheless, it has proved to be a powerful psychic determinant of women's place in society, and has led to a situation where 'women have been encouraged to exclude themselves from the public arena for "the sake of the family" although their educational levels have traditionally been higher than those of their male counterparts' (O'Connor 1998, p. 245). Of course, there have been major, rapid, and hugely positive changes for women in Ireland since O'Connor's assessment two decades ago. However, the function and role of homemaker continues to mostly fall on women.

Martin (2000) is also enlightening in exploring why Irish society retains a strong attachment to women as carers and homemakers. In an interesting examination of how abortion discourse in Ireland is subsumed within mythical associations of Irish women to nation and nationalism—the 'Mother Ireland' motif, in other words—Martin points out that '[t]he memetic links between women and the nation in contemporary Ireland have generally been structured around the Virgin Mary' (p. 69). The May 2018 repeal of the 1983 Eighth amendment to the Irish Constitution, which gave equal right to life of the unborn with the right to life of a pregnant woman, indicates that Irish people have, for decades, been in the process of dismantling the connection of women with her role as mother and homemaker. However, while female students dismissed sexualisation as a tool for female empowerment, they remain unperturbed at the continued association of women with domesticity. In other words, while the sexualisation of women may be construed as undesirable, women's place in the home is thought to be inevitable, if not natural, suggesting that this dismantling process is not yet complete. That is to say, the lack of a sense of unfairness of the domestic burden indicates an ideological complicity with a 'woman's place is in the home' narrative. Furthermore, although students exhibit a critical awareness and express unease with advertising's overly sexualised representations of women, yet fail to find the prevalence of women in domestic settings problematic, this demonstrates a lack of understanding of how this impacts on relations between the sexes. In addition, perhaps students see little wrong with equating women to the private, domestic sphere because of their own personal experience of stay-at-home mothers, or working mothers that undertook the bulk of the housework.

The Turn Towards Men and Boys: *'There Seems to Be a Reverse Stereotype of (Men) Depicted as Bumbling Idiots'*

As already indicated, in discussing with students the topic of gender representations in advertising texts, a concern for men and boys emerges. This thread comes via two narratives: that one sex must lose for the other to win, and also there is a palpable sense of resignation for the way things are in connection to portrayals of women in advertising. The understanding that for an ad to appeal to one sex, whether humorous or otherwise, it necessarily entails ridiculing or manipulating and fooling the other very firmly relies on a 'war of the sexes' narrative that re-emerged with postfeminism, and which in turn is predicated on assumptions about gender and essentialism, and 'naturalised' gender difference. It also echoes, what Gill (2008) calls, the 'vengeful woman' trope in postfeminist advertising imagery, as seen here in this comment by Fiona:

> To get women on board you kind of have to demoralise the man which isn't good for the man, like I think … just be for the fun of it, I'd like a cheeky brief (but) it would just be so hard to get an actual campaign to be towards both sides. (Fiona)

Fiona is referencing here a belief that for advertising to 'work', it must pit women and men against each other. Although expressing relations between the sexes as a 'zero-sum game'[7] scenario was not present among very many students, there was greater evidence of students taking up positions that indicated they were simply resigned to the way things are, in the sense that they assume the inevitability of certain advertising trends, and a perceived lack of agency to make change. It appears that this resignation fuels a complacency, which itself feeds, or indeed results in a lack of awareness of and connection to the real-life and lived implications for perpetuating gender and sexual inequality. This, what may be termed, resignation-complacency-acceptance cycle is especially in evidence in terms of student attitudes to the prevalence of women in domestic settings in adverts, as discussed in the previous section. In other words, a general apathy and numbness is apparent, which is due to overexposure of images of women as either mothers or sex objects:

> I think it's definitely something that's been around a while. I don't really see it going anywhere. I don't see it disappearing from culture any time soon. (Colette)

That indifference and unconcern is absent around the issue of how men are portrayed in advertising. Instead, students' energy and enthusiasm for talking about misandry—which emerged as an unexpected discourse—may be due to the fact that they are not bored or exasperated by such conversations, since the topic has received comparatively little attention; arguably because much advertising content could not reasonably be considered misandrist. Nevertheless, the consequence of students' engagement with such a topic results in them believing this to be a greater issue than it, in fact, is. In general, references to misandry in advertising relates to expressions of concern for the state, status, or treatment of men, boys, and masculinity—by advertising and its imagery or otherwise. There are a few mixed messages within this discourse, namely that while a number of the male students suggest that men are increasingly portrayed in a misandrist manner, some of the young women interviewed express a sympathy with a growing pressure on men to conform to a narrow set of markers of physical attractiveness. There is a perception among some students that men are now being consistently shown as stupid and incompetent in advertising.

Overall, while it is understood that critiques of advertising texts justifiably retain a focus on women, the questionnaire, interview, and observational class data show that the male students, understandably, jostle and argue for acknowledgement that they are also subject to problematic representations—ones that warrant recognition and analysis. However, they then very rapidly eschew the notion that they might be affected by issues such as objectification and sexualisation. The discourse of misandrist advertising is bolstered by a belief that evidence of an exception to a trend disproves the rule. This occurs where one example or illustration is offered as definitive proof that 'the rule', for example, that women are objectified and sexualised far more often than men in advertising, does not really exist or reflect the reality. In other words, given that an 'exception' exists proves that the rule or reality does not, in fact, exist. The Diet Coke adverts were repeatedly referenced, during the interviews, more than any other ad to accompany points being made in this regard.

During discussions with Colette connected to societal beauty pressures on women, she turns to sympathy for men and boys and the fact that the increasing social embrace of curvy women and an unmasking of the artificiality and unattainability of airbrushed women and Victoria's Secret-esque models is a courtesy not extended to men with 'beer bellies', for example. She suggests that men are potentially more subject to constraining beauty standards than women:

> Real women aren't expected to look like that on a daily basis, but you would still kind of expect lads these days to have a six pack and have the perfect hair and all.

Referring to a Lynx advertising campaign and explaining why it remains appealing to young men, Kevin notes that it is because of the attractive woman 'on your arm'. In discussing the supposed misandry and objectification of men in adverts, he believes this to be a concern, and cites the 'macho-ness' of the Lynx advert guy, rather than recognising that it is the woman in this type of ad that is objectified. More generally, however, he does object to the stereotyping of the hypermasculine male who is assumed to love sports and fast cars, but does say that 'there is a bit of a, what's the word, a bit of neglect of focusing on male equality as opposed to just women'.

Bernard more explicitly and definitively raises misandry in advertising as an issue with which he is concerned. In the questionnaire completed by him, he had noted that 'the pendulum has also swung to the other way with men depicted as sex objects'. He talks about taking gender classes and learning about masculinity and femininity, and proceeds to immediately mention that misandry has now crept into advertising. This indicates that this topic had been raised in lectures and, furthermore, suggests that the belief concerning advertising's problematic treatment of men was put forward or endorsed by the lecturer/s. Bernard refers to a discussion on the George Hook[8] radio programme, which covered the topic of gender stereotyping in advertising. While it appears, from Bernard's interpretation of the radio piece, that misandry was taken as being present in a significant way in advertising texts, the reaction of the radio panellists varied. For instance, one contributor 'argued that it was only kind of maybe balancing out the misogynous trend in advertising ... but as Shane Coleman [co-presenter] pointed out just because something has been wrong ... doesn't justify misandry'. In other words, Bernard feels that two supposed wrongs do not make a right. When asked to provide examples of male objectification and misandry in advertising, Bernard alludes to an advert—referring, it is assumed, to the Diet Coke advert—in which a man washing a window is objectified by the women gawping at him. However, similar to Kevin, Bernard demonstrates through this example that he is not aware of the fundamental power imbalances between men and women in society that render any such (questionable) objectification of men fairly benign, given the duration and the extent of the dehumanisation, denigration, and degradation of women in advertising and other forms of cultural imagery.

This misunderstanding of what is meant by 'objectification' and 'misandry' is likewise demonstrated in his assessment of an advert for Equinox Fitness. The ad depicts a life-drawing scene with a male nude being painted by three nuns, while a further nun is present in the background looking on and 'cloistered' behind an ornate gate, suggestive of the setting being a convent. Bernard asserts that the scene amounts to 'objectification of the male body' and as misandrist. In this advert, the male figure is indeed naked but arguably is not objectified necessarily. For instance, he is not in a vulnerable position, such that the nuns are seated and looking up at him demurely, albeit longingly, and he is standing and looks physically stronger. Furthermore, the fact that the women in the advert are nuns and thereby signify virginity and chastity positions him as the more dominant, knowing participant in this scene. Students, arguably, need to be better versed in the visual cues and able to read these signs and how to differentiate misogyny and misandry and to be cognisant of the differential cultural and social impact of both; that is to say that, while students may be proficient at decoding and reading adverts, they are less able to place that knowledge in a context that is mindful of issues of power. Bernard went on to identify a divide in class regarding opinions on the issue of misandry and male objectification. He explains that while male students in the class did not like the trend towards misandry, he says the young women had no issue with it. However, rather than the female students not having an issue with misandrist representations of men, the truth might be closer to Cat's position that instances of male objectification are not commensurate with women's, and therefore cannot be compared.

In discussing the controversial Hunky Dorys 'Tackle These' adverts, which were created in support of Irish Rugby, Paul references the supposed truism that 'sex sells' in order to explain the appeal of the campaign. Although he concedes that a debate about the ads would draw on many diverse and complicated issues, he suggests that a double standard characterises the nature of the conversations, since if the adverts had featured semi-clad male figures, it would not have garnered the same attention or level of critique. Such hypocrisy, Paul believes, may be due to feminists being too primed to express outrage on behalf of women, while simultaneously ignoring similar depictions of men in the media and advertising. By way of illustration, he raises the story of Dr Matt Taylor, the British scientist criticised for his choice of shirt (depicting semi-naked animated women) during a televised interview on the progress of the Rosetta space mission. Certainly, many people—women and feminists included—understood the shirt to be inoffensive and mischievous, and were highly sympathetic towards Dr Taylor, who was left deeply hurt, embarrassed, and apologetic as a result of the backlash. However, Paul's use of this example, and his comparing of male and female objectification, indicates his inability to recognise just how prevalent and pervasive is the issue of the sexual objectification of women: 'I mean if a girl was wearing a t-shirt of just a guy with a six pack on it no one would … whatever, who cares like.' Pushing further on issues of male objectification and sexualisation and misandry, he changes tack somewhat and expresses the view that while he thinks it is probably an issue, he is not especially concerned about it. He contrasts his own reaction to seeing images of muscled, handsome men—which would amount to 'man, it would be great if I was a man like that', but … five minutes later it's gone'—with women's reactions, which is that they cannot let it go because they are far more self-conscious as a result of the wider prevalence of such images targeted to women. He references his girlfriend as constantly repeating the same anguished, self-conscious worries about her looks—a pattern he does not see with his male friends. For instance, on why the Dove campaign is not needed for men, he says:

Maybe males just think they're great the whole time or something like that. I don't know, like. I just don't think it's needed because we don't think that way at the moment, well I don't think that way at the moment.

This perhaps is an expression of what he thinks is an innate and social confidence that men hold about themselves, and, by reverse, a natural or socialised lack of confidence in women, with men, he says, being much more harsh on women and how they look than vice versa. Paul, therefore, advances competing positions on the subject of male objectification and misandry. On the one hand he complains about insufficient attention given to this issue because the focus has heretofore been predominantly on how women have been portrayed by the media. However, on the other hand, he rejects the notion that men are even impacted by advertising that depicts them in ways considered demeaning or sexist. Fiona's recounting of how her male classmates respond in discussions to the Diet Coke ads echoes the sentiment that they want to be considered in analyses and critiques of advertising texts:

The men were giving out and ... saying like nobody has ... like the average man doesn't have a six pack, he doesn't have huge muscles, he doesn't have tanned dark skin and lovely hair, like they were giving out that if women can give out about them things then so can men. That was kind of the general consensus from the Coke ad that came out.

In addition to discussions of misandry and the sexual objectification of the male body, two interviewees—Bernard (a mature, fourth-year student) and Pauline (an art director at a Dublin-based agency)—identify what they perceive as an emerging and concerning trend—the incompetent male in adverts:

There's a pet hate of our creative director ... he hates the way men are always or quite often perceived to be the bumbling idiot in ads next to the woman. You know, juxtaposed with the woman who is the smart, logical one. (Pauline, artistic director)

There seems to be a reverse stereotype of (men) … pictured as bumbling idiots. (Bernard)

It is interesting that the concept of the 'bumbling idiot' is so labelled and referenced by both study participants: one a practitioner with several years of professional experience and the other a final-year student. This is significant, since it suggests that there is potentially a quite widespread belief that such a depiction of men has become widespread in advertising. In fact, such a perception is referred to in the July 2017 report by the UK's Advertising Standards Authority, *Depictions, Perceptions and Harm: A Report on Gender Stereotypes in Advertising*. In one section of the report, which on the whole is to be hugely welcomed for its call to action for advertisers to tackle the issue of gender and sex-role stereotyping, they offer advice which urges advertisers to not create the kinds of adverts that portray 'a man trying and failing to undertake simple parental or house-hold tasks' (ASA 2017, p. 4)—thereby suggesting that adverts of this nature are commonplace. In addition, while there are several, though not many, examples of adverts that portray male protagonists as incompetent at housework, the previous comments by Pauline and Bernard suggest that they believe such adverts represent a broader demeaning of men in advertising. This notion that men are being degraded and humiliated is certainly not an accurate one. In a 2008 study by Debbie Ging and Roddy Flynn on the Irish advertising landscape, they find that men pre-dominantly fill positions of power, authority, and expertise in ads. Consequently, given this misconception, it is crucial to unpick why this may be a common perception.

Throughout the postfeminist period beginning in the 1990s, a grow-ing body of academic literature began to focus on men and masculinity, with theorists such as Connell and Messerschmidt (2005) putting for-ward the view that the promotion and elevation of hegemonic, dominant constructions of masculinity have harmed both men and women. While it is crucial, Connell (2005) notes, that men's experiences of gender, among other issues, be examined and analysed, there are drawbacks to this greater academic and social focus on men and men's issues, which has given rise to a situation where, '[i]n the last fifteen years, in the "developed" countries of the global metropole, there has been a great deal of popular concern with issues about men and boys' (Connell 2005, pp. 1802–1803). Clearly there are legitimate reasons to be worried about a range of challenges that men and boys face, but this turn may also represent a kind of anti-woman and anti-feminist reaction to the gains made by women in the decades preceding the emergence of men's rights activist groups and later the more troubling manifestations of men's groups such as MGTOW (Men Going Their Own Way) (Nagle 2017)—notable for their assertion that men have suffered greatly as a result of the feminist movement. Connell maintains that while life is not always more advantageous for men than women, evidence does not support the notion that men—on the whole—are comparatively now more disadvantaged and disempowered than women. In spite of this, socio-political debates persist in decrying the state and status of men and boys in contemporary Western society.

While growing awareness of constructions of idealised masculinity are, of course, to be welcomed and are helpful in terms of a wider questioning of gender norms, it is important to bear in mind, especially in a postfeminist context, that concerns over masculinity and a shift away from feminist concerns connected to women and women's rights towards a broader rhetoric of gender equality 'risk(s) diminishing or diluting the unfinished business of feminism' (Tasker and Negra 2007, p. 14). In addition, although there have always been pockets of support among men for female liberation and equality between the sexes,

> [t]here is, however, also significant evidence of men's and boys' resistance to change in gender relations ... Research on schools has also found cases where boys assert control of informal social life and direct hostility against girls and against boys perceived as being different. (Connell 2005, p. 1810)

Such animosity results from a reluctance to relinquish the 'patriarchal dividend' that men and boys have enjoyed. This unwillingness of males to give up some of their privilege, and the associated hostility to women and girls, goes some way to explaining the rise of anti-feminist men's movements. Nagle (2017) is illuminating in contextualising a cultural environment that has precipitated and facilitated the growth of men's rights movements, whose advocates suggest that while women now have it all, men are left with nothing. In seeking to explain, in part, the unexpected coalescing of disparate groups of, especially, young White men into online communities that would eventually form what's now known as the 'alt-right' in the US, Nagle compellingly and convincingly offers a harsh, but ultimately fair and helpful, critique of the left. The cohort that now populate this new right-wing 'movement' are acting out, she argues, against a creeping fundamentalism in evidence among some on the progressive left, who articulate positions that are ideologically immovable alongside a tendency to always be in, or on the cusp of, a state of outrage over supposed offensive occurrences. Out of exasperation with being chided by the pejoratively labelled SJWs (social justice warriors) for engaging in behaviours, consuming culture or expressing ideas that are sweepingly tarred as sexist, racist, homophobic, or transphobic, those disenchanted with this version of the left turn to sarcasm, parody, and satire to point out the ridiculous situation where everything is deemed 'problematic'. Nagle also, astutely, is critical of the speed at which this apparently delicate and 'snowflaky' left have demonstrated an eagerness to publicly shame, hound, vilify, and 'no platform' those who do not exactly espouse their viewpoints in the ways that they would like. This is at odds, she argues, with a tendency to fixate on, and to be preoccupied with their vulnerabilities and fragilities. Nagle's point here is that focusing one's energies on legitimising one's oppression and weakness has moved too far away from politically engaged movements that actively work to eradicate injustices and inequalities, particularly those of an economic nature. All of this has facilitated, and for some legitimised, an anti-feminist reaction of such ferocity and vehemence that the backlash to second-wave feminism that characterised the emergence of the 1990s-postfeminist period now seems understated. Nagle's position stands in contrast to Ahmed (2015), who suggests that the tendency to cringe at feminist's 'misguided' instincts to call out supposed inane, innocuous, and benign behaviours and occurrences as 'sexist' plays into the hands of, and maintains, the established male-dominated order. Instead, relentlessness in calling out sexism is precisely what is needed until such a time when sexism is no longer subsumed and assumed in the practices of our daily interactions, institutions, and power structures.

Whatever the cause of the polarised positions of extreme left and right—with, for instance, some on the feminist left inclined to label as 'problematic' any practice or utterance that does not align with their worldview, or the alt-right, who pillory anyone who displays a genuine moral and ethical concern for those who continue to be marginalised and oppressed in our society—it is clear that there is a fine line to tread between engaging in cultural critique while still ensuring that it is politically relevant and meaningful to do so. Hence the tension inherent in this present work, which seeks to offer a constructive critique of student attitudes and how their gendered worldviews might offer clues about what to expect from advertising in the future without harshly condemning them for not being 'woke' enough.

Nevertheless, despite the new round of the sex wars, there is reason to be hopeful, as seen in the fact that gender roles shift and change over time, and social attitudes have changed along with them. A growing awareness and appreciation of the diverse ranges of masculinity and femininity, or indeed a fundamental questioning of those concepts altogether enables a psychic rethinking in society that does not assume hierarchal relations between the sexes to be natural and inevitable. The ideas covered in this discussion are applicable, in varying degrees, to the findings of this study. In particular, the increased focus and anxiety around issues that face men and boys, which appears to necessarily entail a disregard for more long-standing and sustained issues facing women and girls, calls to mind Connell's (2005) analysis of an emerging and increasingly amplified socio-political, masculinist debate about the challenges men face and their experience of deprivation and disenfranchisement. Nevertheless, such concerns as articulated by the student participants of this study are ultimately not deeply held, since any pronouncements that males are seriously disadvantaged and discriminated against are not convincingly made and fade away under closer scrutiny. Even so, it is suggested that the anti-feminist ideology of MRA-style political and social debates which assert the belief that women have gained the upper hand over men have, to some extent, influenced this cohort of advertising students.

Carlsberg Adverts: 'The Crate Escape'—A Case Study

Although not representing a 'concern' as such, there was a 'siding with' men evident in a review of student attitudes to the Carlsberg advert 'The Crate Escape'. This 90-second, 2012 advert[9] is a parody of the classic 1963 film *The Great Escape*, set in a World War II German prisoner-of-war camp. The updated version by Carlsberg is set in a beauty spa retreat, and follows the attempts by the boyfriend character to undermine the weekend break with his unwitting girlfriend by 'breaking out' of the spa, in collusion with the other put-upon boyfriends. Their goal is to capture a crate of Carlsberg. Both the successful break-out and the prize of the beer act as antidotes to the disagreeable aspects of the weekend. The advert was shown to all 12 student interviewees, and was chosen because it offers a compelling example of the kind of advert that is invested in a regressive, old-fashioned, as well as contemporary postfeminist, 'battle of the sexes'. The ad also relies on gendered understandings of women as innately dim-witted, nagging, and narcissistic—traits which are in opposition to men's enterprising, ingenuous, and fun nature. Somewhat counter-intuitively, the majority of the female student interviewees responded really well to the ad, and articulate feelings of commiseration with and support for the male protagonists. The male responses, on the other hand, were more varied, and among other interpretations rejected old-fashioned traditionalist masculine assumptions that men would hate undertaking a spa weekend break.

Below are some reactions from students to the advert:

Colette: Well the first thing that struck me is that the **women are kind of villainised,** like the spa attendants, they're all pushing the men around … they don't want any of that, any kind of spa treatment so I think it kind of **dismisses some of that stuff as a bit trivial and men are beyond this** … So like the **men in this ad have nothing in common with the women, like they're two completely separate groups**, I suppose.

Della: It's **hilarious**. I really liked it but it kind of – it was the stereo … like it's genderised, it really is, like the **girls want to relax**

and have like a great kind of relaxing weekend whereas the **guys just want to go out and have fun** like with their friends and stuff. The way they did it was brilliant, it's hilarious ... I'm more **sympathetic towards the guys** ... **The girl seems like the stereo typical bitch** with the blond hair and she's just treating them like absolute crap like.

Fiona: I think it's **brilliant** ... You know, like **men actually think a spa weekend is torture** ... it looks like they're actually being tortured on a weekend away like they feel like everyone is against them on the weekend because **it's meant to be a women's place** ... I think it's a brilliant ad, it really catches your attention because you want to know what's going to happen and you kind of **you start to root for the men.**

Kevin: I like it in the sense it is **funny** ... and yeah **us lads we much prefer to ... just (be) sitting around and have a Heineken** than be in this crappy spa or something like that ... The **women just seem kind of oblivious**, they're having the time of their life in the spa and the guys are just like 'oh my God I hate this place, it's like a prison get me out of here' ... You kind of **sympathise with the guy.**

Bernard: The **males are very docile but very innovative**; they want their Carlsberg come hell or high water ... it isn't a great representation of males ... The women don't come across very well either ... the **matron or the nurse comes across as quite severe, quite strict**, you know, but yet **gullible** enough that they actually successfully get away with what they were up to ... One gets the impression that it was his partner who decided that he was going there ... So, there's an **emasculation** in terms of **going from being the primary decision maker to in some cases not the decision maker at all** ... he is **reactive rather than being proactive** ... it kind of **belittles** (the men) ... I mean they should be well able to make their own decisions without being told or being frogmarched into a health spa and told that they can't drink.

Gillian: I think it's **hilarious**. I like it ... It's just funny the way they're like trying to get out of it and, I don't know, **the way the**

women are depicted like it's funny I guess … It shows women being all I guess girly, wanting to do **girly things** like going to a spa and the men are like 'no we want to go drink beer and watch the game'. It does show them in like typical roles but it's still funny.

Paul: Yeah no I **hate that ad actually** … like, **I would actually love to go to the spa** and get pampered or whatever … Because I'd be like, it would probably be more likely that my girlfriend might be in the gym, and I'd be in the spa … or something like that **or we would be hanging out drinking Carlsberg together** or something like that you know.

Damien: Eh, I think **it's a 'lads lad' ad, you know, kind of the boyos watching the football**, which eh … I'm not that kind of person, I don't like football first of all, and … yeah, I just think it's eh like 'one for the boys', you know; lads, the banter, having the craic, while the girls are off getting their nails done, and 'what are we gonna do? Go off and have a beer', sort of thing.

Gareth: it's a **nice cultural reference** to The Great Escape … (the women) come across as quite **stern** there but it's played for laughs … there has to be a fall guy for someone to make fun upon … traditionally it tends to be the way with a joke, someone has to be **made to look a fool or ridiculed.** So it seems to be that the fall guy is going to be **women.** But naturally, or sorry not naturally, but they seem to have gone for a very specific kind of stern blonde German woman … The **girlfriend** in the ad is not really given much attention, she's kind of dismissed as a **secondary character.**

Cat: I think **men find this way more offensive** like I think this is really **funny** but I think some of the lads were talking about this the other day saying like they hate it … just like these men who like have to escape like can't … I don't know can't be in a spa or something, I think **they just thought it was really stupid** whereas I actually thought it was very funny.

Nick: It's **not very original**, like it's something that would have been used to … sell beer like 50 years ago something like that ... Like 'cos they are pushing the gender stereotypes ... The one main **woman** seems to be very **strict** ... but she's in charge of the entire place ... She (the girlfriend character) seemed very dolled up, very happy to be there, just her ideal place to be and again that's also **limiting the women as well as the men** even though the focus is largely on the men, 'cos like women may not want to go to a spa.

Des: now I find that **sexist**, the girlfriend is bringing him to the spa, he doesn't really want to go but he'll go because it's his girlfriend. **Like, my girlfriend would never invite me if I didn't want to go. We're on a good wavelength**, if she was like 'do you want to go somewhere?' I'd be like 'no' ... I think they're **both depicted badly** like, even the boyfriend.

Des' take on the advert is significant, since he demonstrates, amongst the student interviewees, the most consistently gender-equal views. He thinks that it is condescending to both men and women and their relationships, which he personally conducts on the basis of mutual respect for each other and not being 'forced' to do something you do not want to do. He says maybe it is a reflection of intimate relationships, but not his own, because 'we're able to talk to each other'. The reactions of the other six male students vary, with Kevin offering the most straightforward reaction in terms of enjoying the advert, finding it funny, and sympathising with the men. Both Paul and Nick do not like the advert for reasons of unoriginality, and for it being stereotypical and reductionist towards men in terms of assuming that men would not enjoy a spa weekend break. While Gareth appreciates the appropriation of the classic film element and reads the ad well, he does not take a personal view, nor does Damien, who explains that he does not relate to the advert because he is not interested in football. Although he did go on to say that he thinks that the ad is reflective of reality, and gave the example of his friends and he watching UFC and the girls 'drinking wine and talking about kittens'. Bernard had the strongest reaction, and expresses concern about the advert belittling the status of men in society, since the male character he interprets as not being the primary decision-maker. Bernard is referencing here long-standing social gendered norms that expect men to be the primary decision-maker for both sexes, and thus he appears highly conscious of why taking that role away from men amounts to 'emasculation'. As a consequence, Bernard endorses the view that women in control equates to disempowerment for men.

With the exception of Colette, who gives an accurate interpretation of the advert but does not offer a personal view, the rest of the young women interviewed liked and enjoyed the advert. Most of their reactions suggest a tendency towards androcentrism, which manifests in them deriding the 'bitchy' and 'strict' beauty therapists, as well as the 'gullible' and 'oblivious' girlfriend character, and instead 'rooting' for the men. It is interesting, although not surprising, that most of the young women interviewed took this position. Such unappealing portrayals of the female characters in the advert, coupled with a more general internalisation of women's inferior status, can reasonably be assumed to result in them taking the side of the men. In addition, the word 'escape' in the ad title, while being a play on the Great Escape film title, also serves to position women as something which men need to escape 'from'—such that wives and girlfriends are a drag, no fun, and serve to spoil and interrupt men's playtime. As previously discussed, this is something Barthel (1992) identified as 'masculine nostalgia' in advertising and represents the uncomplicatedness implied by men being with other men, and without women. This 'siding' with the men in the ad is perhaps explained by McRobbie's (2007) 'sexual contract' and Peterson's (2014) 'Cool Girl', and their assertion that women and girls are compelled to buoy men up, at the expense of calling out jokes, portrayals, narratives, or imagery that they may find demeaning, reductive, or sexist. In examining attitudes to gendered tropes in the Carlsberg advert, the discourse previously discussed of 'I am different' is especially understandable, since the female students interviewed were keen to reject the 'girly', nagging, and emasculating women portrayed. Women implicitly understand that if they do not firmly reject those figures, they are guilty by association. More generally, rooting for the men in the Carlsberg advert perhaps comes easily because of a tendency towards androcentrism, as outlined in the previous chapter.

Mixed Messages in the Classroom

The three strands discussed, which include the sexualisation of women as a consistent issue, equating women to the domestic sphere as inevitable and natural, and a growing concern for misandry in advertising texts, are found to be fuelled by educational gendered discourses and lecturer influence to varying degrees. The idea that advertising campaigns for household and domestic products should and would always be marketed and built around women as a target market was difficult to link with educational instruction. However, the fact that there is so little questioning of this assumption among students points to a silence in the educational setting that there might be alternatives. As previously discussed, the fact that the topic of misandry was raised by several students suggests that this subject was one that has been raised and endorsed in the classroom, although no definitive link can be made. However, more explicitly and positively, students, in numerous exchanges, pointed out that they had learned from their lecturers to be more critically aware of the prevalence and impact of sexual and objectified imagery of women. Colette notes that 'one of our lecturers actually mentioned that sometimes women are … used to sell products to men', while Fiona, in discussing a controversial Dolce & Gabbana advert depicting a woman being pinned down by one male, while a further three men look on, said: 'At the time I just thought it was a bit male dominance … but my lecturer … explained it's actually a rape scene.' Students, thus, appear to be encouraged by their lecturers and class discussions to take up and articulate critical readings of advertising texts.

On the whole, female students adhere to a conviction that women in advertising, more than men, continue to be represented in sexually objectifying ways. Male students, on the other hand, acknowledge that this remains an issue but often deflect such concerns with a 'yeah, but what about men?' response. It is suggested that this deflection elevates and endorses a belief that misandry represents a serious issue in respect to adverts and beyond, albeit a position that is not earnestly felt. It was clear that discussions concerning misandry, sexism, sexualisation, and objectification elicit contradictory responses within some students, which suggests—understandably—that on some issues, they have not fully thought them through or articulated what it is they really believe. Much as was outlined in the previous chapter, while students possess a cognitive awareness of the issue of sexism and stereotyping in advertising, particularly with respect to women and girls, there is a lack of resolution and determination for changing that reality. Instead, the emergence of a slightly androcentric siding with men manifests and seems to necessitate a pushing away of the issues affecting females. Furthermore, the almost complete absence of engagement with the topic of women and their association with the domestic space represents, in part, that androcentrism and results in an indifference at the prospect that women will likely be overrepresented in adverts for household products for many years to come.

Notes

1. This aspect of the findings is covered in Chap. 5 in the section on ethics.
2. SMA is a brand of baby milk.
3. 'Caught yiz rapid' is a slang term for being caught doing something wrong.
4. This report has remained, to date, unpublished. Following the resignation in 2008 of the Chief Executive of the Equality Authority in protest at extensive budget cuts, the Equality Authority went on to be subsumed into the Irish Human Rights and Equality Commission.
5. About 61% of adverts in the sample use a male voiceover, compared to only 36% which had female voiceovers.
6. The concept of humour is discussed in detail in Chap. 5.
7. This is a reference to Michael Kimmel's assertion that encouraging men to invest in gender equality requires challenging the contention that equality for women represents a 'zero-sum game' and therefore a loss for men. Rather, equality should be understood as benefitting both sexes. See Kimmel's TedTalk at: https://www.ted.com/talks/michael_kimmel_why_gender_equality_is_good_for_everyone_men_included#t-54193
8. George Hook is a radio personality on Newstalk FM known for his controversial, 'telling-it-like-it-is' approach to broadcasting.
9. This advert can be viewed at: https://www.youtube.com/watch?v=AtK2qImqBQs

References

Advertising Standards Authority. (2017). *Depictions, Perceptions and Harm: A Report on Gender Stereotypes in Advertising*. Retrieved from https://www.asa. org.uk/asset/2DF6E028-9C47-4944-850D00DAC5ECB45B.C3A4D948-B739-4AE4-9F17CA2110264347/

Ahmed, S. (2015). Introduction: Sexism – A Problem with a Name. *New Formations, 86*, 5–13.

Barthel, D. (1992). When Men Put on Appearances: Advertising and the Social Construction of Masculinity. In *Men, Masculinity and the Media*. Newbury Park: Sage.

Berger, J. (1972). *Ways of Seeing*. London: British Broadcasting Corporation.

Connell, R. W. (2005). Change Among the Gatekeepers: Men, Masculinities, and Gender Equality in the Global Arena. *Signs, 30*(3), 1801–1825.

Connell, R. W., & Messerschmidt, J. W. (2005). Hegemonic Masculinity: Rethinking the Concept. *Gender & Society, 19*(6), 829–859.

Coy, M., & Garner, M. (2010). Glamour Modelling and the Marketing of Self-Sexualization: Critical Reflections. *International Journal of Cultural Studies, 13*(6), 657–675.

Coy, M., & Garner, M. (2012). Definitions, Discourses and Dilemmas: Policy and Academic Engagement with the Sexualisation of Popular Culture. *Gender and Education, 24*(3), 285–301.

Gill, R. (2007). *Gender and the Media*. Cambridge/Malden: Polity Press.

Gill, R. (2008). Empowerment/Sexism: Figuring Female Sexual Agency in Contemporary Advertising. *Feminism & Psychology, 18*(1), 35–60.

Gill, R. (2009a). Beyond the 'Sexualization of Culture' Thesis: An Intersectional Analysis of 'Sixpacks', 'Midriffs' and 'Hot Lesbians' in Advertising. *Sexualities, 12*(2), 137–160.

Gill, R. (2009b). Supersexualise Me! Advertising and "the Midriffs". In *Mainstreaming Sex: The Sexualization of Western Culture*. London: I.B. Tauris.

Ging, D., & Flynn, R. (2008). *Background Paper on the Stereotyping of Women in Advertising in the Irish Media*, 1–91 [unpublished].

Goffman, E. (1979). *Gender Advertisements*. London: Macmillan.

Hilliard, M. (2016, January 2). Remove 'Women in the Home' Clause from Constitution, Says Nash: Minister Says Article that Prioritises Women's Domestic Duties Over Career Is 'Offensive'. *The Irish Times*. Retrieved from https://www.irishtimes.com/news/social-affairs/remove-women-in-the-home-clause-from-constitution-says-nash-1.2483284

Hochschild, A. (1989). *The Second Shift: Working Families and the Revolution at Home*. New York: Penguin.

Kilbourne, J. (1999). *Can't Buy My Love: How Advertising Changes the Way We Think and Feel*. New York/London: Touchstone.

Martin, A. K. (2000). Death of a Nation: Transnationalism, Bodies and Abortion in Late Twentieth-Century Ireland. In T. Mayer (Ed.), *Gender Ironies of Nationalism: Sexing the Nation* (pp. 65–86). London: Routledge.

McRobbie, A. (2004). Post-Feminism and Popular Culture. *Feminist Media Studies, 4*(3), 255–264.

McRobbie, A. (2007). Top Girls? Young Women and the Post-Feminist Contract. *Cultural Studies, 21*(4–5), 718–737.

Miranda, V. (2011). Cooking, Caring and Volunteering: Unpaid Work Around the World. *OECD Social, Employment and Migration Working Papers* No. 116. Retrieved from http://www.oecd.org/berlin/47258230.pdf

Mulvey, L. (1992). Visual Pleasure and Narrative Cinema. In *The Sexual Subject: A Screen Reader in Sexuality* (Vol. 16, pp. 22–34). New York: Routledge.

Nagle, A. (2017). *Kill All Normies: Online Culture Wars from 4Chan and Tumblr to Trump and the Alt-Right*. Winchester/Washington, DC: Zero Books.

O'Connor, P. (1998). *Emerging Voices: Women in Contemporary Irish Society*. Dublin: Institute of Public Administration.

Peterson, A. H. (2014, February). Jennifer Lawrence And The History Of Cool Girls. *BuzzFeed*. Retrieved from https://www.buzzfeed.com/annehelen-petersen/jennifer-lawrence-and-the-history-of-cool-girls?utm_term=.kt3z1Y5bxV#.cr54xgE31o

Pollock, G. (2007). *Encounters in the Virtual Feminist Museum: Time, Space and the Archive*. London: Routledge.

Rose, G. (2001). *Visual Methodologies: An Introduction to the Interpretation of Visual Materials*. London: Sage.

Tasker, Y., & Negra, D. (2007). *Interrogating Postfeminism: Gender and the Politics of Popular Culture*. Durham: Duke University Press.

Williamson, J. (1978). *Decoding Advertisements: Ideology and Meaning in Advertising*. London: Marion Boyars Publishers Ltd.

5

The Catch-22 of Advertising Practice (and Other Deflections): Perceived Challenges to Creating Less Sexist Content

In addition to analysing the gendered worldviews and opinions concerning representations of the sexes in adverts, student attitudes that also relate to advertising practice were explored; specifically of interest were positions taken by students that amount to assertions that the nature of the medium militates against representations that offer greater diversity and less gender stereotyping. The inferred support expressed by students for gender equality, for challenging and tackling issues facing women and girls both in society, and in advertising texts, as well as problematic portrayals of men in adverts, comes under scrutiny in this chapter and is shown to rest on shaky ground. When moving from the level of 'surface' or abstract avowal of the continued need to strive for genuine equality between the sexes, to concrete discussions of bringing that reality about, attitudes counter-productive to that struggle emerge. For instance, while there is certainly a strong awareness of the social responsibility of advertisers to accurately and fairly portray people, as well as a consciousness connected to the need to avoid stereotyping, possible steps towards active efforts to ensure that happens is largely met with one of three reactions: shrugged shoulders, suggesting there is little that can be done; scepticism that any action, regulatory or otherwise, would make a difference; or

© The Author(s) 2019
A. O'Driscoll, *Learning to Sell Sex(ism)*,
https://doi.org/10.1007/978-3-319-94280-3_5

hostility to such measures, which is accompanied by recommendations that a sense of humour dilutes any perceived negative social impact of problematic gendered imagery in advertising texts. However, several students do demonstrate a 'moral imagination' in their musings on how they might avoid sexist and stereotypical representations of the sexes.

Constraints of the Medium: *'Advertising Is a Stereotype Game; You Know, You Have to Play to the Masses'*

It was found that a desire to be more ethically sensitive butts up against certain constraining factors. These include advertisers being caught in a Catch-22 scenario, with several students talking about the fact that advertising campaigns target certain markets because the research and reality dictate it, while simultaneously recognising that this also reinforces a set of behaviours. However, there was not always an awareness of the social impact of advertising on shaping gender roles:

> I could see that like it would be cost effective just to advertise to women because it is women who do the (domestic) things ... but I never thought that maybe society has shaped our views ... that it should be the women doing it. (Fiona)

Also there are constraints associated with the mode of advertising. Given the medium that advertising occupies, it is professed that there is little room for complexity or nuanced 'storytelling':

> I mean advertising, they have a limited budget ... more importantly they have limited time, a certain number of seconds and they have to get their message across within that time ... so if it's more nuance(d) than that, will it achieve its desired effect? (Bernard)

Bernard's hypothesis is borne out in Pauline's explanation that, in her role as art director, she is very aware of the implicit medium-driven limitations that work against infusing nuance into an advert:

> I think with advertising there's often … you're very aware that there might be misrepresentation but you've got such a short amount of time to communicate something to a certain group of people that you kind of have to use shortcuts … you'd love to be able to you know have a broader range of people or colours or shapes or whatever in an ad, (but) sometimes at the end of the day just logistically it doesn't work out but it's never … I don't think it's … it's never, you know, malicious.

In addition to making reference to the limitations of time and narrative space to tell a story, constraints on advertisers also include the onus to give the client what they want, with Paul theorising that the creatives who designed the Hunky Dorys advertising campaign were delivering 'that real masculine image' that the client presumably wanted. Tania Banotti, CEO of the IAPI put it thus:

> If the client says 'I want a woman in an apron presenting this gravy ad', you know and you're like, 'well, no I think it should be such-and-such and such-and-such', but if the client says 'well, no this is what my consumer research is telling me', or 'this is just what I want, period', you are in a difficult situation.

In other words, the nature of the 'conservative client' makes it difficult to be progressive and innovative in the industry. Michelle, an advertising practitioner in the digital arena, suggests that clients may want to be seen as socially conscious not because of a concern for the social impact of the adverts that represent their product, but for more cynical and self-protectionist reasons such that if their brand is attached to an advertising campaign that was perceived as 'wrong, they'd be mortified'. What also makes it difficult to be progressive is the need for definitive 'proof' provided by the market research that doing something in defiance of established trends is a good idea. Consequently, a strong thread of 'the market research tells us …' is present among students, which involves expressing or alluding to the infallibility of what market research advises. This often works as justification for upholding social norms and established gender roles. During the interview with Kevin, he emphasised repeatedly the role of market research. While he expresses concern with issues of accuracy in terms of not perpetuating lazy stereotypes, but rather appealing to various target groups through accurate representations, he does rein-force gender essentialist notions of 'unknowable' women through his adherence to the absolute importance and veracity of market research information:

> I wouldn't have the first idea of how women think or what their stages would be before they actually purchase that so that's where the research would come in. (Kevin)

Connected to this idea of market research is the notion of targeted ads. Students talk about segmented and differentiated target markets and assumptions about men and women, with a degree of acknowledgement and awareness that women are advertised to and targeted by advertisers far more than men. However, some students think that a far greater number of ads are advertised to both sexes simultaneously and are therefore less gendered than in fact they are. The target market is not usually up for debate, they explain, and was found to revolve around gendered assumptions about what appeals to men and women, in terms of product categories and adverts themselves. Additionally, there was a feeling among students that, despite an implied willingness to show or do things differently, the hands of advertisers are somewhat tied or hamstrung because market research and precedence make it less likely that the more risky approach will be taken. In other words, students suggest, advertisers often do not ideologically object to portraying men in a washing-up liquid advert, for instance, with men as the target market, but are 'unable' to do so.

Gareth talked about market research and targeted ads extensively. Advertising, by its nature, he suggests, is attention seeking and therefore has to be inventive. It often reflects other art forms and society generally. It is also aspiration based, and does not, nor should not, fully reflect realities—although just enough to give credibility to people's aspirations. He distinguishes between cosmetic and beauty advertising (which appeals emotively to peoples' desires to be their 'ideal self'; that is to say, attractive and loved) and car advertising (which appeals to one's desire to buy into a perception of functionality). He understands and articulates well the limits of advertising in not being able to introduce 'dramatic tension' or the 'unknown' into adverts, and he surmises that cultural representations of the ideal family being composed of White, husband/wife/children in most American sitcoms have been highly influential in feeding into advertising imagery. Notably, he talks about the lack of single-parent representations in adverts and suggests that this absence reflects the preference of consumers and viewers, since, he suggests, everyone longs for a relationship and therefore appreciates seeing monogamous, committed man-woman relationships depicted on television because it motivates them to seek to achieve that. While this viewpoint is, arguably, condescending and heteronormative, Gareth does think the advertising industry can be a force for positive cultural and attitudinal change. However, this can only come about if done collectively as an industry to reverse or kill a trend, at which point the positive effects could expect to be felt a number of years on from such a concerted effort. He hypothesises that making the moral and ethical case for increasing the representativeness of a minority group in adverts would not be enough for advertisers and the hard research case would need to be made:

> There has to be figures to back it up, so unless that person (the advertiser) can find some evidence from the public, a statistic that proves people want to see this, it isn't just that they approve of homosexuals in advertisements it's that they want to see (it), that they're upset by the lack of representation in advertising.

The major point of contention for advertisers is that they want to appear progressive, while also being fearful of alienating viewers. This desire to be seen as dynamic and modern is tempered by Damien's assessment of the appetites of the viewing public. In his estimation, advertising is a 'stereotype game ... you have to play to the masses, and I think the masses are still pretty much in the "stay-at-home-mam", and the old traditional aspect'. However, he admits to not really thinking much about issues pertaining to sexism in the advertising industry given that, as he explains, his experience of completing a work placement and undertaking training programmes in the industry have mostly put him into contact with high-profile women in positions of authority in the advertising field. On the low levels of representation of women shown in professional positions in advertising, he says, it is surprising that those women working in the industry are not making a change and ponders why they are not 'fighting their corner'. This serves to place the responsibility for challenging the gendered nature of advertising content on the shoulders of women working in the advertising industry—something which discounts the fact that the creative roles, which are most influential in making those decisions, are dominated by men.

Echoing Kevin's belief that market research makes people 'knowable', Cat points out the importance of considering products and campaigns in an open and curious manner that may be outside of one's own interests or frame of personal experience: 'we're supposed just to be open to all kind of influences'. Market research therefore constitutes an important element in educating oneself about an unknown target market group. However, as far as market segmentation goes, Cat believes that 'things are changing, it's going maybe a bit beyond just gender … it's kind of like more specific than that'. That is to say that advertising is employing far more diversified segmentation or targeted marketing tools, so that there is perhaps no longer a single category of 'women', but there are very specific types of women. Conversely, Cat posits that long-established advertising channels, such as television, plays a greater role in perpetuating idealised and narrow representations, whereas online and more targeted advertising has the potential to break down those restrictions and offer much more diverse portrayals. For now, advertising on traditional media will continue to reflect the still mostly conservative views of Irish society, she says—views that are generational and do not apply to the current young generation who grew up with a different set of views: 'I guess yeah maybe like with our generation, kind of, it will completely change or whatever.' Cat, additionally, is conscious of women being extensively advertised to, above and beyond men:

> I suppose I feel like men are probably advertised to less in general because women … there are so many products around women and so many multiple versions of that product so then you're like inundated with ads.

Des reiterates Cat's and Kevin's sentiments in talking about the importance of market research into giving an insight into people. When asked to elaborate on the choice and use of male or female voiceovers in adverts and what that represents or says about gender roles, he says: 'if it's an ad for something soothing, maybe they get a woman's voice; are they being sexist in that way or is it just they know their target audience?' In terms of breaking down differential roles among women and men and encouraging men to do more domestic work, he does think the potential of advertising could be powerful, but that too often the conservatism of clients does not allow for that:

> They (advertisers) could come up with really great ideas and … the agency won't use them. Or they might come up with an idea but they (the client company) are like 'no, just go back to what we do normally'. A lot of agencies are afraid to do anything above the norm because they're in huge contracts, they don't want to lose that contract.

The relationship with the client company is the one, overriding element curtailing the work of, especially, smaller agencies (Nixon and Crewe 2004, p. 133). Tensions exist for the advertising practitioner and especially the 'creative' between pushing boundaries and playing it safe. The client company will often insist on road-testing advertisements on focus groups, and if there is any degree of consumer unfamiliarity with the advertising strategy, structure, format, or content—if it is not tried and tested—then the instinct on the part of the client company may be to backtrack rather than risk it. On the issue of risk and cost, Cronin quotes an IPA spokesperson as saying, 'if that advertisement is novel, challenging, brave, then unless that client is extremely self-confident … they're being asked to make a judgement on something which is going to cost a lot of money to make' (2004, pp. 359–360). In terms of representations of gender, then, 'brave' could refer to, for example, the degree of deviation from the gender norm, and consequently the impulse may be to stick to rigid gender norms and stereotypes.

In addition, and to reiterate the earlier discussion around the advertiser as cultural intermediary, it needs to be considered that the representative from the client company is both producer and consumer, and is therefore also bringing to the table their own worldviews and subjective identities (Cronin 2004). In other words, another client-based constraint comes in the fact that men tend to dominate the top echelons of most organisations, and therefore the client company's vision for its advertising campaign will predominantly represent the male view. A participant in Gregory's (2009) study, who is identified as a female director of research, notes that 'Some multinational clients won't deal with women, even women in top positions. They just don't like women. But in advertising you must keep clients happy' (p. 337). This reflects the kind of restraining effect of satisfying the client; the bigger the client, the more money they will spend, the more power they have to demand a particular 'ad product' and/ or to resist and impose gendered prejudices. The power held by clients to influence advertising campaign design becomes even greater during recessionary periods, when they are under pressure to justify marketing spends and to maximise value for money (Nixon 2003). Clients have also become far more discerning, something reiterated by Mark, a male copywriter at a prestigious Dublin-based advertising agency, who was interviewed for this study. These constraining factors prove to be hugely frustrating for practitioners working particularly in creative roles. In a similar vein, a participant from Nixon's study expresses it like this:

> There's a hell of a lot of businesses (clients) which, seriously, don't want to be edgy, they don't want to be progressive, they don't want the next generation of people to switch onto them, they just want to copy the trends because it's safe. (Nixon 2003, p. 89)

The irony for advertising practitioners is that the kinds of advertisements that win prestigious awards *are* progressive and edgy and artistic, and at industry level, there is less recognition or interest in campaigns that are commercially successful (Nixon 2003). There is, therefore, a clear distinction between what is considered 'creative excellence' and what is deemed effective or money well spent on the client company's side. This is important, since if career advancement is somewhat predicated on winning these awards and being recognised and revered by one's industry peers, then it is going to be worth pushing the client to go in one's desired, potentially 'brave', unconventional, and risqué direction. Therefore, it cannot be assumed that the client company will always dictate the terms of the advertising campaign and win, since there is a high degree of incentive for creatives to not play it safe. This suggests that advertising practitioners, particularly creatives, who are inclined and invested to push the envelope, could offer radically different, diverse, and less stereotyped representations of the sexes.

Awareness of Social Responsibility of Advertisers: *'Everyone Deserves a Fair and Accurate Representation'*

Students were asked questions to gauge their awareness and responses to issues concerning the social impact of advertising imagery on people, and the degree to which advertisers should take responsibility for creating and disseminating images contained in their texts (see Table 5.1).

With equivalent percentages of both sexes answering 'yes' to the question of whether it matters how advertising represents people and various groups of people, almost all male and female respondents in this vein expand on their answer. The most common reasons include references to the social impact of advertising imagery, which was accompanied by implicit or explicit understandings of the wider social implications of representations; the need for accuracy and diversity in depictions of people (the inference being to avoid stereotypes); the necessity to avoid causing offence; that equal treatment of people is imperative; and a concern for brand/ agency/ regulation. Only one male respondent answered 'no' to this question, offering that 'No. Everyone is equal', while the one female respondent who answered 'no', suggested that 'No. I don't think so. Brands who try to be ethically [it is here suggested that she intended 'ethnically'] diverse seem like they are trying too hard. [for example] Benetton.' Nevertheless, despite these two dissenting voices, the vast majority

Table 5.1 Questionnaire question—*Does it matter how advertising represents people or groups of people (e.g. gay people, Black people, women)?*

	Male (%)	Female (%)
Yes	94	94
No	2	2
Left blank/too vague to code	4	4

of respondents adhere to the view regarding the responsibility of advertisers to avoid discriminatory, unfair, racist, or sexist representations of people in adverts. There is a good array and variation of answers, indicating an understanding of why stereotypical and generalised depictions of social groups should be avoided. There is a suggestion by a few that this onus of responsibility on advertisers is because people are 'sensitive', with some more analytical answers suggesting that the ethical side of this responsibility is because if people believe a 'truth' about a group of people, it can lead to real-life repercussions and discrimination.

Students were also asked to reflect on whether they thought advertising had a societal impact and influence beyond its remit to encourage people to buy products (see Table 5.2).

The majority of both male and female respondents answering 'yes' to whether they think advertising has an influence on the public beyond encouraging them to buy the products being advertised expand on their answer. Reasons for answering in this vein include references to advertising's creation of aspirations and/or social norms, and advertising's role in raising awareness in the public domain, for example, with road safety campaigns. There were only two or three respondents suggesting that advertising does not have any major social impact or influence, as people do not 'take it too serious'. Advertising, in the vein of Baudrillard (1998), is seen as a tool for people to benchmark themselves against others, and is understood to conventionalise behaviours and embed social norms. It is also viewed in an altruistic light, something echoed in interview exchanges, where students allude to advertising as being a force for good and positive change. Nick, for instance, expresses the view that engaging with a target market, and better understanding their needs, enables advertisers to give them what they want, which is beneficial for the target

Table 5.2 Questionnaire question—*Do you think advertising has an influence on the public beyond encouraging them to buy the products being advertised? Explain/further comments*

	Male (%)	Female (%)
Yes	94	88
No	2	8
Left blank/too vague to code	4	4

market and for people generally. More broadly, Des talks about advertising campaigns 'starting movements and being really successful' in leading to societal behaviour change for the common good, although explicit examples were not offered. In terms of the charge that advertisers create needs in consumers that are predicated on aspiring to an 'ideal self', Gareth rejects the notion that advertisers should bear full responsibility by saying that concepts of attractiveness are already present in society, and that other media industries are equally culpable. However, he does outline how narrow representations of groups of people, with, for example, the depiction of predominantly White people in adverts, 'warp[s] people's perception of the world'. He feels such narrow representations in ads are 'outdated' and says he sees far more multiculturalism in British adverts, which reflect British society more accurately. This trend has been driven, Gareth suggests, by market research and by recognising a way to be progressive and do something innovative that the competition is not doing.

In the main, the negative social impact of advertising is thought to be connected with, not surprisingly, valorising consumerism above all else, and of creating the myth that material goods equate to happiness. Jhally argues that since 'every ad says it is better to buy than not to buy, we can best regard advertising as a propaganda system for commodities ... (which) is all pervasive' (2011, p. 202). The capitalist underpinning of advertising drives the creation and promotion of images and lifestyles that depict the lives we should be living, rather than the lives we actually are living. Since we are rarely, if ever, living the exalted lives of those represented in advertisements, we have to consume products that bring us nearer to achieving that ideal. However, it is not a clear-cut deception, and Cronin recognises that 'consumers are complicit in its "myth-making" processes' (Cronin 2004, p. 362). The proliferation of consumer choice can make modern life tricky and stressful. Therefore, if we respond to a brand's ethos, we may often remain very loyal because it takes away pressures of having to choose. This chimes with Nick's assertion that understanding the target consumer and delivering what they want is helpful and soothing for people. An opposing view, as Cronin (2004) explains, is that brands explicitly do not seek to make consumers feel safe. Rather, they set out to tug at consumers' insecurities.

Related to this, Coleman (2012) is critical of how women have been constructed as consumers who are vulnerable to advertising, while men assumed to be impervious. While her contention that consumerism is discursively constructed as feminine, with production understood to be a male sphere, is a fair point, she does not account for the fact that this represents more an extension of how gender is socially constructed, with production and its equation to activity associated with men, and consumerism and its connotations of passivity associated with women. Rather she suggests that associations of consumerism with the 'vulnerable' woman amount to understanding women to be intrinsically emotional, passive, or irrational. Specifically, she holds second-wave feminists to task for perpetuating notions about women's lack of agency and their susceptibility to oppressive media images in service of 'attacking advertising's portrayal of women' (p. 8). However, she does not really make a convincing case for why critiques of advertising and marketing as they relate to women are problematic, and seems to misrepresent the 1970s feminist critiques of advertising as essentialising women's innate fragility and weakness. Williamson and Goffman, writing in the late 1970s, however, were criticising advertising imagery and what it denoted and connoted about women's place in society. Coleman's inference that 1970s feminist distrust of the media and its role in women's oppression was somehow ill-founded and misguided does not square with the fact that such writers were not attesting to women's incontestable vulnerability in the marketplace. In other words, these second-wave thinkers were writing from a place of recognition that the images that advertisers were adopting in their advertisements to appeal to women and to 'hail' women were a visual reaffirmation and endorsement of women's inferior status in a patriarchal society—not that women actually were weaker and inferior. Whether Coleman is offering a challenge to literature that deals with the effect of advertising imagery on women and society or the impact of advertising on women's consumer decisions is not clear. In any case, the social impact of advertising and the images and texts it disseminates are, without doubt, a contention well understood by the students of this study. Students also had clearly given thought to how the advertising industry is perceived by a wider public (see Table 5.3).

Table 5.3 Questionnaire question—*In general, do you think the advertising industry is viewed in a positive or a negative light by the general public?*

	Male (%)	Female (%)
Positive	47	40
Negative	44	50
Both positive and negative	9	8
Left blank	–	2

With respect to their understanding of the public perception of the advertising industry, the majority of both male and female respondents who broadly believe that advertising is perceived in a positive light by the public expand on their answer. Common reasons for answering in this vein include references to the enjoyable aspects of good and creative adverts, the important informational aspects of ads, the economic and revenue benefits of the industry, the humorous and/ or emotive appeal of advertising, and a newfound public appreciation for advertisements. There were also some ambiguous references to people not understanding or engaging with advertising. All male and female respondents who thought advertising was probably viewed by the public as negative offered further insight. Common reasons for answering in this vein include references to the perception of advertising as a manipulation, resentment at the intrusive aspect of advertising, its promotion of consumerism, a distrust of the unethical aspects of advertising, adverts as annoying, and the bad production of some adverts. This broadly even split between students speaks to the inner tension that they must navigate in terms of reconciling their own personal enthusiasm and enjoyment for adverts and the industry with a recognition that often it is viewed with disdain and scepticism by the public. Indeed, studies have shown more favourable attitudes to advertising among advertising students than other students, in general. Referencing a study by McCorkle and Alexander (1991), Fullerton et al. (2008) note that their findings:

> indicated that advertising education favorably influenced students' attitudes toward advertising, especially in the areas of entertainment value and support for the media. Students' attitude about the manipulative powers of advertising became less negative after they learned more about the field. (pp. 16–17)

Advertising students, Fullerton et al. explain, are most enthusiastic about advertising's contribution to the economy, while being less engaged by the social and ethical considerations of advertising practice. Consequently, the authors posit that educators need to be more mindful of the need to motivate students to actively consider the sociological side of advertising. The findings of this present research study suggest that students are less concerned with the contribution of the advertising industry to the economy and more complimentary and attuned to the creative and entertainment aspects of adverts. Furthermore, while students participating in the questionnaire and interview component of this study were seen to have strong awareness of the social and ethical implications inherent in advertising, on balance, when moving from the abstract into the realm of practical measures, the student attitudes were skewed towards a neutral/hostile position, as discussed below.

Ethics and the Tolerance for Sexism: *'It's Just a Bit of Humour, a Bit of Fun'*

Several questions were included in the questionnaire and topics covered in the interviews to ascertain the ethical standpoints of students. Ethical concerns and considerations appear to buckle under the weight of their principles (see Table 5.4).

In response to what they would do if asked by their superior, in a professional situation, to create a campaign that was deliberate sexist—regardless of whether it might be ironic or devised intentionally to create controversy—most of the respondents 'get' why a sexist brief is negative. Those who did not have a problem with it answer in terms that people are too sensitive or lack the maturity needed to not be offended by sexism in ads, or they felt it was part of the job, and that they would be just following orders. Likewise, those who did not exhibit any qualms commonly suggest that 'money is money' and that controversy is good:

> I would create the campaign. People need to realise sexism isn't a thing. Diet Coke ads featuring buff men are not indicative of the male population but men do not brand it as sexist. But a topless woman is. How does that work? (Male student, 2nd year, age 19)

Table 5.4 Questionnaire question—*If, in a professional situation, you were told by your boss to create a campaign that was deliberately sexist (whether ironic or to create controversy, or both), how would you feel about that? What do you think you would do?*

	Male (%)	Female (%)
Would do it	**64**	**35**
Unequivocal/undistressed responses	*66*	*33*
Unhappy/anguished responses	*34*	*67*
Would not do it	**27**	**44**
Would offer alternatives	*33*	*39*
Reference to feeling uncomfortable/or to it being morally wrong	*20*	*35*
Unequivocal responses (e.g. 'would refuse'; 'would quit')	*20*	*26*
Concern for reputation	*20*	*–*
Reference to it being poor advertising	*7*	*–*
Depends or don't know	7	10
Left blank/too ambiguous to code	2	11

I don't mind. The goal is to get noticed and get the message across – people should be mature enough to not take personal offense. (Female student, MSc, age 22)

More anguished responses concern being uncomfortable with the idea of creating such an ad campaign, but it being outside of their individual control to resist. References to 'controversy' was sometimes framed in a positive light (e.g. that all publicity is good), and sometimes negative (such that it could lead to alienation of potential customers). Responses on the more morally uncomfortable spectrum range from an expressed ability to problem-solve the dilemma to a supposed individual agency to influence the outcome, either to change the brief entirely or to reframe the sexist campaign in humorous terms. This indicates an internal moral negotiation or trade-off taking place. Others express concern for potential or possible damage to personal reputation, while a few students suggest they would just quit the job altogether:

I would make it. Try to make it funny. (Male student, 1st year, age 19)

I think I would try to create it very ironic, so that everyone recognises that the ad is making fun (without models!) about sexism and doesn't support it. (Female student, 3rd year, age 20)

The differences in female-male percentages here are significant; especially the figures that reveal that, of those students who would do the requisite work on the campaign, more men than women do not express ambivalent feelings about this (66%:33%). This is noteworthy, since the phrasing of the question makes no reference to the hypothetical advertising campaign perpetuating sexism against either women or men, but suggests an understanding among students that women are more widely and likely to be represented in sexist ways by advertising. As such, it is suggested that women are more conscious and concerned with perpetuating sexist images because of a more personal identification with its effects. In addition, recourse to humour among both male and female students as a way to purportedly dilute the sexism of the advert is important, and is elaborated on in the discussion at the end of this section.

Further to ascertain the presence or absence of reluctance to contribute to a sexist advertising campaign, students were asked if they condoned the banning of adverts that had been the recipient of a lot of public complaint and controversy (see Table 5.5).

Only 8 male responses answer 'yes' to this question in condoning the banning of adverts that have been controversial and received complaints by the public, while 14 female respondents answer in this vein. The reasons for answering as such include references to the right to not be offended, to keep the peace, respect for people power, the need to abide by regulations, and that advertising has failed in its duty and function if people are unhappy. For those male and female respondents answering 'no', that controversial adverts should not be banned, common reasons for answering in this vein include references to the 'truth' of the advertising message and/or 'shock' advertising as necessary for the public good (e.g. students make reference to Road Safety Authority campaigns), that controversy is good for publicity, controversial adverts catch attention and/or make people think, freedom of speech should be respected, and/or the need to let people think for themselves. It is also suggested that instead of banning the advert, it could be shown to a more appropriate audience, and that any fallout or reputational damage is punishment enough. Among those responses indicating that controversial ads should not be banned, there is a sense that such advertising maybe be expressing something that needs to be said—a viewpoint that is socially valuable, or that it reflects attitudes that—whether offensive or not—should be reflected in media. Also, some of those on the 'no' side are interpreting this question as, for example, banning graphic road traffic ads which they believe serves a public function. While not very large, the disparity between the male-female responses is significant, such that a greater proportion of women than men are in favour of banning controversial advertising campaigns. This correlates with the greater numbers of female students who are ethically torn at the prospect of having to work on a sexist advertising campaign, and suggests women are more likely to give the social implications of advertising more serious thought than their male peers because of an internalised acknowledgement of advertising's culpability in perpetuating negative gender stereotypes that more negatively impact on women and girls.

Issues of an ethical nature were also discussed during interview exchanges with students. They exhibit aspects of all three ethical categories devised by Drumwright and Murphy (2004), as discussed elsewhere: moral blindness, moral muteness, and moral imagination. An additional category was found to be present among the participants of this study—one of 'moral distancing', such that students were seen to hold ethical concerns at arm's length. In other words, while issues are acknowledged by students, they are brushed aside because they do not really care or feel affected or connected to the ethical and moral implications. There was a strong thread among students of a kind of 'get over it' attitude, that it is up to individuals to not be offended. This occurs because adverts are taken in isolation and are not understood to be part of wider trends. For

Table 5.5 Questionnaire question—*Should adverts that are controversial and /or receive a lot of complaints from the public be banned?*

	Male (%)	Female (%)
Yes	15	27
No	69	48
Depends[a]	16	23
Left blank	–	2

[a]'Depends' relates to answers where participants did not respond broadly 'yes' or 'no' and instead referred to contextual, circumstantial, and determining factors concerning the question being asked

instance, there was significant agreement across students, although not all, that there is no point objecting to an individual advert:

> Like, if it's … actually like (a) trend-trend and it's all you see on TV and you can see it impacting men's view on women, then yeah but I wouldn't say it's the actual ad you need to complain about you just need to say it to – I don't know – the advertising agencies or regulators themselves, saying 'look this is getting out of hand … When you're doing your ads from now on, could you be a bit more conscious of this, that or the other', as opposed to saying 'that ad was disgraceful, take it down now', and blowing a gasket. (Kevin)

There was also adherence to a view of the inevitability of offending someone and that people are too sensitive, something especially prevalent in the questionnaire data. Among male interview participants, in particular, sexism in adverts was thought to be 'lazy', 'uncreative', 'bad taste', and bad for one's reputation rather than they express any explicit concern for women as subjected to sexism as a consequence of sexist advertising. There was frustration evident in having to consider ethical issues, which was thought to stunt the creative process. Additionally, the impact of the client relationship comes to bear on ethical issues in that the client determines what is 'offensive', while also sometimes standing in the way of progressive change. However, there is optimism and hope for change, as evidenced in the presence of a moral imagination or moral compass in several students. Such change, these students articulate, would or could be industry driven through collective action. While it is predicted that this would be slow, it can happen. For instance, as a guiding principle, Nick talks about the benchmark of 'would you show this to your mother?' which offers an opportunity for creatives to resist lowest common-denominator sexism, and means that occurrences of offence are not to be taken as a given. In other words, the notion that people will always been offended is not inevitable if creatives allow themselves to ask how they would feel about showing a proposed advert to their mother. Fiona, however, expresses little-to-no concern with gender stereotyping and sexism. Despite the pretty clear case of objectification of women in the Hunky Dorys adverts, Fiona, while being adamant she 'wouldn't be real like, oh you know, show women as the weaker character or anything', would relish being given a 'cheeky' campaign, such as Hunky Dorys, to work on. The clear contradictions inherent in her position mark a core characteristic of postfeminism and demonstrate how conflicting discourses around independence and empowerment collide with discourses of femininity and attractiveness to men.

Cat much more clearly expresses ethical reservations about the industry and is unsure how those concerns can ever be resolved. She likewise muses on what power or agency she would have as a junior person working in an agency to push back on problematic briefs, but she does say that critical awareness about the industry is high among her and her classmates, and that they are strongly encouraged by lecturers to be critical of the industry and to talk about things they do not agree with or would change if given the chance. She maintains that there are innovative ways to challenge and make change in the industry, thereby demonstrating a moral imagination. She also alludes to organisational cultures and how different agencies have varying approaches and styles towards campaigns, and that it is important to be mindful of the kind of agency one may be going to work for, and to 'try and orientate yourself towards maybe the type of agencies that you like or just become informed about what their atmosphere or ethos might be'. The Catch-22 of lodging complaints about adverts, for example, in discussing the controversial nature of the Hunky Dorys ads, is that it simply adds fuel to the publicity fire for the advert, the product, and the agency, Cat suggests.

Gillian meanwhile, for the most part, subscribes to a 'controversy is good' view. On the Hunky Dorys campaign and complaints levelled against it, she says: 'Yeah I guess you can kind of see why people are outraged but with stuff like that I'd just be like, "oh get over it".' She thus demonstrates that she is not particularly tuned into advertising images and negative representations of people and social groups, and has very little to add, or responds with 'don't know' when asked to reflect or comment on gendered market segmentation and differences among men and women in class. Kevin similarly advises that 'I just think they need to remember it's a fictional film or it's a fictional ad, it's just a bit of humour, a bit of fun'. Likewise expressing contradictory ethical views and a degree of 'moral distancing', Paul agrees with the importance of advertising codes of standards and says he is aware of the impact of advertising in influencing 'the masses'. On the one hand, he says that he would not like to be part of a campaign that is intended to make people feel uncomfortable, but that he might do so if it is required as part of his job. Yet he says of the Hunky Dorys campaign, not that he understands that it might make women uncomfortable, but that it is not very creative. However, even on this basis, he goes on to say that he would not have a problem with releasing that advert, especially since it was probably effective at appealing to its 'laddish', typically masculine target market:

> I guess for me, I don't really take offence very easy or anything so I always find it quite hard to see why someone would get very upset about something like that … I just don't see the point. I've better things to do with my time … They (advertisers) definitely do have a huge responsibility to make sure that everyone's rights are maintained and everything like that, but I think what I was trying to get at there was just they (people who make complaints about adverts) need to ease up… I can understand why complaints were made (in relation to the Hunky Dorys campaign) and stuff like that but I think they just need to maybe lighten up a bit like I don't know, I think everyone just needs to lighten up.

Somewhat similarly, Damien is not especially concerned with being unethical, but thinks the need to be politically correct is more linked to staying out of trouble than an ethical regard for what it attempts to achieve:

> I think everything gets picked up on these days a bit too much. I think getting into the industry, I would say be politically correct just so you don't get in trouble, more so than doing it because I have any strong beliefs that this is right, sort of thing.

Likewise, being sexist in advertising is understood by Damien to be 'lazy' rather than ethically wrong. He clearly feels confused and conflicted about how to do things differently in the industry, given that practitioners are simultaneously compelled to act on the market research while also trying to avoid gender stereotypes. He talks about the challenge of having to admit that some stereotypes might work, and that they not only *don't* offend some women but actively appeal to them; for example, that some women might see an advert for a domestic product and think it looks great. He suggests that a way around the minefield of gender stereotypes is to not feature a person in the advert altogether, but instead to feature, for instance, dancing cartoon detergent bottles, showing here a moral imagination.

When pushed on whether the pressure to conform to an ideal leads to real-life discrimination, Gareth reveals that he believes advertising represents a sort of 'soft' discrimination. Using the analogy of chemical erosion, he says: 'Advertising will never hurt in big clumps and hurt people directly in a big provocative way but slowly it kind of drains away a kind of … worth or … value in something.' However, he is adamant that progress is being made and that we are seeing far greater diversity than ever before in ads. Ethics was an important consideration from what Nick saw in the agency at which he completed a work placement, especially the onus to be honest and truthful. He brings up what he considers to be unethical rape-culture references in adverts like the Bud Light tagline 'The perfect beer for removing 'no' from your vocabulary for the night', and he puzzles over how the advert was conceived: 'they may claim stupidity or whatever else but like you really can't do things like that to sell a beer'. He takes a strong moral stand on this in asserting that ignorance is not an excuse. As an explanation for why that particular Bud Light advert made it to final production stage, Nick theorises that there were no 'fresh eyes' on it before dissemination to the public, and agrees that it was right to pull it in sensitivity to people who have suffered the trauma of rape. Nick's assessment of the slogan for Mother advertising agency in London—'would you show this to your mother?'—is that it is helpful as '*a sort of way to step away from the cop-out of … "sex sells"*'; again, like other students, he shows a capacity for moral imagination. Des similarly believes that reverting to sexism in advertising represents the lowest-common-dominator advertising practice and a lack of creative imagination. However, the ability to sidestep the easy, expected approach is constrained by the conservatism of the client companies, who may often say 'no' to innovative ideas. Nevertheless, the smaller the brand, and the smaller the agency, the more scope there is to be risky and try to do something outside of the norm, because there is less at stake, and there is not such a big precedence of 'tried and tested' and a sense of what has worked in the past. Des takes up a stance of optimism about the capacity for ethical practice in advertising.

The feasibility and desirability of being idealistic and principled in advertising, especially as it pertains to more diverse representations in adverts, meets with contradictory opinions by two female practitioners interviewed for this study. Anna, a strategic planner, is all for 'tokenism' in adverts, if that is how it needs to start out. She talks about the perceived need for 'token' characters being met with resistance by others working in the industry. She notes that especially those who are White and male 'don't get it'. Her response to her male colleagues who do not appreciate the function served by the presence of 'diverse' characters in an advert, if even for tokenistic reasons, is 'of course you're not going to get it because you're everywhere, you are represented fully in a multitude of roles'. The idea of the token character was also raised by art director Pauline, who positioned herself differently to Anna and said:

> The thing that kind of grates on me sometimes is when people do it really on purpose, when you know that that's the token character in that ad because they're trying … like sometimes it's a little bit too 'there's a character of a different ethnicity' or 'there's a character with something …', and they've just done it just because … I think when it's part of the story, it's nice because it's more natural.

Anna's point that it needs to start in a more contrived manner with a 'token' character introduced very consciously before it can become 'natural' and just part of the story is not fully appreciated or considered by Pauline.

Although citing research dating from the mid-late 1990s, Fullerton et al.'s (2008) assertion that 'men (are) … less offended by advertising and less inclined to regulate it' (2008, p. 16) and that 'women tended to agree more strongly with the statement "there should be less emphasis on sex in advertising"' (p. 19) speaks to and squares with the findings of this study. Particularly, the questionnaire responses reveal that far fewer men than women would have qualms about working on a sexist advertising campaign, and also fewer male respondents than female agree that offensive and controversial advertising should be banned, thereby demonstrating a reticence among men who participated in this research to resist sexist advertising and/or take action to regulate it. In addition, the evidence of recourse to humour among both male and female students as a way to purportedly dilute the sexism of the advert is important. Resorting to humour is hugely relevant when considered alongside gender stereotypes and sexism in advertising imagery. This chimes with Mallia (2008), who identifies the importance of a specifically masculine style of humour in advertising. It also echoes Whelehan's (2000) contention that postfeminism, Lad Culture and humour are inextricably tied in ways that mean sexist banter enjoys immunity to critique, and instead can be injected into advertising texts and imagery with impunity.

More specifically, answers to questions and discussions of an ethical nature with students raise issues of personal responsibility and perceived agency. Embracing or rejecting personal responsibility, as exhibited in student questionnaire responses about taking on work to design a deliberately sexist ad campaign, can be understood—as already indicated—using Drumwright and Murphy's (2004) research study, and their three categories of ethical response: moral myopia, moral muteness, and moral imagination. For instance, present within the category of moral muteness, there is the sentiment that the client is always right and that the advertising practitioner could not or would not challenge the client company on its desired direction. In the student responses, those exhibiting a 'moral muteness' were clearly aware of the ethical implications entailed in devising a sexist campaign. However, rather than references to the client company, they made reference to a 'the-boss-is-always-right' kind of narrative. This differentiation can perhaps be explained by students being at the pre-peripheral stage of membership of professional advertising practice, thereby looking to their hypothetical 'boss' rather than the client as the authority or definitive voice on moral and ethical considerations. Some of the student responses demonstrate attempts to devise innovative and imaginative ways to get around ethical concerns, and therefore fit the description of displaying a 'moral imagination'. For instance, in answering what they would do if asked to work on a sexist ad campaign, one student responded, 'I would advise against it and suggest ethical and moral views and how it could potentially damage brand image and perceptions' (female student, 2nd year, age 20).

An additional category that could be added to Drumwright and Murphy's framework is one of 'moral distancing', fitting somewhere between moral myopia and moral muteness. Moral myopia, the authors explain, skews one's reactions to ethical considerations and results in varying justifications for problematic practices. These range from the only imperative for advertisers is to operate within the regulatory system to assertions that advertising is merely reflecting back to society already established dynamics and social structures, as well as the 'ostrich syndrome', which entails brushing aside and shutting one's eyes to ethical issues. Moral muteness, moreover, implies simultaneous recognition of ethical issues alongside a refusal to speak up about them. The features of this position, including 'ethics is bad for business', 'the client is always right', and the ability to 'compartmentalise', were not present in any significant way among this study's student participants. This is why a fourth category has been devised to capture a trend that shows itself to be present in how students—in both questionnaire and interview data—navigate ethical issues. 'Moral distancing', similar to both moral myopia and moral muteness, implies acknowledgement, justification, complacency, and inaction with respect to ethical considerations. However, the underlying reason for belonging to this position is one not identified by Drumwright and Murphy, or by Tuncay Zayer and Coleman (2015). This is one of emotional disconnect and apathy in relation to the ethical implications of advertising practice. For the purposes of this study, such ethical considerations concern issues of gender representations and gender stereotyping in advertising texts. This absence of interest in or concern for the social impact of problematic gendered tropes in advertising imagery reveals itself in the numerous contradictory responses expressed by students. On the one hand, they adhere to the view that, for instance, sexual objectification of women in advertising is both prevalent and undesirable; however, on the other hand, they assert the view that the appropriate response for those who are concerned with such is to 'get over it'. While this attitude bears the hallmarks of Drumwright and Murphy's 'ostrich syndrome', it is distinct in the sense that students are not so much shutting their eyes and ears to ethical considerations; rather, they are looking those issues square in the face and pushing them away at arm's length.

Creativity and Humour: *'It Just Seems to Be More a Defining Aspect of Male Culture to Make Each Other Laugh'*

Throughout both the literature covered in this book and the topics considered, discussed, and raised by student participants, the concepts of creativity and humour have emerged as key considerations in addressing the research questions of this study, as well as more generally understanding salient issues connected to gender and advertising practice. This section deals with constructions, understandings, and attitudes to both creativity and humour, specifically as they pertain to gender. It begins by considering how students responded to a question that was included to ascertain whether there is a perception that certain tasks and roles tend towards sex segregation (see Table 5.6).

Only 18 out of the total of 107 male and female respondents answer 'yes' to the question of whether there are certain roles that male and female students were more likely to adopt. Reasons for answering in this vein include references to women being drawn to the organisational, supporting, or 'quieter' roles, with the young men positioned as risk-takers, and as more humorous and creative. With the majority answering 'no' to this, the suggestion is that people fulfil the roles they are interested in. Most of the 'no' answers refer to an assumption that students are all equal now, or that personality type and individual strengths override gender. This sentiment is summed up in the quote 'I think my generation is mature enough not to be sexist.' Despite assertions by students that there is no discernible sex-based divide in terms of roles undertaken, the reality is vastly different, and reveals that there is far greater skewing of male students towards creative roles and female students towards executive

Table 5.6 Questionnaire question—*When you are working on group projects in college, are there specific roles that males and females are more likely to adopt? Explain/further comments*

	Male (%)	Female (%)
Yes	14	19
No	82	77
Left blank/not sure	4	4

Table 5.7 Questionnaire question—*What role in the advertising industry would you most like to have?*

	Male (%)	Female (%)
Creative[a]	53	23
Executive[b]	29	35
Don't know/left blank	14	36
Too ambiguous/vague to code	4	6

[a]Creative = copywriter, art director, creative director, more general references to interest in the creative roles
[b]Executive = account manager/planner/handler roles, media planner, events, CEO, client services, marketing, media

roles at the undergraduate level. In addition to attendance at the BA end-of-year showcase, which showed this to be true (discussed later in this chapter), students were asked what role they are interested in taking up in the advertising industry. The answers indicate that male students are more firmly self-positioned in the creative sphere (see Table 5.7).

The breakdown of answers that veer towards creative jobs, which is articulated in answers such as copywriter, art director, creative director, 'making ads', and more general references to interest in the creative roles or to being on the creative side, shows that 53% of male respondents indicate a desire towards a creative role, compared with only 23% of female respondents who answer in a similar vein. A significant proportion of 36% of female respondents answer that they are 'not sure', 'don't know', or left the answer blank. This indicates a lack of conviction on the part of young women entering the field in terms of career options and career longevity. Aspects concerning the concept of creativity were also raised by and with student interviewees. Such exchanges reveal their understandings of, or interest in, the creative aspects of advertising work, or creativity in general, as well as expressions of perceived creative competence and some gendered connotations connected to creative endeavour. The lack of female creatives in the industry was seen as affecting the career choices and path for one female student, while all of the students, with the exception of Bernard and Des, express excitement and enthusiasm for the creative opportunities that advertising work affords. Della and Fiona both reveal their eagerness to take up creative work, and are both confident about their abilities to contribute creatively to the industry. Fiona, in particular, mentions the 'fun' of advertising work a number of times and is really fired up about the possibilities and creative aspects of the work. She displays an infectious enthusiasm around her involvement in group efforts that lead to creating innovative ideas. Revealingly, she associates the guys in her class as taking the 'cool' creative approach and the girls with taking the 'sensitive' approach, echoing findings about assumptions connected to creativity and gender by Windels and Mallia (2015).

Early in the interview with Kevin he affirms his creative proficiency—'I was told I was creative'—and divulges that he is motivated by the perception of the 'fun' of advertising as a career choice. He exudes a confidence in his ability to create adverts that are funny, witty, and intelligent. Gillian also looks forward to the scope to be creative and is keen to be involved in the kinds of campaigns that are not run-of-the-mill television adverts, but something more innovative and more memorable. She expresses disillusionment with the lack of dynamism and innovative ideas emerging from her classmates, and is not really attracted to the idea of working for an agency in an office. She is more drawn to the events-planning side of marketing work, and, consequently, although she is unsure what role she may take up, it is unlikely that working as a creative would fulfil those conditions. Paul, meanwhile, came to advertising through his interest in the film industry and discovering that some of his favourite directors had started their careers in the advertising field. In other words, the precedent set by role models for Paul was an influential factor in him applying to do the course—something the female students did not identify, which is unsurprising when one considers the distinct lack of celebration and recognition of creative women, in the film industry and in other creative fields.

Paul talks about his perceptions of the industry being 'cool', 'hip', 'trendy', and 'creative' and 'everyone says advertising is like a young person's game and everything'. Advertising, he says, is partly coming up with 'awesome ideas', but is also clearly knowledge-directed through research. Nevertheless, he demonstrates lots of excitement and enthusiasm about the scope to be creative, with less interest apparent for the business side of increasing sales of a client's product. He defines 'hip', 'fun', 'trendy' as 'super modern, everything being like super sleek and super cool', with a very idealistic view of what contemporary advertising can mean or represent: 'a lot more free thinking and open mindedness I guess as well, like there's no barriers, you can be whoever you want to be it doesn't matter or you can think whatever you want to think'. This echoes perceptions, as previously discussed, about the CCI's being populated by non-conformist, progressive, and liberal types. While he regards with disapproval retro-sexist celebrations of the lifestyles and careers of Mad Men and that era, he holds strong gendered notions of creativity. He sees women in his class as drawn to events management and account handler roles, with men preferring the creative aspects, and argues that this is because women are more 'social'. The suggestion here is that women's supposed more natural sociality makes them, therefore, less creative:

> You can be really creative and you can be a complete reclusive like you don't really have to talk to anybody … as long as what you're doing is good. But if you are engaging with the public you have to be a real figure, like, so yeah. I think generally women are, women do seem to be better at that, like I mean I don't know I think they can hide when they're in a bad mood or something like that, men can't really do that.

This aligns to and echoes views held by male creatives interviewed by Nixon (2003), and by implication, Paul is positioning women in the role of emotional labourers and normalises female socialisation which compels women to put the emotional needs of others above their own.

Being drawn to, and enjoying the creative elements of advertising work, Damien talks about being especially interested in working on humorous campaign. He makes reference to 'quirkiness' and to Monty Python as the style of humour he likes. He suggests a gender divide in terms of competence and interest in certain roles among classmates, and believes—echoing Nick's assertion that women have a civilising influence on men—women to be more mature and organised, and not as much interested in creative roles. Men, he thinks, are slower to mature, are 'messers', and are a bit flaky. Damien constructs creativity in terms of not taking things too seriously, but recognises that this has its drawbacks and therefore the working process needs a firm hand to keep the creatives on track—that firm hand being the more organised, serious, and mature female classmates:

Like, four lads working in a group, it can get a bit kind of 'did you do that?', 'no', 'me neither', so you know. Whereas, had Sarah (female class-mate) been there we would have been in trouble, we would've got (it) done.

In discussing gendered roles in her master's class, Cat notes that she sees the guys being more 'laid back' and relaxed, with the girls more likely to be organisers and taking care of logistical concerns. Interested in taking up a creative role in the industry, she sees creativity as 'not doing the obvious thing'. She thinks that creatively 'pushing boundaries' does not have to be overtly or explicitly shocking, but more that it offers up something unexpected, such as the Cadbury's campaign devised around a drum-playing gorilla. In terms of future career plans, she reveals:

I'm kind of gravitating more towards copywriting because I know there is more women copywriters and there's less women art directors or creative directors ... It's harder to, sort of, ascend that side of things ... That would play on my mind is where women are distributed in agencies and stuff.

However, despite an awareness of the paucity of women in certain creative roles in the Irish advertising industry and a sense that this might create barriers to her being 'taken seriously' in a male-dominated space, she bears the sole burden of that, and says that this is just something she should 'get over'. Thus she demonstrates adherence to a neoliberal, meritocratic belief that the onus to surmount obstacles to progression rests on the individual. Likewise, and counter-intuitively, Cat goes on to say that during a class discussion of gender representativeness of various roles in the industry, despite knowing that there is a clear gender gap among male-female creatives, and a lack of women in higher positions of the industry, the issue of quotas came up, with 'people ... stanchly anti-quotas', on the basis that the best person should get the job.

This anti-quota sentiment was discussed by both Pauline and Tania, in their respective roles as Art Director at a Dublin-based agency and CEO of the IAPI. While Tania, who was instrumental in launching the Doyenne Awards in Ireland, which is aimed at promoting career progression for women in the advertising industry, expresses disappointment that there is such resistance to the initiative, Pauline positions herself as firmly against the notion:

I don't think I should be acknowledged for any achievements in my career because I have a set of ovaries or anything else. I can see why they're doing it but I kind of feel in a way it's a sexist award because men can't enter.

For Nick, creativity allows for 'freedom' and 'bouncing ideas back and forth'. He clearly understands it in 'craft' terms, and not as something teachable. The creative process should be totally uncensored and involve completely open, frank, and off the wall, potentially offensive associations. He posits that advertising's aim is to be remembered, but that 'you're not going to be memorable if you're not making people uncomfortable or laugh'. However, despite espousing the need for total freedom to play with any idea, regardless of how controversial, he is very adamant that these things should not necessarily make it to idea, concept, or pitch stage. If it does and if it is inappropriate and unfairly offensive, he thinks it is reflective of a symptom he calls the 'sitting in a room too long syndrome':

> because, like, you can sit in a room for two hours with creatives and go like 'that makes total sense' and then when you say to someone who hasn't heard any of it before they're like 'lads, you're off the wall, you've been sitting in that room too long'.

Closely tied to creativity is the concept of humour. The presence of humour was, at times, understood to act as an agent that cancels out any sexism infused in adverts. Fiona and Nick both identify humour as functioning in this capacity, with Nick positing that, much like comedy, saying something provocative is more easily 'brushed off' when it is funny. Fiona, meanwhile, says that couching sexism in adverts in funny terms means that the viewer understands that the advert is 'taking the mick[1] out of… men being the upper-class or the upper sex'. Mark, a copywriter working in Dublin, similarly talks about fusing humour and sexism, and, much in the vein of Lad Culture, notes that

> it's almost like you feel if the advertising doesn't take itself too seriously that it's okay to sort of tread into slightly dodgy territory when it comes to say sexism … it's done in the kind of acknowledgement that look 'we may

recognise that this is wrong but boys will be boys', so you know to some extent there's a naughtiness and a fun to be had in that naughtiness.

However, not all interviewees condoned the use of humour in this capacity. Cat expresses the view that if humour is used as 'a crutch' or to cloak something offensive, then those types of adverts tend not to appeal to her.

Evident among several student participants is a thread of humour as integral to masculinity, and as a defining feature of the male experience. There is simultaneously an acknowledgement that women are often the butt of the joke, as seen in attitudes to the Carlsberg advert discussed in the previous chapter. This recognition, however, sits alongside an insistence to 'lighten up'. When men are the butt of the joke, some of the male students say it is not an issue for them, that they do not take it seriously and can laugh it off. In contrast, Bernard was of the view that laughing at men is not to be taken lightly and that it is both denigrating and detrimental to the status of men to belittle them:

> There is a clear difference between laughing with someone and laughing at them. And unfortunately too many of the advertisements now that we see they seem to laugh at men rather than with them, which can create … a trend over time that is not favourable.

There are gendered constructions of both comedy and humour, with an implicit understanding that women and girls are never, or at least, rarely funny. Present here too, although more tenuously, is a sense that men can often afford to have a sense of humour, and indeed give voice to it. In other words, having not been the more oppressed of the two sexes and having not been at the receiving end of sexist advertising in the ways women have had to contend with, arguably men have the greater luxury of not being so invested in advertising imagery, and therefore are more inclined to suggest that an appropriate response to problematic adverts is to laugh it off. This trend was evident in exchanges with Kevin, who also demonstrates a lack of appreciation and understanding of the social impact of advertising, in particular the implications of sexually objectified tropes of women in advertising. This coincides with his argument that women need to find a sense of humour, and he advises women to 'remember it's a fictional film or it's a fictional ad, it's just a bit of humour, a bit of fun'. When discussing the Carlsberg advert, in the knowledge that women are the butt of the joke, Kevin was asked to reflect on and provide examples of humorous advertising that centres on women. The aim of the question was to ascertain if Kevin could identify adverts in which women are portrayed as funny and humorous themselves. He calls to mind a Yorkie advert:

> The one that comes to mind is the Yorkie ad. They're going to a football match wearing their jerseys and the girl turns around and says, 'you're going to have to take me home', he says 'why?', 'that girl over there is wearing the exact same top as me'.

When asked who the advert is targeting, and who we are laughing at and with, Kevin concedes that it is an ad targeted to men, and the viewer is being cued to laugh at the silliness and cluelessness of the female protagonist who fails to understand that everyone wears the same jersey to matches. While admittedly this is a funny and humorous advert, it was revealing that this ad sprang to Kevin's mind, in which clearly the woman is decidedly not the funny character. Indeed, when asked again to try to identify an advert that revolves around women actually being funny, he has to admit to not being able to think of one. Likewise, Della said that 'there's definitely really funny ads with both like, it's not defined by one gender. I can't think of any really now.' This inability to think of adverts that portray women as fun is testament to the dearth of such advertising, and is reiterated in an exchange with Gareth, in which he explicitly makes the connection between male-targeted adverts and the element of comedy and humour. In so saying, he observes that when men are used in adverts, it always has to be done in a 'laddish' manner:

> It's unrealistic if you're going to have a group of men on screen and not for there to be humour … they have to put in some humour because it's such a definition of what … men are like.

Humour, Gareth believes, is far less a feature of women and women's experiences, in terms of growing up and communicating with each other.

He talks about the skill and capacity that men and boys have for creative 'jeering' and insults, and marks out the 'inventive' witty put-down as a male phenomenon. However, conceivably, what may be deemed a 'humorous', witty 'put-down' in male circles may be considered 'catty' when applied to women. While this is something Gareth does not consider, it echoes a position taken by Della, when she said 'girls can ... be catty and guys can ... be their, like, mocking kind of self, you know, prankster kind of person'. Clearly 'cattiness' has negative connotations, associated with a supposed innate 'bitchiness' in women, and the other one positive, such that 'prankster' calls to mind juvenile and fun-loving male behaviours. In addition to denying that women possess the capacity for witty and clever teasing, Gareth thinks male-female creative advertising practitioners bring different perspectives and approaches to humour. However, he notes that in cases where women are being humorous, 'it seems to be more a subtle thing and... naturally that doesn't lend itself to comedy because comedy tends to be more overt and obvious'. By implication, therefore, he suggests that women cannot and are not funny or comedic. In terms of the disproportionate numbers of male creatives over women who take up creative roles, he posits the theory that women leave the workforce to have children and find it difficult to break back in, and that the impression becomes one of 'there's a sense that, maybe rightly or wrongly, is that "oh well she's obviously not that interested in her job compared to her child"'. Gareth's articulation that women creatives are not adept at creating funny advertising is hugely significant in terms of advertising practice, since humour is, as explained by Gareth, a massively important strategy in advertising because it disarms people, meaning that they are therefore more open to the advert's message.

As previously outlined in this book, focusing on the creative role in advertising remains crucial because of its influence as an ideological actor (Soar 2000). Marchand (1985) argued that those creating advertising were far more inclined to 'portray the world they knew, rather than the world experienced by typical citizens' (cited in Soar 2000, p. 425). Cronin (2004) likewise notes from her study participants that professional decisions, creative and otherwise, are driven and influenced significantly by their personal opinions, attitudes, and engagement with advertising and the consumer space, as much as established working practices. Cronin concludes from her study that 'their practices are more reactive than proactive' (2004, p. 365). This is significant when considering the lack of diversity among industry creatives, who are typically male and White. Rather than being proactive, pushing boundaries, and presenting new, progressive ways of being, or, for example, 'doing gender', advertising practitioners tend towards rehashing established and understood norms, while also getting inspiration from newly emerging trends and adapting those into their campaigns. If this accurately represents the role of the advertising practitioner, as Cronin (2004) suggests, it is probable that such creatives will focus on 'new' trends that are more closely aligned with, and reaffirm, their own—mostly young, White, male, middle-class—worldviews, than readily appropriate perhaps uncomfortable, unfamiliar radical thought movements, which challenge the very status quo and structures, such as racial and gender privilege, that have gone in their favour. An article appearing in the *New York Times* in May 2016 focuses on the fact that the advertising industry remains male dominated, and that women make up only 11% of creative directors. As noted by a female creative director at Doyle Dane Bernbach (DDB) Chicago, 'If all the advertising is being created through that dominant male lens and you look at what the result is, there's a bias in that and there's only one perspective' (Ember 2016). Similarly, in a profile piece in *The Guardian* in June 2016, Cindy Gallop, former president of Bartle Bogle Hegarty (BBH) agency in New York, predicts that until and unless parity is reached between the sexes in terms of creative positions, 'you will not see anything change in terms of gender stereotypes in advertising' (Saner 2016). Therefore, practitioners' perceptions of gender roles and behaviours can, and indeed does, influence advertising content.

Being proactive and progressive in creative advertising work may require traits that Schweizer (2006) identified as crucial for creativity. Among others, she notes that expressly resisting established norms, taking risks, and exhibiting an 'openness' are foundational to creative work. The findings of this study indicate that students, with the majority of those interviewed interested in taking up a creative role, do not, for the most part, display attitudes that are highly critical of social and cultural norms. This, perhaps, is not surprising when considered alongside discussions by Peck (2005) and Taylor and O'Brien (2017), who suggest that creative cultural workers are no more likely to be critical of normative prescriptive roles for the sexes than the general population. Nevertheless, the capacity for creativity, and its associated attributes of openness and psychological androgyny, which represents the ability to transcend sex- and gender-based assumptions about men and women, can be encouraged, taught, and nurtured (Schweizer 2006; Keller et al. 2007; Windels and Lee 2012). Nurturing a creativity that is underpinned by a rejection of social norms could prove favourable to questioning, critiquing, and offering alternatives to the kinds of gendered representations that currently make up advertising imagery. Encouraging a nascent creativity in advertising students must also include future female creatives and practitioners, in order to tip a balance that has heretofore resulted in predominantly male-created advertising texts.

This is especially urgent given the findings outlined in this section which indicate, among other things, a disproportionately male drive in the questionnaire answers towards the creative roles as compared with answers from female respondents. This result is not surprising in light of the fact that creativity is socially and culturally understood to be a male trait (Nixon 2003; Windels and Lee 2012; Hesmondhalgh and Baker 2015), the effect of which, as evidenced in the findings of this study, is to largely reserve the creative roles in the advertising industry for men. This was reinforced by several male students interviewed, as well as being understood by Cat, who was reluctant to pursue an art director role in the knowledge that men dominate in that position. This not only has a potentially massive impact on the content emanating from the industry, but as Hesmondhalgh and Baker (2015) point out, there is a degree of esteem and status implicit in creative roles that is thereby mostly only afforded to male workers in the industry.

In addition to assumptions of women's competence lying in the direction of communication and caring skills, Hesmondhalgh and Baker identify another unhelpful supposition in the realm of the cultural industries: that being a belief that women are better organisers and logisticians than men. Where this impacts female creatives is that these skills are thought to be in direct contrast to those needed for creative work. Certainly, comments by Damien and Paul, and a view more implicitly expressed by Nick, reveal that they held such a conviction of women's strength for whipping the boys into shape, but not necessarily for immersion in creative work. So too, the centrality of humour to notions of advertising creativity has been constructed by some study participants as male and as more a feature of male-directed advertising. Indeed, a content analysis study by Eisend, Plagemann, and Sollwedel (2014) shows that when men and women are portrayed in gender stereotypical roles in advertising, humour does not tend to be present in the female scenario, unlike the male-focused adverts, which do apply humour and comedy. This study largely tallies with findings by Ging and Flynn (2008), as well as comments made by Gareth, and attitudes by students that sexist content is 'just a bit of fun'. It serves to reinforce notions that women and the ways they engage with each other, themselves, their work, and the world are not fun, funny, or fun-filled, while the reverse is reinforced in understandings of men.

Cultural and social constructions of creativity and humour as male are something female advertising students have also, perhaps, intuitively internalised. However, the crux of the issue centres on the perception that all possible barriers to advancement have apparently been removed and equal opportunities are supposedly open to all, in which case the poor representation of women in creative roles is merely a reflection on them, and nothing more. This was the position taken by Cat. In the creative and media industries, the 'rhetoric of the meritocracy prevails and "not making it" is interpreted through a toxic discourse of individual failure' (Gill 2011, p. 63). This discourse is highly evident in an article featured in the *Irish Times* weekend magazine of 29 March 2014. The article offers a profile of 12 women working in various roles within the Irish advertising industry, although notably with only one female creative (copywriter). The other women occupied a mixture of positions, some being very successful and having reached managing director level, as well as mid-level executive roles. In addition to constantly reverting to discussions of the motherhood role throughout the article, and qualifying statements of ambition, drive, and power that involve depictions of women as narcissistic, vain, and insecure—for instance, one disadvantage highlighted in the ambitious career plans of a 26-year-old account executive was that it meant she 'has put on a stone in weight'—there is also a neoliberal and meritocratic narrative expressed by the women. This manifests through the scant regard for structural, cultural, or attitudinal biases and barriers that impact women operating and working in the industry. For example, a female copywriter notes that while the creative roles remain male dominated, agencies are making adjustments to allow for women to join the ranks. She also adds that 'if you are good enough, the agency should adapt to you' (Gallagher 2014, p. 10). Such allusions to merit and talent alone sufficing in order to succeed make it difficult to tangibly point to discrimination, and therefore it does not get articulated or spoken about. These issues are worthy of attention and, echoing Mallia (2008), need to be expressly communicated to students who are about to commence a career in advertising.

The Educational Role in Students Ethical Stances and 'Creating' Future Male Creatives Starts at Third Level

The educational role and influence on the themes and discourses discussed in this chapter vary. While it seems that lecturers have done their best—and have succeeded—in instilling some sense of moral responsibility into students, it is not 'sticking'. Such concerns remain too abstract, and at an intellectual rather than at a 'felt' level. Therefore, students need more specific guidance, and for pressure to be put on them to apply their ethical principles, along with greater awareness of the real social impact of stereotyping, which disproportionately has an impact on women and girls. However, this is not without its challenges, given that the moral responsibility for advertisers to do more to combat stereotyping and related ethical concerns is tricky, since advertising is ultimately and fundamentally a capitalist enterprise and profit remains the driving factor. The educational role in students' propensity to 'laugh off' sexist advertising content is less evident, and likely this attitude does not arise from lecturer influence. However, in addition to wider social discourses that reserve creativity and humour as male traits, the influence of the educational sphere in constructing creativity as a male preserve is partly in evidence in student responses and opinions, as well as on actual designation of creative roles, as outlined below.

End-of-Year Student Showcases

An invitation was extended to attend the undergraduate, BA final-year student project showcase. As part of their fourth-year requirement to graduate, students are divided into a team with three fellow classmates. They are allocated a client, with which they work on developing an advertising campaign. Conceptually speaking, regarding the campaign design, there was not much to report in terms of how gender was conceived of and represented in the adverts that were designed by the students. There were, however, two campaigns of note: an advert designed around a make-up product which was pitched as an 'aspirational' product, thereby echoing student perceptions of beauty as something women want to work to achieve. There was also another campaign whose client was a financial services representative body. This organisation specifically stated that students should devise the advert and the campaign around a young male professional as opposed to a woman. On the evening of the final-year student's showcase, during which a stand was allocated for each of the eight teams, 30 students were encountered. There were two students absent at the event, meaning that for Team 6, there were only two members present at their stand: male and female. Additionally, the opportunity to ascertain the division of tasks for these two students was not possible (see Table 5.8).

Across the 4 mixed-sex teams of 4 students each (which includes Team 3, Team 4, Team 7, and Team 8), totalling 16 students, there were 8 female and 8 male students. Within these four teams, there were eight creative roles and eight executive roles. Male students were allocated seven out of eight of the creative roles. Consequently, there was only one male in a non-creative role in a team of two other males where both were creatives, and a female classmate who was likewise allocated an executive role. This skewing of the creative role towards the male students is something that is noteworthy and concerning. Indeed, considering that the questionnaire data reveals that more male students than female plan to take up creative roles, but that far more young women than men express uncertainty about desired roles in the industry, more attention needs to be paid by programme coordinators and course lecturers towards encouraging female students, who might otherwise believe they are not capable of going on to be creatives in the industry. Lack of recognition, encouragement, and underrating women's creative abilities prove damaging to women's confidence and creative competence, leading to—among other factors—lower representation of women in these roles in the advertising industry (Grow and Deng 2015; Windels and Mallia 2015; Mattern et al. 2013; Windels and Lee 2012; Windels 2011; Mallia 2008).

The MSc students likewise hold an annual, end-of-year showcase of the work undertaken with a client company. The entire master's class is divided into two for this task, and each team is given a separate client with which to work and devise an advertising campaign based on a developed brief. In the class there were 28 students, evenly divided between male and female students. There were 2 teams made up of 15 creative roles and 13 executive roles across both teams. The allocation of creative roles was, gratifyingly, more evenly assigned than at undergraduate level, with 6 out of 14 female students taking up creative roles, and 9 male creatives out of 14 male students (see Table 5.9).

For Team 1, whose client was a national television network company, they were working with the brief of raising the profile and viewership of one of the client's soap opera shows. The campaign was notable for its distinctly overt masculine tone. However, there was no mention of gender in the entire presentation, specifically with no explicit reference to whether the team were seeking to target and attract men and/or women, when it seemed quite clear that they had developed their campaign around raising the show's 'coolness'—in the sense that the 'vibe' of the campaign had a distinctly laddish, masculine tone—and by implication hoping that this would attract male viewers. The second team were allocated a national broadsheet newspaper as their client. This campaign came across as more gender neutral than Team 1's campaign, and was noteworthy for its polished and sophisticated concept. When compared to the first team's approach, Team 2's chosen direction might have been due to the influence of the 'seriousness' of the brand, as much as, or perhaps more than, the specific approach of either team. An online overview on the institution's website of the MSc content delivered during the course of the year describes creativity as being about 'great ideas that sell'. Ideas are conceived of as 'the foundation of advertising ... Ideas matter when they disrupt, surprise, engage, challenge, connect and change, and

Table 5.8 Creative vs. Executive role breakdown by sex (final-year BA class)

Role	Team 1	Team 2	Team 3	Team 4	Team 5	Team 6	Team 7	Team 8
Creative	Male ($n = 2$)	Male ($n = 2$)	Male ($n = 1$) Female ($n = 1$)	Male ($n = 2$)	Male ($n = 2$)	–	Male ($n = 2$)	Male ($n = 2$)
Executive	Male ($n = 2$)	Male ($n = 2$)	Female ($n = 2$)	Female ($n = 2$)	Male ($n = 2$)	–	Male ($n = 1$) Female ($n = 1$)	Female ($n = 2$)
Unknown	–	–	–	–	–	Male ($n = 1$) Female ($n = 1$)		

they matter because they do these things.' If this is how the institution frames creativity, then the notion of ideas that 'disrupt' offers exciting and wide scope for pushing away and rejecting staid and expected gender norms and stereotypes.

In summary, both a willingness to recognise the issue of gender stereotyping and the drive to do something about it were found to be somewhat absent among study participants. Various justifications are put forward to explain that reticence and inaction, including assertions that the medium of advertising does not allow for 'nuanced' storytelling and therefore, by inference, is incompatible with more diverse and alternative representations of the sexes. Perhaps more understandable and justifiable, students and practitioners express a constricted sense of agency to be progressive and 'brave' in their practices given the need to satisfy and please the client. In addition, advertising strategies, especially the use of market research, work to further 'ghettoise', polarise, and essentialise women and men, who alternately only become knowable to each other through these tools. While there was extensive awareness and tacit support for the advertising industry to own and take seriously its responsibility for the social impact of its content, this openness appears to close down when students are asked to apply these principles and predict what actions they would or could take when working in this sphere. Rather, students buckle under the weight of making ethical decisions, and revert to a 'moral distancing' that enables them to abdicate responsibility. This stance also facilitates claims about the usefulness of humour in diluting the negative implications of sexist advertising. Indeed, humour, and its associated concept of creativity, is discursively constructed as male skills and attributes in student attitudes and discourses, and actually manifests in creative roles being reserved for male students in the educational setting. This thereby implicitly and explicitly discourages women from taking up these

Table 5.9 Creative vs. Executive role breakdown by sex (MSc class)

Role	Team 1	Team 2
Creative	Female ($n = 3$) Male ($n = 4$)	Female ($n = 3$) Male ($n = 5$)
Executive	Female ($n = 5$) Male ($n = 2$)	Female ($n = 3$) Male ($n = 3$)

roles. Far greater numbers of female students need to be encouraged and nurtured into the creative space. This would offer the potential, at the very least, of a greater diversity and array of perspectives and worldviews shaping the gendered content of contemporary advertising imagery. Furthermore, a decidedly postfeminist utilisation of humour to excuse and often promote sexism and stereotyping in adverts, which disproportionately impacts women and girls, requires direct and significant challenge by lecturers and course module material.

Note

1. 'Taking the mick' is a slang expression meaning to make fun of.

References

Baudrillard, J. (1998). *The Consumer Society: Myths & Structures*. London: Sage.

Coleman, C. A. (2012). Construction of Consumer Vulnerability by Gender and Ethics of Empowerment. In C. C. Otnes & L. Tuncay Zayer (Eds.), *Gender, Culture, and Consumer Behavior*. New York: Routledge.

Cronin, A. M. (2004). Regimes of Mediation: Advertising Practitioners as Cultural Intermediaries? *Consumption Markets & Culture, 7*(4), 349–369.

Drumwright, M. E., & Murphy, P. E. (2004). How Advertising Practitioners View Ethics: Moral Muteness, Moral Myopia, and Moral Imagination. *Journal of Advertising, 33*(2), 7–24.

Eisend, M., Plagemann, J., & Sollwedel, J. (2014). Gender Roles and Humor in Advertising: The Occurrence of Stereotyping in Humorous and Nonhumorous Advertising and Its Consequences for Advertising Effectiveness. *Journal of Advertising, 43*(3), 256–273.

Ember, S. (2016, May 1). For Women in Advertising, It's Still a "Mad Men" World. *The New York Times*. Retrieved from http://www.nytimes.com/2016/05/02/business/media/for-women-in-advertising-its-still-a-mad-men-world.html?_r=0

Fullerton, J., Kendrick, A., & Frazier, C. (2008). A Nationwide Survey of Advertising Students' Attitudes About Advertising. *Journal of Advertising Education, 12*(1), 15–25.

Gallagher, A. (2014, March 29). Meet the Mad Women. *The Irish Times Magazine*, pp. 10–14.

Gill, R. (2011). Sexism Reloaded, or, It's Time to Get Angry Again! *Feminist Media Studies, 11*(1), 61–71.

Ging, D., & Flynn, R. (2008). Background Paper on the Stereotyping of Women in Advertising in the Irish Media, pp. 1–91 [unpublished].

Gregory, M. R. (2009). Inside the Locker Room: Male Homosociability in the Advertising Industry. *Gender Work and Organization, 16*(3), 323–347.

Grow, J., & Deng, T. (2015). Tokens in a Man's World: Women in Creative Advertising Departments. *Media Report to Women, 43*(1), 6–11 & 21–23.

Hesmondhalgh, D., & Baker, S. (2015). Sex, Gender and Work Segregation in the Cultural Industries. In B. Conor, R. Gill, & S. Taylor (Eds.), *Gender and Creative Labour* (pp. 23–36). Chichester: Wiley-Blackwell.

Jhally, S. (2011). Image-Based Culture: Advertising and Popular Culture. In G. Dines & J. M. Humez (Eds.), *Gender, Race, and Class in Media. A Critical Reader* (3rd ed.). Thousand Oaks: Sage.

Keller, C. J., Lavish, L. a., & Brown, C. (2007). Creative Styles and Gender Roles in Undergraduates Students. *Creativity Research Journal, 19*(2–3), 273–280.

Mallia, K. E. (2008). New Century, Same Story: Women Scarce When Adweek Ranks "Best Spots". *Journal of Advertising Education, 12*(1), 5–14.

Marchand, R. (1985). *Advertising the American Dream: Making way for Modernity, 1920–1940*. Berkeley: University of California Press.

Mattern, J. L., Child, J. T., Vanhorn, S. B., & Gronewold, K. L. (2013). Matching Creativity Perceptions and Capabilities: Exploring the Impact of Feedback Messages. *Journal of Advertising Education, 17*(1), 13–26.

McCorkle, D. E., & Alexander, J. (1991). The Effects of Advertising Education on Business Students' Attitudes Toward Advertising. *Journal of Education for Business, 67*, 105–110.

Nixon, S. (2003). *Advertising Cultures: Gender, Commerce, Creativity*. London: Sage.

Nixon, S., & Crewe, B. (2004). Pleasure at Work? Gender, Consumption and Work-Based Identities in the Creative Industries. *Consumption Markets & Culture, 7*(2), 129–147.

Peck, J. (2005). Struggling with the Creative Class. *International Journal of Urban and Regional Research, 29*(4), 740–770.

Saner, E. (2016, June 26). Advertising Is Dominated by White Guys Talking to White Guys. *The Guardian*. Retrieved from https://www.theguardian.com/media/2016/jun/26/cindy-gallup-advertising-white-men-sex-tapes

Schweizer, T. S. (2006). The Psychology of Novelty-Seeking, Creativity and Innovation: Neurocognitive Aspects Within a Work-Psychological Perspective. *Creativity and Innovation Management, 15*(2), 164–172.

Soar, M. (2000). Encoding Advertisements: Ideology and Meaning in Advertising Production. *Mass Communication and Society, 3*(4), 415–437.

Taylor, M., & O'Brien, D. (2017). 'Culture Is a Meritocracy': Why Creative Workers' Attitudes May Reinforce Social Inequality. *Sociological Research Online, 22*(4), 1–21.

Tuncay Zayer, L., & Coleman, C. A. (2015). Advertising Professionals' Perceptions of the Impact of Gender Portrayals on Men and Women: A Question of Ethics. *Journal of Advertising, 44*(3), 264–275.

Whelehan, I. (2000). *Overloaded: Popular Culture and the Future of Feminism.* London: Women's Press.

Windels, K. (2011). What's in a Number? Minority Status and Implications for Creative Professionals. *Creativity Research Journal, 23*(4), 321–329.

Windels, K., & Lee, W.-N. (2012). The Construction of Gender and Creativity in Advertising Creative Departments. *Gender in Management: An International Journal, 27*(8), 502–519.

Windels, K., & Mallia, K. L. (2015). How Being Female Impacts Learning and Career Growth in Advertising Creative Departments. *Employee Relations: The International Journal, 37*(1), 122–140.

6

Conclusions and Reflections

The resurgence of a vibrant and active feminist movement has resulted in increasing social discourse and discussion around issues that affect the sexes, and particularly concerning the ways in which women and girls continue to be systematically oppressed, silenced, and marginalised. In Ireland, the preceding few years have witnessed a successful referendum to legislate for same-sex marriage, a far larger percentage than previous of Irish people indicating support for liberalising the country's restrictive abortion laws, and the widely publicised and much supported grass-roots theatre-based and arts movement #WakingTheFeminists, which began life as a critical response to the Abbey Theatre's lack of inclusion of women playwrights in its year-long 'Waking the Nation' programme. The similarities shared by these movements and campaigns echo a wider-world conversation that is, once again, turning attention to issues of women's visibility, voice, equal rights, and representation. Considering the microcosm of the context examined in this book, calling advertisers to task for their portrayal and perpetuation of gender stereotypical advertising texts and imagery capitalises on that energy and implies a timely potential for change.

© The Author(s) 2019
A. O'Driscoll, *Learning to Sell Sex(ism)*,
https://doi.org/10.1007/978-3-319-94280-3_6

Advertising and its outputs are especially worthy of attention given its undeniable omnipresence, not just across multiple media platforms but also in our physical environment in the form of billboard and poster campaigns. The universality of adverts also testifies to advertising's social influence and impact. Jhally's (2011) assertion that *all* advertising demands attention from *all* people, not just the target market, means that a continuous computation, interpretation, and internalisation of advertising images, texts, and messages—both at a conscious and at an unconscious level—is ongoing. Therefore, how advertisers choose to frame gender, gender roles, and relations between the sexes becomes part of the psychosocial landscape which impacts people's attitudes and behaviours towards women and men. Like other media forums, advertising is far from immune to the gender ideologies that pervade our societies. Indeed, the notion of whether the media breeds and feeds certain beliefs about the sexes or simply reflects them is not an easy case to answer. Nevertheless, it is clear that such ideological attitudes to gender and gender roles that are characterised by patterns of domination and subordination, which dichotomously position men in a privileged position over women, are excessively concentrated in advertising texts (Williamson 1978; Goffman 1979; Kilbourne 1999; Gill 2007; Lazar 2006).

The postfeminist era, and its distinct discursive constructions and expressions of women and men and gender roles, changed the landscape of advertising imagery (Gill 2007). Postfeminist tropes became highly infused and enmeshed in advertising texts from the mid-1990s, right through the first decade of the twenty-first century. In particular, this period is marked by a return to biological essentialism, characterised by a supposed playful 'men-are-from-Mars, women-are-from-Venus' narrative. Significantly, the rebirth of a naturalised gender differences rhetoric occurred in simultaneous conjunction with an eschewing of the legitimacy of both feminism and 'political correctness' and fostered a tongue-in-cheek, jokey, retro-sexist bent in media in general, and advertising in particular. This was especially facilitated by a Lad Culture humour and aesthetic, which continues to be felt today in certain types of adverts that pervade the medium, such as the Hunky Dorys campaign, which students of this study referenced extensively. As Lazar (2007) has noted, the 'discourse of popular postfeminism requires urgent need of critique, for it lulls one into thinking that struggles over the social transformation of the gender order have become defunct' (p. 154). Although postfeminism appears to be loosening its grip on gendered attitudes or at the least is being challenged in a concerted fashion, depictions and representations of gender in advertising remain problematic. Whether influenced by postfeminist discourse or not, the challenge inherent in interrogating the prevalence of hierarchical gender representations in advertising is in the hegemonic nature of gender ideology and the fact that 'it often does not appear as domination at all, appearing instead as largely consensual and acceptable to most in a community' (Lazar 2007, p. 147). This masking of inequality between the sexes is abetted by what Lazar calls the 'pervasiveness of tacit androcentrism' (2007, p. 147), which crucially and fundamentally is supported and endorsed by women as well as men. This assertion is much like McRobbie's (2004, 2007) and Bourdieu's (2001) theorisations about women's role in her own oppression and subordination. Among other attitudes prevalent among the student participants of this study, skewing towards an androcentric position was one of the significant findings.

The proliferation of sexist content in advertising is testament to the fact that problematic adverts do not occur by chance. Rather sexist stereotyping in advertising is pervasive and systematic, and one of the logical places to launch an exploration of why such reductive tropes persist is with the personal opinions and attitudes of those embarking on a career in the industry. Consequently, the objectives and aims of this research project were to ascertain the predominant attitudes to gender, gender roles, women and men's relationships to each other, and perceptions of gender in advertising texts among advertising students. Some analytic limitations implicit in the research design and the resulting large body of qualitative data collected meant that more in-depth comparative analyses and a more nuanced examination of contradictory discourses were unfortunately beyond the scope of this study. Nevertheless, garnering a sense of the predominant attitudes was deemed central to answering the study's central questions and in the potential to offer conclusions based on the attitudes and opinions held by the students, as a whole. It is argued that the attitudes that rose to the surface, and that represent the majority viewpoint, will come to bear on future advertising campaign design when students are practitioners in the industry. Furthermore, documenting and understanding those opinions and worldviews offers the opportunity to address and challenge the position of students, and represents scope to make recommendations and suggestions for an alternative way forward, particularly pertaining to the educational field.

Considering that this study is concerned with investigating general attitudes to gender norms among students, and whether postfeminism retains a stranglehold on gender ideological discourses, it was found that adherence to postfeminist discourses was less than predicted in some respects and holding steady in others. For instance, postfeminism continues to exert an influence on gendered attitudes, particularly those connected with a naturalised gender differences discourse. However, other features of a postfeminist culture were less present, such as overtly antagonistic attitudes to feminism, which perhaps is due to a resurgence of feminism and an emergence of a fourth wave, especially in the visibility of popular cultural figures identifying as feminist. Some of the findings were unexpected and somewhat counter-intuitive to what was expected, such as female students responding in positive terms to the Carlsberg 'Crate Escape' advert more than their male classmates, while others broadly aligned to long-established assumptions about women and men, such as the domestic space as reserved for women, and therefore did not offer any such surprises.

Across all three platforms that formed the bases for discussing the results of this study, namely attitudes to gender, attitudes to gender in advertising texts, and attitudes to gender in advertising practice, an androcentric thread was found to be present. Women are discussed in ways that mark them out as 'problematic' and that privilege men and the male experience as aspirational, sympathetic, and relatable. This was seen in how students talk in subtle ways that denigrate traditionally associated female traits and interests. Issues such as objectification, sexualisation, and sexual harassment of women, and especially social pressures concerning beauty, perfection, and body image are decontextualised and framed in such ways that the onus is on women to change their behaviours, deal with their insecurities, and empower themselves, thus, amounting to an individualisation of the issues facing women as a whole. Male students, in particular, exhibit a disinterest and a disregard, especially during discussions of sexism in advertising and what could or should be done to address that trend. Such exasperation manifested in suggestions to 'lighten up' and to recognise that sexist representations of women in advertising is just a bit of fun and should not be taken seriously. This position is more often taken by the male students arguably because they have the luxury of not having to be concerned with sexism, since men have historically not been subjected to discrimination based on their sex in the systematic ways that women have. Consequently, men can afford, as it were, to have a sense of humour about sexist or risqué content in advertising. Having said that, however, both male and female students were found to articulate and subscribe to feminist views, but this was found to be a 'theoretical' or abstract adherence to feminist principles. 'Abstract', in this context, refers to an emotional distancing, or a lack of emotional connection and investment in gender equality issues. This indicates a perception versus behaviour rupture in that students may aspire to be feminist and progressive, but they do little to consciously enact and live their feminism. In fact, when probed, the 'abstract feminist' often reveals themselves to be 'androcentric' at heart. It is suggested that this is abetted, in particular and very effectively, by students' tendencies towards postfeminist essentialist thinking. For instance, given that they, for the most part, dichotomously position girls and women as rarely cool or funny, as clueless, high maintenance, and interested in the 'wrong' things, while men and boys are understood to be funny, cool, chilled out, and low maintenance, it is therefore explicable and understandable that both sexes align themselves to the male experience.

While students did get animated around a number of issues, especially evidenced during an in-class discussion around men as supposed doubly victims of violence and feminist denial of that phenomenon, an emotional disconnect exhibited by students pervades many issues covered within this research study. Lack of emotional investment was particularly evident and noteworthy around discussions of unequal sharing of domestic tasks. While there was acknowledgement that working women and mothers continue to retain the burden for the 'double shift' in the home, there was an almost complete or total lack of a sense of unfairness that this continues to be the case. That a sense of outrage or injustice is missing points, perhaps, to Bourdieu's concept of 'symbolic violence', and may also be in evidence among this study's cohort because they are young. In other words, for those young women who are heterosexual and have not yet embarked on a co-habiting intimate relationship, they have not felt first-hand the frustrations of that reality and therefore lack a personal frame of reference in which to rail against the unfairness and its impact on achieving full equality with men.

It was found also that an emotional connection and investment in wider gender issues is largely absent. This apathy, it is asserted, manifests from a kind of numbness due to overexposure to feminist issues connected with women's rights generally, and sex stereotyping in advertising texts in particular. This also explains why students became far more animated when they raised issues of misandry in advertising, and society more generally, since it is a less referenced social discourse. Facilitating this apathy also is an underlying belief that gender equality, for the most part, has been achieved, and that contemporary culture is more progressive. This leads to complacency—itself an effect of postfeminism, such that the veneer of equality eclipses the reality. Students talk about the state of the sexes in a kind of 'we're progressing' narrative, and they make assumptions on the extent of changes happening in society at large, and advertising in particular, that leads to the contention that 'it's not so bad'. However, there is a possibility that the attitudes exhibited by students, especially those in connection with gender essentialist sentiments, are not as complex as being argued here, but perhaps point to the possibility that students are just more conservative than expected.

While there is not a malicious sexism running through the opinions, attitudes, and behaviours of this study's participants, and students were found to be articulate, thoughtful, intelligent, and engaging subjects of this study, there is a sort of 'sexism' through taking up a stance of 'moral distancing', as well as a 'sexism' borne out of an exasperation and boredom with feminist concerns. In addition, as per other authors, it is suggested that students—as creative cultural workers in training—are possibly simply no more and no less progressive than wider society (Peck 2005; Taylor and O'Brien 2017). While student's espousal of feminist views was genuine on some level, the contradictions that emerged in this study indicate that students are misinformed and misguided. The contradictions evident are also indicative of the continued influence of postfeminist discourses, with Gill (2016) arguing that this points to— among other reasons—the sustained imperative of feminist media research to interrogate postfeminism. In addition, the educational instruction received by students was found to be offering mixed and contradictory messages. It is tentatively suggested that lecturer influence perpetuates certain unfounded falsehoods, such as the fact that misandry now represents more of a concern than misogyny in advertising; the fact that students believe this indicates that such ideas and notions have been endorsed, approved, backed up, or left unchallenged by lecturers. Taking all such student viewpoints, opinions, and attitudes together and attempting to proffer predictions of what can be expected from these future advertising practitioners is difficult. Nevertheless, given that they are— on the whole—unlikely to be highly critical and motivated to resist gender norms and stereotypical depictions of the sexes, it is suggested that it is unlikely for the content of advertising to change substantially in the near future.

Having said that, why should the advertising education sector and the advertising industry reflect on these findings? And how may it respond in ways that are constructive and proactive? Firstly, at industry level, it is essential that practitioners have a professional stake in pushing more diverse and less stereotyped representations of gender. In other words, incentivising industry players and especially creatives would create a motivation and drive to do things differently. The potential of engaging organising committees of industry awards on this issue has not yet been exploited, but it represents an opportunity to bring about real and substantive change. For instance, organisers of the annual Irish 'Kinsale Sharks' awards that recognise outstanding creative work in the advertising field could include a category that celebrates advertising that offers unexpected, complex, and multidimensional portrayals of women and men. Thus, creatives would be explicitly encouraged to push themselves and their clients to reconceptualise standardised and staid gendered advertising texts and imagery.

In a broader capacity, practitioners from the industry alongside the third-level educational institutions tasked with instructing and preparing students for careers in the advertising sector could join Hearn and Hein's (2015) call for alternative gendered theorisations of the market in contemporary marketing and consumer research (MCR). In particular, these stakeholders could urge advertising academics to reconsider their current framing of the sexes in gender essentialist terms in ways that would repoliticise the hierarchical power differentials that are at play in wider society and that resist an overreliance on cultural specificities to account for and justify inequalities between women and men (Hearn and Hein 2015). The strong case to be made in doing so speaks to the anachronistic biological determinist bases of much MCR, such that predetermined, prescriptive, and defined gender roles not only serve to impede progress towards full equality between the sexes but also position advertising research and practice outside of a zeitgeist that is engaged and invested in the fight for equality. A shift in the academic conversation about women and men would allow for a different and more diverse way of conceptualising the sexes, and enable both a challenge to assumptions concerning gendered consumer behaviours and a rejection of gender stereotypical advertising strategies. At an educational institutional level, there is much to hope from convincing advertising programme coordinators, chairs, and lecturers to become invested in engaging students in a broad array of critiques of the industry and also concerning inherent ethical and moral challenges they are likely to face (Drumwright and Murphy 2004). Moreover, pressuring the advertising educational sector to pave the way for cementing diversity as a mainstay of advertisements begins with sensitising students to that need at the very outset of their educational instruction (Golombisky 2003; Rios 2003). On that basis also, in terms of gender and its connection to advertising texts and design, increasing awareness among advertising students of the social impact of their choices offers greater likelihood for change to occur with respect to gendered advertising.

There are reasons to be hopeful and optimistic for change occurring in the Irish advertising landscape, not least because the spokesperson for the Irish advertising industry, Tania Banotti, was confident about the willingness of the industry to engage with academic research that documents the prevalence of gender stereotypes in adverts, and believes that there would be an interest among creatives in being given that information. The advertising educational sector may well, likewise, invest itself in the insights provided here, since this book represents the first comprehensive survey of the gendered attitudes of advertising students, and therefore future practitioners, in Ireland. Thus, it offers a useful jumping-off point from which a teaching guide could be developed in order that the advertising educational sector can play its part in working to eliminate sexist content and gender stereotyping emanating from the advertising industry.

References

Bourdieu, P. (2001). *Masculine Domination*. Stanford: Stanford University Press.

Drumwright, M. E., & Murphy, P. E. (2004). How Advertising Practitioners View Ethics: Moral Muteness, Moral Myopia, and Moral Imagination. *Journal of Advertising, 33*(2), 7–24.

Gill, R. (2007). *Gender and the Media*. Cambridge: Polity Press.

Gill, R. (2016). Post-Postfeminism?: New Feminist Visibilities in Postfeminist Times. *Feminist Media Studies, 16*(4), 610–630.

Goffman, E. (1979). *Gender Advertisements*. London: Macmillan.

Golombisky, K. (2003). Locating Diversity Within Advertising Excellence. *Journal of Advertising Education, 7*(2), 20–23.

Hearn, J., & Hein, W. (2015). Reframing Gender and Feminist Knowledge Construction in Marketing and Consumer Research: Missing Feminisms and the Case of Men and Masculinities. *Journal of Marketing Management, 31*(15–16), 1626–1651.

Jhally, S. (2011). Image-Based Culture: Advertising and Popular Culture. In G. Dines & J. M. Humez (Eds.), *Gender, Race, and Class in Media. A Critical Reader* (3rd ed.). Thousand Oaks: Sage.

Kilbourne, J. (1999). *Can't Buy My Love: How Advertising Changes the Way We Think and Feel*. New York/London: Touchstone.

Lazar, M. M. (2006). Discover the Power of Femininity! *Feminist Media Studies, 6*(4), 505–517.

Lazar, M. M. (2007). Feminist Critical Discourse Analysis: Articulating a Feminist Discourse Praxis. *Critical Discourse Studies, 4*(2), 141–164.

McRobbie, A. (2004). Post-Feminism and Popular Culture. *Feminist Media Studies, 4*(3), 255–264.

McRobbie, A. (2007). Top Girls? Young Women and the Post-Feminist Contract. *Cultural Studies, 21*(4–5), 718–737.

Peck, J. (2005). Struggling with the Creative Class. *International Journal of Urban and Regional Research, 29*(4), 740–770.

Rios, D. I. (2003). Diversity in Communication Education: The "D" Word is All About Including Others. *Journal of Advertising Education, 7*(2), 15–16.

Taylor, M., & O'Brien, D. (2017). 'Culture Is a Meritocracy': Why Creative Workers' Attitudes May Reinforce Social Inequality. *Sociological Research Online, 22*(4), 1–21.

Williamson, J. (1978). *Decoding Advertisements: Ideology and Meaning in Advertising*. London: Marion Boyars Publishers Ltd.

Index[1]

---

[1] Note: Page numbers followed by 'n' refer to notes.

© The Author(s) 2019   **209**
A. O'Driscoll, *Learning to Sell Sex(ism)*,
https://doi.org/10.1007/978-3-319-94280-3

Printed by Printforce, United Kingdom